If you are a worshiper of Jesus, challenge you to worship not c 4:24). Kelly has somehow managed to marry in-depth, scholarly research with heart-depth sisterly love. One minute I was reading a detailed account of the queen of heaven and her influence thousands of years ago and the next I was examining my own heart for her influence today. Ever direct, but never judgmental, this book will not only teach you, but show you how Jesus has liberated us from the queen of heaven's influence and made the Church His true Queen. May His consuming fire of love so evident in this book burn away everything that hinders His love.

BRENT PARKER
DESTINY FOURSQUARE CHURCH LEAD PASTOR

Isaiah 59:14 says, "Justice is turned back, and righteousness stands far away; For truth has stumbled in the street, and uprightness cannot enter." Kelly is a seeker of truth and a lover of righteousness. The love that Holy Spirit has shed abroad in her heart will not allow her to stand idly by and watch brothers and sisters stumble down dark streets of half-truths. She was born to see wrongs made right. Page after page of this timely book, you will experience the heartbeat of not just Kelly but also of her savior, Jesus. Together they turn on lights that will set you free and allow you to behold who you really are in Christ. Kelly, raise your banner high until the glory of the Lord dwells in our land and the true bride arises and shines brightly, without spot or wrinkle.

TANI PARKER
DESTINY FOURSQUARE CHURCH LEAD PASTOR
AND DISCIPLE OF KELLY WHITAKER

Kelly has written a fascinating book. *Jealous* reveals an ancient spirit that has been opposing the heart of God for His people since the beginning of time. Through faithful stewardship of prophetic revelation, intensive research, and unique personal encounters, Kelly describes the queen of heaven's destructive influence throughout history, even into our present day. *Jealous* identifies a foe the church has not known well and equips believers through a word of wisdom to overcome this enemy of our souls. I highly recommend this book. It will empower you to reach people lost in the chaos of our culture with the compassionate heart of the Father.

DAVID BEDELL
FOUNDER OF DESTINY WRITERS

Kelly's book is groundbreaking! I could find no other book covering God's jealousy as it relates to the queen of heaven to the extent that this book does. It is a must read for anyone interested in the subject.

BILL BOYLAN, Ph.D.
LIFE ENRICHMENT SERVICES, INC.

JEALOUS

You shall not worship any other god,

for the Lord, *whose name is Jealous,* is a jealous God.

Exodus 34:14

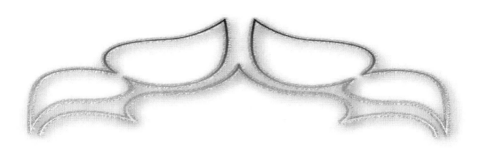

JEALOUS
EXPOSING THE QUEEN OF HEAVEN

KELLY JEAN WHITAKER

RED
DOOR
SENTINEL

Published by
Red Door Sentinel
Rapid City, South Dakota

ISBN: 978-0-9980909-0-0

Cover and graphics by Undercover Press
(writeundercover@gmail.com)
Author picture by Infinite Creations Photography
(https://www.facebook.com/icsphoto2)

Revision 2

I dedicate this book to my Grandmother. After devotedly reading every one of my dry college papers she would say, "You should write a book!" She prophesied over me without either one of us knowing it at the time.

Gram, I have no doubt that you are cheering me on from heaven the same way you did while you were still on this earth.
I will always love you.

TABLE OF CONTENTS

TABLE OF FIGURES

PREFACE

YOU MAY WONDER why the *queen of heaven* merits such close study since the term is only mentioned a handful of times in the Bible by the prophet Jeremiah. I thought the same thing, but have since learned that the queen of heaven goes by many different names throughout the Bible and secular world history.

This Old Testament liar is still active today, having a profound influence on many nations and religions. Manipulating modern people is no different than it was in ancient times when kingdoms succumbed to cultural destruction under her dark powers. The queen of heaven has savagely weakened the people of God through-out all time and in every culture.

In 2011, I had a vision that launched me on a journey of discovery, laying the foundation for this book. Its purpose is to reveal how the queen of heaven is hiding not only in our society, but also in the lives of the Bride of Christ.

This is a call to action for believers to purify their devotion to the Lord. God is saying,

> "This is not a call for rejoicing; but a call of urgency, of compassion, and of mercy. This is a time for the Bride of Christ to turn away from the false queen and expand My kingdom. The time is coming soon for the

bride to realize her place in My kingdom as the True Queen."

Please do not change anything in your life because of what you read in these pages. Instead, let the Lover of your soul move you to respond to Him. He did this for me by opening the eyes of my heart and guiding me closer to His heart. Throughout the coming chapters I share the stories of my journey that I hope will encourage you.

This book exposes the dark schemes of the devil. My number one goal while writing was to do it in such a way that does NOT condemn anyone. If you sense any form of self-condemnation as you read, I encourage you to immediately pray and let Holy Spirit minister to you. God loves you and does not want you trapped by the queen of heaven. His name is Jealous because He longs for your pure worship and love.

If you are not a believer, please know how precious you are to God. He desires to have an intimate relationship with you. The way to His heart is through His Word; the only way to understand His Word is through the guidance of Holy Spirit. This book includes many Bible verses. Reading it without the help of His presence will be like trying to read a foreign ancient artifact: you will not be equipped to understand the meaning of its unfamiliar language. Therefore, I encourage you to seek out a relationship with God before reading further.

I recommend being in a constant attitude of prayer as you go through this book. It is an important, but complicated topic. Close communion with Holy Spirit is essential for ensuring spiritual protection, understanding revelation, and discovering God's desires for you.

Do not be surprised if exposure of the queen of heaven occurs in your own life. Interwoven throughout the following chapters I share my dealings with the queen of heaven both in my own life and in the lives of others in order to help you know how to react to that exposure.

I encourage you to have your Bible out to reference often. There is a Kings Chart in Appendix B that can help you understand the text better.

I pray God's blessing over you as you go through this book.

Peace to you.

Kelly

ACKNOWLEDGMENTS

MY DADDY GOD is the sole One responsible for the whole idea behind writing this book. He provided the vision, and everything that followed. It is my hope that I was able to create all that He had planned. I thank Him for teaching me so much during in the five years it took to complete this work and for the persistence to get it done.

Without my husband's gracious support this book would not be possible. Thank you baby for being so understanding and for sharing your time with this project. I love you more than anyone else in this world!

My son Brent was the best sounding board I could have ever had. Thank you for supporting me from the very beginning and for proofing my endnotes! Thank you to my daughter-in-law, Alysha, for being my second set of eyes during the design phase of my cover and for taking such a wonderful author picture of me. I love you both!

Thank you to my pastors, Brent and Tani Parker. You have been with me since that Sunday morning of my vision. Pastor Brent, I will never forget your reply when I told you about it and thought I was supposed to share it during worship that morning. "I understand what you're saying, but this is too big for the short three minutes that we could give you. However, I'm willing to see if God wants you to share." I was so happy that you never called me forward because I barely understood the message myself. Thank you both for believing in this project, for your many prayers, and for supporting me all the way through it.

Thank you to David Bedell for taking a risk in being an editor for such a unique topic. Thanks to you, I have learned more about grammar than I did in grade school! Thank you for going above and beyond in helping me out until the very end. I could not have put out such a high quality product without your help.

Thank you to Monae Johnson and Shela Maijala for being by my side in the very beginning, encouraging me and asking me fun questions like, "What's the name of your ministry?"

Thank you to Kay Anderson, Valerie Link, and Bill Boylan for being the first to read my earliest manuscript and providing excellent feedback.

Thank you to my many test readers who provided some great input and to my Facebook group for all their encouragement!

Without the talent of Undercover Press and their excellent work in designing my cover, this book may not be in your hands right now. Thank you!

JEALOUS

EXPOSING THE QUEEN OF HEAVEN

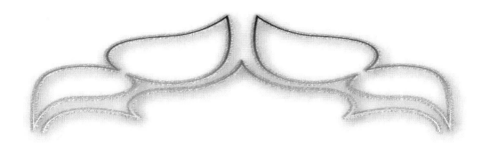

THE VISION

MY VISION CAME on Sunday morning, September 11, 2011 shortly after I woke up. I sat up in bed, put my Bible in my lap, and was about to read a couple chapters. My thoughts turned to my marriage. Thanking God for my husband, I praised Him for the many years we have been together.

Then I heard God say to me, "It is time to come from My courts, into My throne room."

Immediately, a vision of a large ornate room with a long gold-carpeted aisle leading to a gold throne appeared before me. A king dressed in an English style military uniform with a red shirt was sitting on the throne. A multitude of happy people were standing on either side of the aisle in Renaissance style clothing that bore breathtaking jewel tones.

The king's glowing, relaxing demeanor had everyone's attention as he stood up and headed down the aisle. Strolling slowly with one hand in his pants pocket, he met the eyes of many with a smile. A pair of wooden, arched doors stood as tall guardians before him.

Settling his hands on the ornate handles, he slowly pulled the doors open. Brilliant light began spilling into the room, revealing a tall, slender woman. Her glimmering ivory gown and gracefully swept up brunette hair accentuated the kindness in her eyes. Immediately catching her attention, the king's eyes locked on hers. The timeless, adoring love between them touched everyone's heart.

Going to her side, the king gently laid her hand on his. Her loving gaze lingered on him as he led her into the room. Beaming from overflowing emotions, he took her in his arms and began to waltz her gently down the golden aisle. In a significant gesture of love, he put his hand on the small of her back, pressing her closer to him.

A grand waltz slowly unfolded with elegant strides of grace, leaving those present with a breathless sense of anticipation. Radiating a deep joy, the couple's eyes were transfixed on one another as if they were completely alone. The room remained breathlessly quiet as the crowd looked on in awe.

Finally arriving at the throne, they faced the people. Tenderly placing his beloved's left hand on his right hand, the king lifted her hand up high. In this royal display, he presented her to all of those in the room.

In a crisp, loud voice he announced, "This is my bride, my queen!"

Then, just as abruptly as it began, the vision ended. God said to me, "This will happen soon, share this with everyone."

Although it was a beautiful vision and seemed to be biblical, I sought out confirmation in Scripture right away.

CONFIRMATION

After writing the vision in my journal, I turned back to my Bible. Doubt crept in as I began my daily reading that was currently in Jeremiah. The words of a weeping prophet are not exactly the wedding fare found in Esther.

I picked up the story where Jeremiah was trying to turn the children of Israel back to God after they fled to Egypt. Scripture says they had dealt deceitfully toward God within their own souls. Jeremiah was telling them what God's judgment would be if they did not come back to Him.

Then the following verses containing their response caught my attention:

"As for the message that you have spoken to us in the name of the LORD, we are not going to listen to you! But rather we will certainly carry out every word that has proceeded from our mouths, by burning sacrifices to *the queen of heaven* and pouring out drink offerings to her, just as we ourselves, our forefathers, our kings and our princes did in the cities of Judah and in the streets of Jerusalem; for then we had plenty of food and were well off and saw no misfortune.

But since we stopped burning sacrifices to *the queen of heaven* and pouring out drink offerings to her, we have lacked everything and have met our end by the sword and by famine." "And," said the women, "when we were burning sacrifices to *the queen of heaven* and were pouring out drink offerings to her, was it without our husbands that we made for her sacrificial cakes in her image and poured out drink offerings to her?" (Jeremiah 44:16-19, italics added)

God answered my request by showing me the antithesis of my vision. There are two queens: the true queen of my vision and the false queen described in these verses.

Returning to the scene of my vision, I seemingly zoomed out of the throne room and into the darkness outside. There I could make out shadows of rebellious people who were causing trouble while under the influence of the queen of heaven. This was taking place at the same time as the scene in the throne room described earlier.

Trying to take this all in, my thoughts turned toward heaven where the throne room of God is. Suddenly, I remembered a blog post I wrote the day before. It began with, "Why is it that more people believe in heaven than in God? And why is it that no matter who you talk to, be it a hardened criminal or your grandmother, they all think everyone is going there?"[1] The timing of this post was not coincidental. I believed it was a definite precursor to my vision.

For the next few days, I methodically went through every part of my vision to make sure it lined up with Scripture. This is recorded in Appendix A / Vision Elements.

In the coming months confirmations continued to occur. The most significant one came the following year when I was considering going on a mission trip. In March God said to me, "You will get more answers about the queen of heaven in Brazil."

Ironically, I was not even certain of going on the trip until the airline ticket was in my hand a few weeks before leaving in July. While in South America I learned about the Brazilian queen of heaven, which I will share about in the chapter titled, "Catholic Mary."

God taught me about the queen of heaven for the following four years after my vision. At one time it got so intense that I told God, "Enough already! When are you going to give me more about the true queen?"

His response was, "I have been teaching you about the true queen for the last 25 years." I could not argue with that! In the past few decades, I learned much about the Bride of Christ, but it never occurred to me that upon marrying her King, Jesus Christ, she will be his queen.

TWO QUEENS

The Bride of Christ and the queen of heaven are polar opposites. The only thing they have in common is that they are both known throughout the world.

Adored by the One True King, the status of the Bride of Christ in God's kingdom assures her of a blameless identity. She operates in His light through love, joy, peace, patience, kindness, goodness, faithfulness, gentleness, and self-control (see Galatians 5:22-23). She clothes herself in royal garments as she accomplishes good works (see Appendix A / Vision Elements section titled, "Bride"). She guides lost people to their Savior, heals the sick, raises the dead, and loves the unlovable. The true queen rules and reigns with her King from a sure place in heaven where she is established by redemption in righteousness.

The queen of heaven goes by many names and operates in the deeds of the flesh that include hatred, discord, jealousy, rage, selfish ambition, dissensions, envy, drunkenness, idolatry, witchcraft, sexual immorality, and gluttony (see Galatian 5:19-21). Her gender cannot even be referred to as female because of her confused identities; being male, or female, or both.[2] (Even so, I will use the feminine form throughout this book to refer to the queen of heaven). She has held many kings under her manipulative power. Purity is not what defines her virginity; instead, it is a result of her refusal to come under a male influence in marriage. Working her dark deeds in secret, she prostitutes herself publicly while showing off her nakedness. Deceitfully brought under her dominion, naïve victims suffer confusion, oppression, physical assaults, and many other horrendous torments.

Who is the queen of heaven? Is she still present in society today? How does she influence the lives of believers? What can you do if ever faced with her? I will answer these questions in the coming chapters.

---

[1] Kelly Whitaker (2011), "To Heaven and Back" [Online]. http://kwinrc.blogspot.com/ 2011/10/to-heaven-and-back.html [2014, Jan].

[2] Those who make up the Bride of Christ are often referred to as sons in the New Testament, however the original Greek word also means descendants.

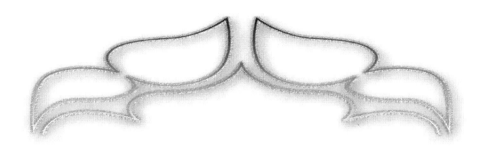

THE QUEEN OF HEAVEN

THE QUEEN OF heaven manifests satanic behavior that is violent, pornographic, murderous, emasculating, sexually immoral, abusive, and extremely feminist. She confuses gender, mutilates human flesh, causes disease, traffics human beings, and aborts babies. To put it plainly, the queen of heaven is attempting to annihilate the human race, thus accomplishing the devil's scheme to kill, steal, and destroy.

MANY ALIASES

It is not easy to distinguish between the many that carry the name, Queen of Heaven. Many sources conflict with one another about who is who and some experts are admittedly confused. This is even more reason to conclude that there is one sole evil presence behind it all - a Wizard of Oz behind the curtain, that is the master deceiver playing all the different characters. Each character has their own chapter in this book and will hereby be referred to as "aliases."

Dr. David Brown's article entitled, *Iraq in the Bible*, has a theory of why there are so many aliases of the queen of heaven.

According to ancient writings, Semiramis was the wife of Nimrod. She became the high priestess of the Babylonian religion and was called the queen of heaven. As the ancient legend says, Nimrod died and became the sun god. His wife Semiramis was impregnated by a sunbeam and gives birth to her son Tammuz (a counterfeit miraculous birth). Later Tammuz is killed by a wild boar.

However, after Semiramis cries for 40 days, Tammuz comes back to life again, which is a counterfeit of the resurrection. In fact, this is the origin of a counterfeit religious system that revolves around the worship of a mother and child....This diabolical worship spread across the world. In Egypt Semarimis is called Isis and her son is Osiris. In Assyria it was Ishtar and Bacchus...In ancient Greece it was Aphrodite and Eros and in ancient Rome it wasVenus and Cupid.[1]

TARGETS GOD'S PEOPLE

The Old Testament prophet, Jeremiah, risked his life to provide God's warning to the remnant of Israelites who had fled to Egypt. The rest of the nation was in captivity in Assyria and Babylon because of their worship of the queen of heaven. In a last ditch effort by the prophet, he did not sugar coat God's message as he exclaimed, "Why are you harming yourselves? Have you not seen how your family who lived before you turned themselves and your land into a curse? Your magic, rituals, and devotion to idols are turning you into an object of horror!"[2]

These people worshiped God just like you and me. They memorized Scripture just as we do and they went to the temple, the same as we go to church. Yet, God said to them,

> Will you steal, murder, and commit adultery and swear falsely, and offer sacrifices to Baal and walk after *other gods* that you have not known, then come and stand before Me in this house, which is called by My name, and say, 'We are delivered!'—that you may do all these abominations? (Jeremiah 7:9-10, italics added)

"Other gods" included the queen of heaven. Theft, murder, adultery, and lying are ancient forms of evil worship, as we will soon learn.

Jeremiah worshiped God, memorized Scripture, and went to the temple, but he also had a relationship with the One True God. Jeremiah's message came from a heart of pure devotion to God. Hearing God's voice was a part of his everyday life. By seeing with his spiritual eyes, he was able to expose the treachery that had ensnared his people. We can do the same.

DESTROYS THROUGH LACK OF KNOWLEDGE

Despite many warnings, God's beloved children suffered destruction due to their lack of understanding. These verses are about them, but also apply to us:

> If they do not hear, they shall perish by the sword and they will die without *knowledge*. (Job 36:12, italics added)

My people are destroyed for lack of *knowledge*.
(Hosea 4:6, italics added)

My people go into exile for their lack of *knowledge*.
(Isaiah 5:13, italics added)

Gaining this knowledge requires a two-fold process. First, we must seek to know God intimately through meditating upon His Word and spending time alone with Him, listening to what He has to say and seeing what He has to show us. Second, through this intimate relationship with Him, He gives us knowledge about the enemy.

The enemy's intent is always to steal, kill, and destroy. However, in God's battle plan, the enemy is already defeated. We only need to partner with God to find out how.

To understand this, imagine that you have a tiny army and that your enemy fills the valley below your position. God tells you to go down into that valley under the cover of night, and there He will tell you His plan. You obey. The first group of soldiers you sneak up on are talking about a dream one of them had in which you destroy them all! The next day, that dream comes true as you execute the plan God laid out for you.

God could have given you that dream, but He would much rather have a relationship with you that results in your partnering with Him in the victory. God loves you and wants to excite you by sharing His plans with you, just as He did in this instance with Gideon (see Judges 7:9-14). Gideon did not suffer destruction because he obtained that knowledge.

The children of Israel did not seek after the relationship that Gideon had with God; therefore, they lacked knowledge. This is what caused their ultimate ruin. The queen of heaven led them to devote their time, land, possessions, and children to their own desires. Worshiping the queen of heaven caused their nation to split, their northern tribes to be taken captive by Assyria, the southern ones to be taken away by Babylon, and for the entire nation to be wiped off the map.

The influence of this evil principality has spread destruction and death down through the ages, right to today. The queen of heaven is on our doorstep splitting churches and destroying the lives of believers. If you love God and follow His ways, then you are in her crosshairs. Proverbs 9:15-18 tells us that the adulteress (same word as *idol* in the original Hebrew language) calls out to those who are making their paths straight and seduces those who lack understanding into the depths of hell.

In the New Testament, many people came to Jesus because they knew the reality of demons and of the afflictions they caused. The evil assignments of the devil have not changed since then. Paul tells us, in 2 Corinthians 2:11, that if we are ignorant of the devil's scams and tricks, he will take advantage of us. Staying ignorant of the queen of heaven only empowers her dark spiritual forces and keeps us blind to spiritual treachery.

POLLUTES THE TEMPLE

The queen of heaven's presence in Solomon's temple polluted its purity and holiness. Watching it being torn down was a heavy consequence for the people of Israel. In the same way that this temple held the Spirit of God, so too does our physical body. If we allow the queen of heaven access to our temple, it will also be torn down through sickness, physical violence, emotional instability, and constant spiritual attacks.

DAUGHTER OF SATAN

In the *Apocryphal Acts of the Apostles*, '*The History of John the son of Zebedee, The Apostle and Evangelist*," the Apostle John refers to Artemis (queen of heaven) as the "daughter of Satan."[3] John did not see the queen of heaven as just an idol or demon, but as one of the highest-ranking powers of darkness. Famous psychologist, Carl Jung, also called the queen of heaven the "daughter of Satan" when talking about Lilith.[4]

Whether or not the queen of heaven is literally the daughter of satan is unknown. However, there is strong evidence that suggests this is true. One such supporting fact is that just as satan exalts himself as God, the Father, the queen of heaven disguises herself as Jesus, the Son of God. I will bring your attention to this in the coming chapters in the sections titled "Jesus Christ Imposter."

We will also discover evidence of the queen of heaven sharing many attributes of the devil as described in the Bible. Just as Jesus is one with God as his Son, the queen of heaven appears to be one with the devil as his daughter.

HIGH RANKING DARK PRINCIPALITY

The queen of heaven is a powerful, high-ranking, dark principality that operates directly under satan. She has the ability to influence the world as a whole and has control over multitudes of demonic spiritual rulers and demons. She causes wicked spirits to harass as well as enter into objects, people, animals, and regions.

In the *Three Battlegrounds*, Francis Frangipane explains:

> The word principality as used in Ephesians, means, "beginning, government, rule" and is used to describe

a class of spirit-beings in the satanic hierarchy. Principalities rule over powers as well as the more numerous subcategories of demons. Principalities influence countries, regions within countries, states, cities, and even churches. These are Governmental spirits in the system of hell...Principalities are not "cast out," for they do not dwell in people; they dwell in "heavenly places."[5]

During his travels, Peter Wagner made the following observation in *Confronting the Queen of Heaven:*

One discernible pattern from continent to continent was frequent references to the "queen of heaven"...I was beginning to realize that she must be one of the most important principalities under the command of Satan. Because God is a God who is not willing that any should perish (see 2 Peter 3:9), my hypothesis is that He hates the queen of heaven so much because she is the demonic principality who is most responsible under Satan for keeping unbelievers in spiritual darkness.

It could well be that more people are in Hell today because of the influence of the queen of heaven than because of any other spiritual influence.[6]

NOT TO BE FEARED

Wagner also states, "Confronting the queen of heaven is not fun and games. It is an advanced, high-risk assault against the powers of evil."[7] However, there is no reason for you to be afraid. If you are a child of the Most High God, then you are seated with Him above all principalities, powers, dominions, and every name that is named in both this world and the one to come (see Ephesians 1:21).

Drawing closer to God will allow you to learn about the enemy of your soul without making the mistake of the Israelites in Jeremiah 44. They decided, to their own detriment, to return to worshiping the queen of heaven instead of purifying their devotion to God. God is Jealous for you in the same way He was for them. He will not share your devotion with another.

Learning about this false queen might make you uncomfortable. It may even cause you to get defensive. Although we may not have little idols or shrines in our homes, we share the same societal norms as the Old Testament idolizers. Unless we are aware of the identity of the queen of heaven and recognize her influence over our culture, this adulteress will take advantage of us too. Joel C. Rosenberg has said, "To misunderstand the existence and nature of evil is to risk being blindsided by it."

Subsequent chapters will distinguish each queen of heaven alias by exposing their modern references, tracing their origins, and providing evidence about who they are as found in historical literature and Scripture. We will begin the oldest deity, Inanna, whose name literally means "queen of heaven."

---

[1] David L Brown, PhD, "Iraq in the Bible" [Online] http://logosresourcepages.org/OurTimes/iraq.htm [2015, Sep].

[2] Author's own questions devised from Jeremiah 44.

[3] W. Wright, LL.D., PH.D., *The History of John, the son of Zebedee, The Apostle and Evangelist. Apocryphal Acts of the Apostles. Vol. 2.* (London: Williams and

Norgate, 1871. 3-60.) 11,56 [Online] http://www.tertullian.org/fathers/apocryphal _acts_02_john_history.htm [2016, Sep].

[4] Pravin Thevathasan, "Carl Jung's Journey From God" [Online] https://www. catholicculture.org/culture/library/view.cfm?recnum=4676 [2015, Aug].

[5] Fragpane, *The Three Battlegrounds*, Kindle, A Short Glossary, 95%.

[6] Wagner, *Confronting the Queen of Heaven*, 25.

[7] Ibid., 7.

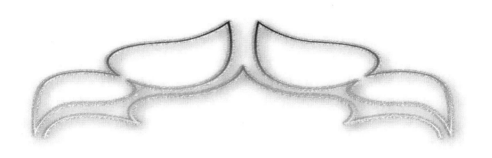

INANNA

Shocking was the best word to describe the news I received about a friend and coworker who I had not seen in a long time. The man I had long respected was now identifying himself as a woman. It was heart breaking to hear how his colleagues persecuted him in the name of religion. With this news, I struggled with the Old Testament law of emasculated men not being able to enter God's temple and the many verses that tell men to "be a man." Jesus calls us to love, yet I could not figure out how to approach my friend sincerely at an upcoming leadership conference. In the days right before our meeting, God answered my prayers and guided me through this delicate situation.

TODAY

In 2009, the child-friendly *Inanna and the Huluppu Tree* opened at Miami's Playground Theater. The Miami New Times described it, "as pagan as pagan gets, and in the best possible way."[1] The play began with Inanna descending from heaven and followed the story set forth in the famous poem of the same name found in the ancient work, *The Epic of Gilgamesh*. Although, sexual immorality was not a part of this production, we will soon discover the potential spiritual damage imposed on hundreds of unsuspecting young minds attending the play on school field trips.[2]

ORIGIN AND LOCALE

Inanna, whose Sumerian (Iraq) name literally means "queen of heaven," was the preeminent goddess among the Mesopotamians. Mesopotamia was the area between the Euphrates and Tigris rivers in Figure 1 (area below "FERTILE CRESCENT").

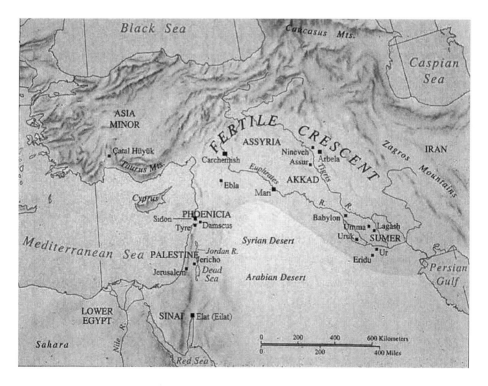

Figure 1. Map of Fertile Crescent

Inanna's lineage is unclear since she has three different fathers in Mesopotamian literature: the sky-god; Nanna, the moon god; and Enki, the god of wisdom.

Figure 2. Mask of Warka [3]

All the other queen of heaven aliases originated from Inanna. In *Inanna, Queen of Heaven and Earth,* Wolkstein claims,

> female deities were worshiped and adored all through Sumerian history…but the goddess who outweighed, overshadowed, and outlasted them all was a deity known to the Sumerians by the name of Inanna, 'queen of heaven,' and to the Semites who lived in Sumer by the name of Ishtar. Inanna played a greater role in myth, epic, and hymn than any other deity, male or female.[4]

DESIGNATIONS

Worshiping Inanna required offerings of incense, sheep, cakes, dairy, fruit, flowers, honey, or beer. As a goddess of love, procreation, and war, those in her cult believed her power extended over plants, animals, human fertility, death, and rebirth.[5] She was called: first daughter of the moon; Evening Star (Venus); Queen of Heaven and Earth; woman of the gods; and goddess who rules over the sky, earth, and underworld.

ICONOGRAPHY

The Mask of Warka from 3,100 BC (see Figure 2) is one of the earliest representations of the human face and believed to be a depiction of Inanna.[6]

Figure 3. Akkadian Seal [7]

As a sovereign goddess, who bore the crown of steppes on her head, Inanna either sat on a throne or stood with her foot on the back of a lion. Her symbol was the eight-pointed star, representing her astral form of Venus. An Akkadian cylindrical black-stone seal, dated between 2334 and 2154 BC display Inanna with her crown, star, and lion (see Figure 3). *Goddesses Who Rule* states that these "cylinder seals...were rolled in the wet clay used to seal storage jars and to make clay tablets.[8]

JESUS CHRIST IMPOSTER

During the first dynasty of Uruk, the Sumerian king list shows Gilgamesh reigning for 126 years. He is best known from *The Epic of Gilgamesh*, the great Sumerian poetic literature from 2100 BC. This work includes many hymns about Inanna that insinuate biblical text.[9] The most notable is *The Huluppu Tree* that contains similar elements to the Genesis creation account. The story includes a holy garden, the Euphrates River, a revered Huluppu Tree, a dragon (snake), and a flood. This hymn is central to the development of the queen of heaven and will be discussed throughout this book.

In another Gilgamesh hymn, *Inanna and the God of Wisdom*, her father, the "god of wisdom" while in a drunken stupor gave her things that you will recognize belong to Christ alone. These included the high priesthood, an enduring crown, the throne of kingship, the staff, the holy measuring rod/line, shepherdship, truth, descent into the underworld, ascent from the underworld, the sheepfold, and procreation. He gave her many other things too vulgar to include here.[10]

The Descent of Inanna, The Great Above to The Great Below is a hymn about her descent into the underworld where she loses her status as high priestess of heaven, is stripped naked, beaten, and dies. Flies created by her father bring her back to life and she ascends three days and three nights later.[11] This is a horrid counterfeit resurrection, schemed by the devil who is known as Beelzebul, meaning "lord of the flies" (see Luke 11:15).

In *The Holy Priestess of Heaven* hymn, her names include Holy

One who appears in heaven, Great Lady of Heaven, and First Daughter of the Moon. In the *Loud Thundering Storm* hymn she is also Proud Queen of the Earth Gods and Supreme Among the Heaven Gods.[12] *The Holy One* hymn states, "the male prostitutes comb their hair before you [Inanna]."[13]

The kings of Uruk were also considered husbands to Inanna upon their coronation which would include a *hieros gamos* ritual (similar to consumation of marriage) that was completed with a priestess who represented Inanna. The union would result in powers of sovereignty bestowed on the king followed by a great feast. Elisabeth Bernard explains how the king's identity was changed:

> The insignia of kingship were kept in Inanna's temple. These included the scepter and the crown, each resting on a separate altar. After proceeding to the temple, the new king would approach the throne, take up the scepter, and place the golden crown on his head. Discarding his personal name, he assumed a new royal name, a new identity.[14]

This union and change of identity is a counterfeit process of the marriage between the Bride of Christ and her Bridegroom, Jesus Christ (Isaiah 62:2-3, 5c-d).

SEXUAL IMMORALITY

Inanna's display of both female and male characteristics encouraged sexual immortality. Prostitutes, adulterers, transvestites, homosexuals, and pedophiles worshiped her. Transgenderism and cross-dressing was also common in the temples of Inanna. An ancient text attributes Inanna with changing the gender of men and women: "To turn a man into a woman and a woman into a man are yours, Inanna."[15] The famous hymn, *Inanna-Dilibad*, dating from 1976 BC, shows how men worshiped Inanna:

> They walk before the holy Inanna,
> Their right side they dress with men's clothes,
> They walk before the holy Inanna,
> Their left side they cover with women's clothes.
> They walk before the holy Inanna,
> To the great Lady of Heaven, Inanna, I would say:'Hail!'[16]

Many have been, and still are, Inanna's victims. The queen of heaven has grown bolder, evidenced by the loud voice of the LGBT community around the world today. These people have not only convinced themselves and many others of how harmless their lifestyle is, they now hold prominent positions in many churches.

While working at a previous job, I spent many breaks with a gay gentleman who was a local pastor. We had many conversations about homosexuality as presented in the Bible. He believed that the many verses that refer to it as sexual immorality are outdated and not meant for today.

PROSTITUTION

Ancient Babylonian texts say that Inanna "has sent the beautiful, unmarried and seductive prostitute Lilitu (Lilith) out into the streets and fields in order to lead men astray."[17] This Babylonian passage shows that Inanna was a pimp of sorts, acting as a superior figure over prostitutes. "Her temples throughout Mesopotamia were numerous, and sacred prostitutes of both genders were employed to ensure the fertility of the earth and the continued prosperity of the communities."[18] We will see that worship through prostitution is a common thread among all the queen of heaven aliases.

Proverbs 7 is a warning from King Solomon to his son about these seductive ones who lead men astray. This advice takes on more meaning now that we know the spiritual adulteress is the queen of heaven:

> Say to wisdom, "You are my sister," and call under-standing your intimate friend; that they may keep you from an adulteress, from the foreigner who flatters with her words. For at the window of my house I looked out through my lattice, and I saw among the naive, and discerned among the youths a young man lacking sense, passing through the street near her corner; and he takes the way to her house, in the twilight, in the evening, in the middle of the night and in the darkness.

> Behold, a woman comes to meet him, dressed as a harlot and cunning of heart. She is boisterous and rebellious, her feet do not remain at home; she is now in the streets, now in the squares, and lurks by every corner. So she seizes him and kisses him and with a brazen face she says to him: "I was due to offer peace offerings; today I have paid my vows. Therefore I have come out to meet you, to seek your presence earnestly, and I have found you. I have spread my couch with coverings, with colored linens of Egypt. I have sprinkled my bed with myrrh, aloes and cinnamon. Come, let us drink our fill of love until morning; Let us delight ourselves with caresses. For my husband is not at home, he has gone on a long journey; he has

taken a bag of money with him, at the full moon he will come home."

With her many persuasions she entices him; with her flattering lips she seduces him. Suddenly he follows her as an ox goes to the slaughter, or as one in fetters to the discipline of a fool, until an arrow pierces through his liver; as a bird hastens to the snare, so he does not know that it will cost him his life.

Now therefore, my sons, listen to me, and pay attention to the words of my mouth. Do not let your heart turn aside to her ways, do not stray into her paths. For many are the victims she has cast down, and numerous are all her slain. Her house is the way to Sheol, descending to the chambers of death. (Proverbs 7:1-27)

Proverbs chapter nine says that this same adulteress sits "by the high places of the city." High places in this context are associated directly with the worship of the queen of heaven (see chapter titled, "Asherah").

TAMMUZ

Inanna's husband was supposedly Dumuzi, a king of Uruk, who transformed into Tammuz, the god of vegetation. As a pagan god, he died at the end of every summer season due to his wife, Inanna, having him carried off to the underworld. After repenting of being ungrateful, he would be allowed to rise to the earth at the time of the Sumerian New Year. His sexual reunion with Inanna made everything bloom again.

The women of Israel would weep for Tammuz every year at the gate of God's temple. God shows Ezekiel these women in a vision.

> Then He brought me to the entrance of the gate of the Lord's house which was toward the north; and behold, women were sitting there weeping for Tammuz. He said to me, "Do you see this, son of man? Yet you will see still greater abominations than these." (Ezekiel 8:14-15)

Although Inanna's name never appears in Scripture, Israel's first patriarch was very familiar with who she was.

INANNA IN THE BIBLE

Inanna's main city was Uruk, located southeast of Baghdad, twelve miles from the Euphrates River. Uruk is believed to be the city in the Bible called Erech that was established by Nimrod (see Genesis 10:10). It is important to remember that Nimrod was a cursed man because of his grandfather, Ham (see Genesis 9:25). Perhaps Inanna was birthed in this place due to the curse.

Inanna's temple in Uruk was called Eanna, which means "House of Heaven." Figure 4 is a wall from the temple that is in the Berlin Museum. This temple was a prominent place in society. According to *Goddesses Who Rule*, "archaeological evidence suggests that it served as the center of economic, industrial, and intellectual life as well as a religious shrine."[19]

Besides Uruk, Nimrod also established Babylon, Akkad, Calneh, Nineveh, Rehoboth-Ir, Resen, and Calah. These cities along with Ashur, Ur, and Arbela had temples for Inanna (see map at Figure 1).

28

Figure 4. Wall of the Eanna temple [20]

Abraham, who was from Ur (see Genesis 11:31), was certainly familiar with Inanna.

> Joshua said to all the people, "Thus says the Lord, the God of Israel, 'From ancient times your fathers lived beyond the River, namely, Terah, the father of Abraham and the father of Nahor, and they served *other gods.* Then I took your father Abraham from beyond the River'...
>
> Now, therefore, fear the Lord and serve Him in sincerity and truth; and put away the gods which your fathers served beyond the River and in Egypt, and serve the Lord. If it is disagreeable in your sight to

serve the Lord, choose for yourselves today whom you will serve: whether the gods which your fathers served which were beyond the River, or the gods of the Amorites in whose land you are living; but as for me and my house, we will serve the Lord." (Joshua 24:2-3a, 14-15, italics added)

Abraham was righteous because he put away the other gods, including Inanna, and believed in the One True God. However, the queen of heaven krept back into the the lives of Abraham's descendants as is evident during Joshua's era.

ENCOUNTER WITH TRANSGENDERISM

Continuing with the story at the beginning of this chapter, three days before my encounter with my transgender friend, God broke through my unsettled thoughts with a question, "What is the worst sin ever committed by mankind?" I know we would all offer different answers, but for me it would definitely be Judas' deception. He is forever known as "the one who betrayed Jesus." As I read John 13 in my hotel room, the text suddenly took on new meaning for me.

Now before the Feast of the Passover, Jesus knowing that His hour had come that He would depart out of this world to the Father, having loved His own who were in the world, *He* loved *them to the end.* During supper, *the* devil *having already put into the heart of Judas Iscariot, the son of Simon, to betray Him.* Jesus, knowing that the Father had given all things into His hands, and that He had come forth from God and was

going back to God, got up from supper, and laid aside
His garments; and taking a towel, He girded Himself.
(John 13:1-4, italics added)

Jesus loved Judas to the very end. The true love of Christ came
pouring out for all to see when He washed Judas' feet.

My difficulty in this matter was settled. If Jesus could do that,
then I could certainly be sincere with my friend, who I had not seen
since before the change. My only desire was to share Jesus' love for
him. God moved my heart to compassion.

God not only settled my issue, He also put it on my heart to
wash my friend's feet. This was no small matter since it would
happen in a business environment with coworkers and people I
barely knew. Entirely swept away with the revelation of Judas, I did
not care what others would think. God, being the master of details,
helped me accomplish my task in an honoring way.

After giving a speech about what leadership means to me and
how my ultimate leader is Jesus Christ, I knelt down in front of my
friend. We were both in tears as I gently washed, anointed, and dried
his feet. I told him how much I appreciated him and wished him well
in retirement. It was a moment I will never forget. I was thankful for
the silence of any disapproval that may have been in the room.

As a counterpart to Inanna, Ishtar was nearly identical to her.
However, just like the other aliases, Ishtar morphed in order to fulfill
the needs of the cultures she was introduced to.

---

[1] Brandon K. Thorp, "Playground Theatre's Inanna and the Huluppu Tree Resurrects
Ancient Myths" December 2009 [Online] http://www.miaminewtimes .com/arts/

playground-theatres-inanna-and-the-huluppu-tree-resurrects-ancient-myths-6366174 [2015, Oct].

[2] Manuela Gabaldon, "The Playground Theatre. Inanna and the Huluppu Tree" Jan 28, 2010 [Online] http://www.miamiartguide.com/the-playground-theatre-inanna-and-the-huluppu-tree-2/ [2016, Mar].

[3] "File:UrukHead.jpg" [Online] https://commons.wikimedia.org/wiki/File:UrukHead.jpg [2016, Sep].

[4] Wolkstein, *Inanna*, xv.

[5] Ibid., xvi, 105-106.

[6] "File:Part of front of Inanna temple of Kara Indasch from Uruk Vorderasiatisches Museum Berlin.jpg" [Online] https://commons.wikimedia.org/wiki/File:Part_of_front_of_Inanna_temple_of_Kara_Indasch_from_Uruk_Vorderasiatisches_Museum_Berlin.jpg [2014, Jul].

[7] "Inanna/Ishtar (Isis)" [Online] http://www.whale.to/c/inanna.html [2014, Oct].

[8] Benard, *Goddesses Who Rule*, 75. Kindle Chapter 4, 31%.

[9] "Dating of the oldest fragments of the Gilgamesh account originally indicated that it was older than the assumed dating of Genesis. However, the probability exists that the biblical account had been preserved either as an oral tradition, or in written form handed down from Noah, through the patriarchs and eventually to Moses, there-by making it actually older than the Sumerian accounts which were restatements (with alterations) to the original...The most accepted theory among evangelicals is that both have one common source, predating all the Sumerian forms. The divine inspiration of the Bible would demand that the Genesis account is the correct version. Indeed the Hebrews were known for handing down their records and tradition. The Book of Genesis is viewed for the most part as an historical work, even by many liberal scholars, while the Epic of Gilgamesh is viewed as mythological. The One-source Theory must, therefore, lead back to the historical event of the Flood and Noah's Ark. To those who believe in the inspiration and infallibility of the Bible, it should not be a surprise that God would preserve the true account of the Flood in the traditions of His people. The Genesis account was kept pure and accurate throughout the centuries by the providence of God until it was finally compiled, edited, and written down by Moses. The Epic of Gilgamesh, then, contains the corrupted account as preserved and embellished by peoples who did not follow the God of the Hebrews." Frank Lorey, "The Flood of Noah and the Flood of Gilgamesh" 1997 [Online] http://www.icr.org/article/noah-flood-gilgamesh/ [2014, Aug].

[10] Wolkstein, *Inanna*, 12-27.

[11] Ibid., 52-73.

[12] Ibid., 93.

[13] Ibid., 97.

[14] Benard, *Goddesses Who Rule*, 72. Kindle Chapter 4, 28%.

[15] Leick, *Sex and Eroticism in Mesopotamian Literature* 62.

[16] Ibid., 157.

[17] Hurwitz, *Lilith, the First Eve*, Kindle, Part I, 18%.

[18] Joshua J. Mark, *Ancient History Encyclopedia*, "Inanna" 15 Oct 2010 [Online] http://www.ancient.eu/Inanna/ [2016, Mar].

[19] Benard, *Goddesses Who Rule*, 75. Kindle Chapter 4, 31%.

[20] Marcus Cyron, "Part the front of the Inanna temple of the Kara Indasch from Uruk" [Online] https://commons.wikimedia.org/w/index.php?curid=1542454 [2016, Sep].

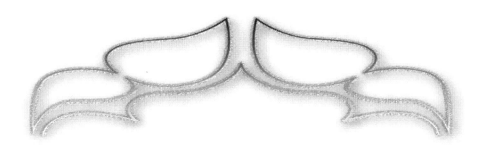

ISHTAR

Bigger than the mountains, I am
Empress of the gods, I am
Queen of heaven, I am
Mistress of Earth, I am
- Ishtar of Ancient Babylonia [1]

TODAY

THE IRAQI TELEVISION station, Ishtar TV, states on their website that they chose the name Ishtar because the goddess is a symbol of love, fertility, beauty, and tenderness. This media outlet "disseminates the principles of harmony, love and peace and renounces all forms of violence and discrimination in Iraq" on behalf of the name of Ishtar.[2] Ironically, Ishtar is anything but the wholesome goddess they make her out to be.

ORIGIN AND LOCALE

In 2330 BC, Sargon was the king of Akkad, in Mesopotamia. (Akkad is in the middle of the Fertile Crescent area on the map at Figure 1). According to the *National Geographic Magazine*, "Sargon of Akkad was born in secret to a priestess mother...In his youth, Sargon was visited by Ishtar...who loved him. Inspired by her, he rose from obscurity and took the world by storm."[3]

After becoming king and defeating the Sumerians, "Sargon made his daughter...the high priestess of the goddess Inanna in Ur...known to the Akkadians as Ishtar."[4] Besides the Akkadians, numerous other ancient people groups worshiped Ishtar, including the: Mittanians, Assyrians, Babylonians, Hurrians, Chaldeans, and Hittites.[5]

Ishtar temples were in the Assyrian cities of Assur, Arbela, Nineveh, Mari, Carchemish, and Babylon (see map at Figure 1). In these temples, she "was ministered to...by a large band of girls and women who were known as her consecrated or 'sacred' priestesses."[6]

The earliest archaeological evidence of a temple devoted to Ishtar, found in Mari, Syria, dates back to about 2500 BC. The Louvre Museum website states, "Many worshipers placed votive statues in their own image in the temples of Mari, thus perpetuating their prayers to the deity."[7]

DESIGNATIONS

Ishtar was a chief goddess of Babylon whose likeness was paraded through the streets of Babylon every year. In the following verses the apostle John describes the queen of heaven's appearance and brutal behavior as Ishtar:

The woman was clothed in purple and scarlet, and

adorned with gold and precious stones and pearls, having in her hand a gold cup full of abominations and of the unclean things of her immorality, and on her forehead a name was written, a mystery, "Babylon the great, the mother of harlots and of the abominations of the earth." And I saw the woman drunk with the blood of the saints, and with the blood of the witnesses of Jesus. (Revelation 17:4-6)

Worshipers considered Ishtar a goddess of nature, passion, war, love, sex, fertility, and mothers. She was known as: first born of heaven and earth; first born of the gods; the creator of gods and beings; Gracious Mother of Creation; giver of plenty; hearer of the supplications of the sinner; the mistress of battle who breaks the weapons of the enemy; healer; and purifier.[8] Many of these designations belong to Jesus Christ alone.

Different locales had unique ancient names they used for Ishtar including:

- Attar by the Arameans
- Belat-ekallim and Innin by the Sumerians
- Atargatis by the Hittites
- Mulliltum and Mullissu by the Assyro-Bablyonians

In each of these cultures, she is the wife of their chief god and considered "goddess par excellence." As a supreme deity, all other gods bowed to her as their queen.

She was called Holy Virgin and Virgin Mother long before the Catholic Mary was, but Ishtar's virginity was due to her freedom from never being married, not her sexual purity.

Assyrians worshiped Ishtar as the divine mother, protector of kings, and the guarantor of oaths and treaties. Her cult members sought her out to take violent action on those who broke their word. In a hymn written by the Assyrian king, Assur-Banipal, he praises her power and strength in defeating his enemies.

Figure 5. Ishtar relief at the Louvre Museum [9]

Isaiah prophesied about Assyria being the rod of His anger against Israel and describes it as a kingdom of idols "whose graven images were greater than those of Jerusalem and Samaria" (Isaiah 10:10). These Assyrian graven images included Ishtar. We will talk further about the graven images of Jerusalem and Samaria in the chapter titled, "Asherah."

GENDER

Although referred to as female, this deity's gender is not specific. Sometimes portrayed with facial hair, an ancient text praises the beard of Ishtar.[10] Inscriptions from two Ishtar temples located on the upper Euphrates support Ishtar being simultaneously male and female. The following quote is from a French article about Assyrian prophecies by Simo Parpola. In translation, the male and female pronouns used for Ishtar are intermingled throughout the article, perhaps due to her seemingly dual gender.

> In the prophecies, the king is presented as the son of the goddess Ishtar, a semi-divine being, part human, part god. In an oracle, the goddess says: "I am your father and mother, I brought you into my wings."[11]

ICONOGRAPHY

Inanna's metamorphosis into Ishtar was due to Sargon's defeat of the Sumerians. This explains why these two queen of heaven aliases resemble each other so closely. The eight-pointed star and lion are symbols of Ishtar also.

The following is a conversation the king of Assyria, Assur-Banipal, had with another god that reveals another form of Ishtar.

> You were a child, Assurbanipal, when you sat in the lap of the Queen of Nineveh. Her four teats are placed in your mouth (Ishtar is often pictured as a wild cow, so four teats are normal for her); two you suck and two you spray milk on your face.[12]

This is not the only alias of the queen of heaven who took on the form of a cow. We will discuss this further in the chapter titled, "Isis/Hathor."

JESUS CHRIST IMPOSTER

Many stories of Inanna were passed down to Ishtar. These closely parallel many narratives of the Bible. *The Descent of Ishtar* is a vulgar counterfeit story of Jesus' death, descent to Hades, and resurrection. In this story, many of Ishtar's names are similar to those attributed to Jesus Christ alone. They include: the first and the last; ruler of heaven and earth; morning star; all seeing; life giver; light bringer; exalted light of heaven; forgiver of sins; and shepherd(ess).

It is important to keep in mind that satan always counterfeits the truth by twisting the Word of God. God exists outside of time and so does His truth.

SEXUAL IMMORALITY AND PROSTITUTION

A plaque illustrating sexual activities along with writings by Assyrian kings, Shalmaneser I and his son, Tukulti-Ninurta I, indicate that sexual immorality had specific functions in the cult of Ishtar. Sacred prostitution was central to Ishtar temple worship since Ishtar was venerated as a goddess of prostitutes. Simo Parpola says, "We know that the Assyrian princes were entrusted, even children, to the temples of Ishtar, almost certainly to be nursed and raised by hierodules (sacred prostitutes) who embodied aspects of the maternal Goddess."[13]

Book 1, section 1999, of *Herodotus* gives an explicit explanation of a law for all females in Babylon to participate in temple prostitution. They could not return home until they fulfilled their obligatory temple duty.[14] These women were required to forfeit their virginity to a stranger who would in return make a payment to the temple. This coupling was an enactment of a sacred wedding; a joining to the deity of the temple.

Ishtar, as the Mother of Harlots, has spread her cultic forms of worship over the entire world and throughout history, including today's generations. Do not be mistaken, harlotry is not an act of anyone's free will. Fashioned by the devil and propagated through the queen of heaven, prostitution is one of the most severe forms of bondage for the human race.

TAMMUZ

Like her predecessor Inanna, Ishtar also had a relationship with the biblical Tammuz. In Tablet VI of *The Epic of Gilgamesh*, Gilgamesh says to Princess Ishtar, "Tammuz, the lover of your earliest youth, for him you have ordained lamentations year upon year." Ezekiel 8:14 talks about this yearly mourning as we read in the previous chapter.

SPLIT PERSONALITY

Assyrian king Assur-Banipal wrote about the Ishtar of Arbela and the Ishtar of Nineveh as separate deities. He claimed Ishtar of Arbela was his creator who gave him everlasting life and the Ishtar of Nineveh was his mother who gave him unparalleled kingship. In the *Rise and Fall of the Assyrian Empire*, Ragozin explains Ishtar's multiple identities:

> [In the city of Arbela] she was worshiped pre-eminently in her martial character as the goddess of war and battle, the inspirer of heroic deeds, and the

41

giver of victory; while in Nineveh, it was her feminine, voluptuous aspect which predominated, and she was essentially the goddess of love, of nature and all delights. So marked became this division, that she, so to speak, split herself into two distinct deities.[15]

OFFERINGS

The cake and drink offerings made to the queen of heaven as recorded in Jeremiah are evident in the worship of Ishtar. A paper about Ishtar's multiple identities, published by the British Institute for the Study of Iraq, says that ancient Assyrian texts describe a royal ritual in which the Assyrian king and a priest gave gifts of drink and food to the gods worshiped in both Assyrian and Babylonian temples belonging to different versions of the goddess Ishtar. They included Ishtar of the stars, Assur-Ishtar, Assur-Ishtar of Arbela, Ishtar the panther, and Ishtar Lady of Nineveh.

A Babylonian hymn about Ishtar mentions *kamanu* sacrificial cakes offered to Ishtar. A panel found in an Assyrian palace shows the king making a drink offering to Ishtar after killing a lion that says,

> I, Ashurbanipal [Assur-Banipal], king of the universe, king of Assyria, whom Assur and Ninlil have endowed with surpassing might. The lion which I slew, the terrible bow of Ishtar, lady of battle, I aimed at them. I brought an offering, I poured wine over them.[16]

BRUTALITY

Ishtar's influence as a deity of war caused kings and generals to be brutally cruel, handing out all forms of torture for those who chose to defend themselves. The Assyrians fierceness and disregard for human suffering were why their conquests were so successful.

Bringing captured kings to their capital city of Nineveh in order to skin them alive was a common practice. This is no doubt, why many of Israel's kings chose to pay a tribute to the Assyrian kings. In doing this, Israel feared the queen of heaven more than God.

In *The Goddess Revival*, Ishtar's own words reveal her savagery.

> Ishtar, descending into the netherworld, shouts: "I will smash the door, I will shatter the bolt, I will smash the doorpost, I will move the doors, I will raise up the dead, eating the living, so that the dead will outnumber the living."[17]

The spiritual ramification of this statement is clear when you consider the significance of the first Passover in Egypt. The death angel, on assignment to kill all that were first born, could not enter through any door that had the blood of an unblemished lamb on the doorpost. The only ones covered by the blood were God's elect. In the New Covenant, the blood of Jesus also covers God's elect (believers).

Considering this, the above quote of Ishtar could be worded as, "I will smash Jesus (who calls Himself the door in John 10:9), I will smash the purifying work of Jesus' blood, I will raise those He considers dead, eating those who are alive in Him so that my followers will outnumber His."

Unfortunately, the falling away of believers will occur, but not due to the queen of heaven causing any harm to Jesus. The falling away occurs because of the devil's deception in making his queen of heaven appear as something charming and satisfying.

Revelation 17:2 explains, "kings of the earth committed acts of immorality, and those who dwell on the earth were made drunk with the wine of her immorality." This can happen when believers muddy their faith in God by having connections with the queen of heaven. 1 Timothy 4:1 states, "the Spirit explicitly says that in later times some will fall away from the faith, paying attention to deceitful spirits and doctrines of demons." This is why it is so important for believers to keep their faith in God completely pure.

In the end Jesus is the One who will smash the queen of heaven.

> For she says in her heart, 'I sit as a queen and I am not a widow, and will never see mourning.' For this reason in one day her plagues will come, pestilence and mourning and famine, and she will be burned up with fire; for the Lord God who judges her is strong. (Revelation 18:7-8)

HUMAN TRAFFICKING

Modern day sex slavery reflects many aspects of the Ishtar cult including split personality disorder, physical violence, and submission through brutality. The queen of heaven operates through a cycle of seduction, monetary profit, abuse, and ultimately death. We saw this pattern in chapter seven of Proverbs and as described throughout the Ishtar cult. This same cycle is also evident in the global prostitution of today.

The film, *Nefarious, Merchant of Souls,* is a documentary that uncovers the disturbing trends within modern sex slavery around the world. Victims restored from human trafficking tell their stories throughout the film.

Most of them have the same story of being charmed in some

form either by a stranger who feigns falling in love with them, or by the promise of a good job from a fake employment agency, or by the glamour of prostitution in Las Vegas. Then their pimps or kidnappers broke them down physically, emotionally, and spiritually. These women were more fortunate than many of their fellow prostitutes who ended up dead. No matter how it appears in public, it is a life of bondage.

Ishtar held great influence over many people and places in the Bible, including the city of Nineveh.

ISHTAR AND NINEVEH

I watched a documentary about the Hanging Gardens of Babylon, which was one of the Seven Wonders of the Ancient World.[18] It showed how archaeology proves these gardens were in Nineveh, not the famed Babylon. The narrator mentioned the "goddess of Nineveh," which of course sparked my attention. I was not surprised to find out that this goddess was the queen of heaven's alias, Ishtar.

In the Bible Nimrod established the city of Nineveh (see Genesis 10:11). It was also Jonah's dreaded destination and the target of Nahum's oracle. It is likely that Nineveh was named in honor of the Sumerian deity Nin. Nineveh was located across the Tigris River from Mosul, and in its heyday, was the largest city in the ancient world.

Ishtar's history in Nineveh goes back to the Akkadian King Manishtushu, son of the famous Sargon, who built a temple and ziggurat to Ishtar during his reign from 2269-2255 BC. Known as the Temple of Emenue, it was located in the district of Emashmash.[19]

About 400 years later the Assyrians overtook Nineveh and the love affair with Ishtar transcended empires. The city became home and capital to most of the Assyrian kings, until its capture in 607 BC by the Babylonians.

There is currently a large excavation site in modern Turkey where Nineveh once thrived. Thompson, one of the original excavators, concluded that a portion of this site was the Temple of Emenue that was rebuilt by the Assyrian King Shamshi-Adad I who died in 1776 BC.[20] The pomp and devotion of this king are made clear in his own narcissistic words.

> Shamshi-Adad, the strong one, king of the universe
> ...beloved of the goddess Ishtar: The temple
> Emenue...which Manishtishu, son of Sargon, king of
> Akkad, had built, had become dilapidated. The temple
> which none of the kings who preceded me – from the
> fall of Akkad until my sovereignty, until the capture of
> Nurrugu, seven generations have passed – had rebuilt.
> I laid the threshold of the temple, the equal of which
> for perfection no king had ever built for the goddess
> Ishtar in Nineveh. I raised its ziggurat. Thus I
> eminently completed it and named it Ekidurkuga,
> "The Storehouse of Her Treasure"...Therefore the
> goddess Ishtar, my mistress, has given me a term of
> rule which is constantly renewed.[21]

There are records of twelve Assyrian kings, all taking credit for restoring the Ishtar temple in Nineveh, from the period beginning about 1809 BC and ending around 626 BC. This Ishtar temple housed a library and a bank, making it an important community site. These commerce activities of pagan temples were carried over into the house of God and frowned upon by Jesus (see Matthew 21:12).

JONAH

Jonah was a prophet during the reign of Israel's King Jeroboam II. Debate lingers about whether Jonah wrote the Book of Jonah or if it was written later in the third century BC. In his article, "Who was the 'King of Nineveh in Jonah 3:6?" Paul Ferguson provides compelling proof that the author was indeed Jonah. This helps us understand who the man was that heard and heeded Jonah's prophecy:

> There is an intriguing body of evidence that suggests the 'king of Nineveh' in Jonah 3:6 may not have been the head of the entire kingdom of Assyria but only the governor of the province of Nineveh. Governors of Nineveh held this office in 789 and 761 BC. Their names were Ninurta-mukin-ahi and Nabu-mukinahi respectively.[22]

When the governor and people heard Jonah's proclamation that Nineveh would be overthrown, they believed in God. "When God saw their deeds, that they turned from their wicked way, then God relented concerning the calamity which He had declared He would bring upon them" (Jonah 3:10).

This might be why the Assyrian records are silent about the Ishtar temple during Jonah's lifetime. Unfortunately, King Sargon II of Assyria revived the temple in the early seventh century BC when Nineveh became the official capitol city of the Assyrian Empire.

NAHUM

The Medes and Babylonians burned and permanently destroyed

all of Nineveh, including the Ishtar temple, in 612 BC.[23] The prophet Nahum foretold this:

> The Lord has issued a command concerning you [Nineveh]: "Your name will no longer be perpetuated. I will cut off idol and image from the house of your gods. I will prepare your grave, for you are contemptible." (Nahum 1:14)

The third chapter of Nahum explains that it was the harlot who destroyed Nineveh. This harlot was none other than Ishtar, whose cultic savagery comes alive in these verses:

> Woe to the bloody city, completely full of lies and pillage; her prey never departs. The noise of the whip, the noise of the rattling of the wheel, galloping horses and bounding chariots! Horsemen charging, swords flashing, spears gleaming, many slain, a mass of corpses, and countless dead bodies — they stumble over the dead bodies!

> All because of the many harlotries of the harlot, the charming one, the mistress of sorceries, who sells nations by her harlotries and families by her sorceries. (Nahum 3:1-4)

Nineveh was not the only place the Assyrians clashed with God's people. The Assyrians constantly terrorized the children of God in their own land. The map at Figure 6 will give you an idea of the extent of the Assyrian Empire. I recommend using Appendix B, Kings Chart as reference while reading the next section.

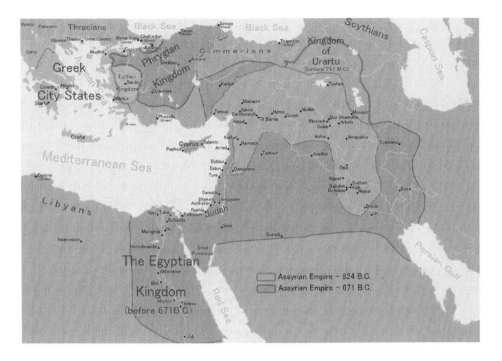

Figure 6. Map of Assyrian Empire [24]

ISHTAR, ASSYRIA, AND GOD'S PEOPLE

MENAHEM AND PEKAH (ISRAEL)

The Assyrian king Tiglath-Pileser III, who is called "Pul" in the Old Testament, played an important part in Israel's history. When Pul came against Israel's northern tribes, King Menahem offered him a large tribute in hopes of quelling the advance and forming an alliance that would strengthen Israel's kingdom (see 2 Kings 15:19).

Pul bided his time until Pekah became king, at which time he conquered the land of Naphtali (one of Israel's twelve tribes). The first captives were taken to Assyria where they were most certainly integrated into the Ishtar cult (see 2 Kings 15:29).

After that, King Pekah, along with the king of Aram, went on a rampage against Judah, fulfilling the prophecy of the Lord against King Ahaz. The army camped just north of Jerusalem, causing Ahaz and his people to shake with fear "as the trees of the forest shake with the wind" (Isaiah 7:2).

AHAZ (JUDAH)

The prophet, Isaiah, brought God's counsel to King Ahaz saying there was no need to fear, but added, "If you will not believe, you surely shall not last" (Isaiah 7:9). Ahaz did not believe the prophet and the northern kingdom waged war on Jerusalem, killing 120,000 men and leading captive 200,000 of women and children of Judah.

Following this devastation, attacks on Judah continued from other foreign kings. Ahaz turned to Pul, instead of God, for help. After giving the Assyrian king silver and gold from God's temple as payment, Pul defeated Damascus in Aram (see 2 Kings 15:17-16; 1 Chronicles 28:20).

King Ahaz then went to Damascus, saw the altars of the Aramean gods, and commissioned his priest to build identical ones in Judah.

> He [Ahaz] sacrificed to the gods of Damascus which had defeated him, and said, 'Because the gods of the kings of Aram helped them, I will sacrifice to them that they may help me.' But they became the downfall of him and all Israel. (1 Chronicles 28:23)

In doing this, Ahaz introduced the Ishtar cult to Israel.[25] Perhaps this is how temple prostitution was instituted in the land of Israel.

King Ahaz demonstrated how the queen of heaven could

interfere with rational thought and make something evil appear as if it is good. Just like forbidden fruit, the queen of heaven can be desirable, no matter the situation. She can morph quickly in order to maneuver an unsuspecting soul into her clutches.

HOSHEA (ISRAEL)

Pul claims to have chosen Hoshea as the next king of Israel's northern tribes. When Pul's son, Shalmaneser IV, became king of Assyria, he threatened Hoshea who responded by paying him tribute. However, Hoshea made the mistake of withholding a regular payment, which was met by the wrath of the new Assyrian king.

Shalmaneser invaded the northern kingdom, imprisoned Hoshea, and led Israel into Assyrian captivity (see 2 Kings 17:1-6).

> Now this came about, because the sons of Israel had sinned against the Lord their God...they walked in the *customs* of the kings of Israel which they had introduced. The sons of Israel *did things secretly* which were not right against the Lord their God. (2 Kings 17:7-9, italics added)

The customs and things done in secret included worshiping the queen of heaven. The northern tribes removal from their homeland was due to the influence of the queen of heaven and personal choices to not have a pure devotion to God alone.

HEZEKIAH (JUDAH)

After the Assyrians captured the northern tribes of Israel, they set their course for Judah. Unlike Ahaz, King Hezekiah sought God's help. The prophet Isaiah also turned to God on behalf of the nation:

Truly, O LORD, the kings of Assyria have devastated all the countries and their lands, and have cast their gods into the fire, for they were not gods but the work of men's hands, wood and stone. So they have destroyed them. Now, O LORD our God, deliver us from his hand that all the kingdoms of the earth may know that You alone, LORD, are God. (Isaiah 37:18-20)

God responded, "*She* has despised you and mocked you, the virgin daughter of Zion; *She* has shaken her head behind you, the daughter of Jerusalem!" (Isaiah 37:21-22, italics added).

Why would God use the pronoun "she" is these verses? Some may say it is a pronoun used to reference the country of Assyria, but I propose "she" refers to the queen of heaven. Due to Hezekiah's faith in God, the Assyrians were destroyed and their king ran home.

Unfortunately, future kings of Judah were not convinced of God's superior power over the queen of heaven. A pattern in the Old Testament emerges with Israel's leaders: they experienced decisive victory when trusting God or devastating defeat when mixing their worship of God with the queen of heaven.

Let there be no strange god among you nor shall you worship any foreign god. I, the Lord, am your God, who brought you up from the land of Egypt; open your mouth wide and I will fill it. But My people did not listen to My voice, and Israel did not obey Me. So I gave them over to the stubbornness of their heart, to walk in their own devices. Oh that My people would listen to Me, that Israel would walk in My ways! I would quickly subdue their enemies and turn My hand against their adversaries. (Psalm 81:9-14)

It is not surprising that the Babylonians also revered Ishtar, since Assyria defeated and ruled Babylon many times. In the next section, we will find out how the queen of heaven's influence caused destruction to God's people through Babylon, as well.

ISHTAR, BABYLON, AND GOD'S PEOPLE

Jeremiah prophesied before and during Babylon's three sieges of Judah. Babylon was the predominant world power that God used as a rod of judgment against His adulterous wife, Israel.[26]

Figure 7. Ishtar Gate replica in the Pergamon Museum, Berlin [27]

Nebuchadnezzar was the king of Babylon when Jeremiah prophesied to Israel about returning to the Lord. Jeremiah 44 records their response of rededicating their worship to the queen of heaven. (This was the immediate confirmation to my vision.)

Nebuchadnezzar restored Babylon to the glorious city it was more than a millennium earlier when Hammurabi proclaimed the Mesopotamian province of Babylonia as "supreme in the world." Nebuchadnezzar defeated Egypt and controlled all of Syria and part of Palestine, but it is his siege of Jerusalem in 597 BC and subsequent deportation of the Hebrews to Babylon that made him famous.

Figure 8. Babylon Processional Way and Ishtar Gate model [28]

The land did not see the Jews again until seventy years later. During those seven decades, they lived in one of the most prominent kingdoms of Ishtar.

ISHTAR GATE AND PROCESSIONAL WAY

Nebuchadnezzar built the enormous Babylonian Gate of Ishtar (see Figure 7). At one time it was one of the Seven Wonders of the

Ancient World. Constructed around 575 BC, it was the eighth gate to the inner city of Babylon on the north side. In the 1980s, Saddam Hussein reconstructed a smaller replica of the Ishtar Gate in Iraq, where Babylon once was. It survived the recent US war in Iraq. Lions, dragons, and bulls cover the blue gate.

Parading an idol statue of Ishtar through the Ishtar gate and down the Processional Way (see Figure 8) occurred each year during the New Year's celebration. Excavated in the early 1900s, much of the original gate is currently in the Pergamon Museum in Berlin. Other parts of the gate are in museums around the world.[29]

The Ishtar gate was at one end of the Processional Way and the Etemenanki ziggurat stood at the other.[30] Built at some point in the second millennium BC, Etemenanki could be the original tower of Babel referred to in Genesis 11.

The tower of Babel ziggurat represented all nations when they were still only one nation (see Genesis 11:1-9). A modern version of this was at the opening ceremony of the 2012 Olympic Games in London. A huge ziggurat-shaped hill was at one end of the stadium with a looming tree at the top. The ceremony included parading flags of every nation up the ziggurat and planting them from the bottom all the way up to the tree. The tree is also symbolic of the queen of heaven, which we will explore in the chapter titled, "Asherah."

The chapter about Lilith was one of the last chapters I wrote simply because this alias is not obvious in Scripture. God Himself exposed her to me. Just as she is hidden in the Bible, her dark presence works as a powerful undercurrent in our society.

[1] Temple Yani Matre, "Celebrating the Goddess, Attributes :: Ishtar " [Online] http://www.celebrerladeesse.net/attributs-dishtar.html [2014, Jan].

[2] Channel Asteralvdhaiah [Online] http://ishtartv.com/about.html [2016, March].

[3] National Geographic Partners, LLC. "The Most Influential Figures of Ancient History." National Geographic Time Inc. Specials (2016): 112. Magazine. 11.

[4] Ibid., 13.

[5] Reade, *The Ishtar Temple at Nineveh*, 368-369.

[6] Ragozin, *The Rise and Fall of the Assyrian Empire*, Kindle, Chapter 1, 11%.

[7] Iselin Claire "Ebih-Il, the Superintendent of Mari" Department of Near Eastern Antiquities: Mesopotamia [Online] http://www.louvre.fr/en /oeuvre-notices/ebih-il-superintendent-mari [2015, Apr]. Shortly after learning about this temple, I came across a Japanese video game character with the name Marik Ishtar. The name seems to be a play on the Ishtar temple in Mari. Marik Ishtar is a multiple-personality anime (Japanese adult cartoon) that shares the same cruel traits as his namesake.

[8] Morris Jastrow, "Ishtar" [Online] http://encyclobooks.com/The-Religion-of-Babylonia-and-Assyria/ISHTAR-1-GODDESS-ARBELA-ASSYRIAN.htm [2014, Jan] and Simo Parpola, Collège de France, "The God Assur/The Goddess Ishtar" 2008 [Online] http://annuaire-cdf.revues.org/413?lang=en#authors , http://www.digitorient.com/wp/wp-content/uploads/2008/12 /Parpola-Istar.pdf [2014, Jan].

[9] "File:Ishtar Eshnunna Louvre AO12456.jpg" [Online] https://commons.wikimedia.org/wiki/File:Ishtar_Eshnunna_Louvre_AO12456.jpg {2016, Dec].

[10] Reade, *The IshtarTemple at Nineveh*, 347.

[11] Simo Parpola, Collège de France, (2008). "The God Assur/The Goddess Ishtar" [Online] http://annuaire-cdf.revues.org/413?lang=en#authors [2014, Jan].

[12] Porter, "Ishtar of Nineveh and Her Collaborator, Ishtar of Arbela, in the Reign of Assubanipal" 42.

[13] Parpola, "The God Assur/The Goddess Ishtar."

[14] "Herodotus Book 1: Clio [190]" [Online] http://www.sacred-texts.com/cla/hh/hh1190.htm [2014, Jul].

[15] Ragozin, *The Rise and Fall of the Assyrian Empire*, Kindle, Chapter 1, 6%.

[16] Gordon Franz MA, (May 28, 2009)."Nahum, Nineveh and Those Nasty Assyrians." [Online] http://www.Biblearchaeology.org/post/2009/05/Nahum2c-Nineveh-and-Those-Nasty-Assyrians.aspx [2015, Apr].

[17] Spencer, *The Goddess Revival*, 58.

[18] Secrets of the Dead, Unearthing History (May 6, 2014) "The Lost Gardens of Babylon" [Online] http://www.pbs.org/wnet/secrets/the-lost-gardens-of-babylon-watch-the-full-episode/1203/ [2015, Oct].

[19] Grayson, *Assyrian Royal Inscriptions,* 23.

[20] Reade, *The Ishtar Temple at Nineveh,* 355.

[21] Grayson, *Assyrian Royal Inscription,* 24.

[22] Paul Ferguson, "Who was the 'King of Nineveh' in Jonah 3:6?" Tyndale Bulletin 47.2 (Nov. 1996), 301-314.

[23] Reade, *The Ishtar Temple at Nineveh,* 385.

[24] Ningyou, "File:Map of Assyria.png" [Online] https://commons.wikimedia.org/ wiki/File:Map_of_Assyria.png [2016,Nov].

[25] It appears from their inscriptions as well as from their names that Arameans worshiped Assyro-Babylonian gods such as...Ishtar (whom they called 'Attar). Wikipedia, "Arameans" [Online] http://en.wikipedia.org/wiki/Arameans [2014 Jan].

[26] *International Inductive Study Bible,* 1195.

[27] Rictor Norton [CC BY 2.0 (http://creativecommons.org/licenses/by/2.0)], via Wikimedia Commons. [Online] .https://en.wikipedia.org/wiki/Ishtar_Gate# /media/File:Ishtar_Gate_at_Berlin_Museum.jpg [2016, Sep].

[28] "File:Pergamon Museum Berlin 2007109.jpg" [Online] https://commons. wikimedia.org/wiki/File:Pergamon_Museum_Berlin_2007109.jpg [2016, Sep].

[29] Wikipedia, "Ishtar Gate" [Online] http://en.wikipedia.org/wiki/Ishtar_Gate [2014, Jan].

[30] Ancient History Encyclopedia, "Lion's Head from the Processional Street, Babylonia" [Online] http://www.ancient.eu.com/image/2106/ [2014, May].

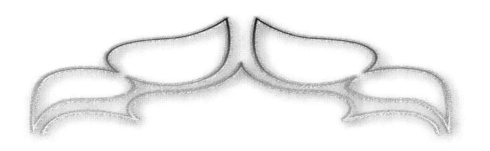

LILITH

GOD REVEALED LILITH to me at a quilting convention, of all places. In a room filled with quilters, I sat within feet of a quilt that, until then I had admired through instructional YouTube videos. We were all eager to learn the detailed techniques used to create this work of art. Little did I know, that by the end of the day this award-winning quilt would transform into an object of horror right before my eyes.

TODAY

In Jewish mystical literature, Lilith was the first spouse of Adam. She became the first feminist of all time when she refused to lie beneath Adam and fled Eden. Over time, painters, poets, and playwrights have shared her story as the first Eve. The Metropolitan Museum of Art in New York and the Sistine Chapel are two of the more famous places around the world that bear the image of Lilith.

The name of Lilith has headlined operas, festivals, dance

productions, books, movies, songs, and even a popular online Jewish magazine that claims to be "frankly feminist." *Cheers* was always a favorite TV show of mine, but little did I know the significance of the powerful female character's name, Lilith.

The soft pornographic Victoria Secret Angels became such a sensation with their undergarment commercials that they now have their own annual TV show. They bear a stunning resemblance to Lilith, described in the Talmud with big wings, long hair, and seductive body language. The name "Dark Angel," refers to both Lilith and a Victoria Secret angel.

The video game, *Final Fantasy*, has a character named Lady Lilith, who has a light and a dark presence. The figure of light is a female angel with big wings and has what appear to be miniature male genitalia. Its dark figure has bat wings, pointed ears, and goat's horns. This reveals the tactics of the ancient goddess who first appears as seductively innocent, but quickly turns into a man-eating monster.

Lilith's popularity even reaches into environmentalism as revealed in the *The Goddess Revival:*

> Much of the interest in earth-centered, goddess worship has arisen as a result of a freshly-empowered feminist spirituality, a repackaged witchcraft, and a concern for the environment. Unfortunately, Judaeo-Christainity is perceived, with its emphasis on the biblical mandate to "subdue" the earth, as to blame for the world's ecological crisis and the oppression of women. Faced with what many see as an inequitable present and a bleak future, some are looking back to the early history of humanity for answers for today.

Archaeologist Marija Gimbutas has been key in reviving praise for supposed prepatriarchal civilization in which, she claims, matristic, goddess-worshiping cultures held nature in higher esteem and thus lived in greater harmony with the environment.

Author Elinor W. Gadon concurs: "In the late twentieth century there is a growing awareness that we are doomed as a species and planet unless we have a radical change of consciousness. The reemergence of the Goddess [queen of heaven] is becoming the symbol and metaphor for this transformation...(and) has led to a new earth-based spirituality."[1]

Lilith made an appearance on the HBO series, *True Blood*, as a character who was the root ancestor of the vampire race. According to the show's Fandom website, this character was "made in God's image" and worshiped as a god. Aside from the name Lilith, the character is also called, "the First, the Last, the Eternal." This stolen Biblical reference of Jesus is unmistakable.

ORIGIN AND LOCALE

Originally worshiped in Greece, Spain, Babylon, Germany, and Persia (Iran) Lilith's fame has spread throughout the entire modern world. Babylonian and Jewish artifacts, the Talmud, the *Testament of Solomon*, the Dead Sea Scrolls, the Zohar, and more than one Jewish Midrash (collection of Jewish commentaries and stories) expose Lilith's history. Just like Inanna and Ishtar, archaeological evidence shows her possible origins as the ancient Mesopotamian civilization, as described in *The Hebrew Goddess*.

The earliest mention of a she-demon whose name is similar to that of Lilith is found in the Sumerian king list which dates from ca. 2400 B.C.E. It states that the father of the great hero Gilgamesh was a Lillu [Lilith] demon. The Lillu was one of four demons belonging to a vampire or incubi-succubae class...Originally these were storm-demons, but because of a mistaken etymology they came to be regarded as night demons.[2]

DESIGNATIONS AND GENDER

The term Lilith is the singular form, whereas Liliths, Liliathas, and Lilin are the plural forms. The Babylonian Lilu was male while the Talmudic Lilith was female.

Lilith was called: Ancient Mother; Ardat Lili; Matronit; First Eve; Queen of Heaven; Heavenly Queen of Israel; Black Madonna; Veiled Bride; Maid of Desolation; the great goddess of death; serpent (that deceived Adam and Eve); the strangler (of children); end of all flesh; Mother of Demons; Queen of Sitra Abra; and end of days. Her association with prostitution was clear with her names of Mother of All Prostitutes and Woman of Harlotry.

Known at times as a virgin or an angel, Lilith was deceptively enchanting, seductive, and fatally destructive. Her reputation included infecting people with illnesses, diseases, and death. Many Christians believe they are sick because it is God's will.

This false thinking is rooted in Calvinism (a major branch of Protestantism); however, coming into agreement with sickness and disease is also another form of worship to the queen of heaven. I discuss this further in the chapter titled, "Defeat the Queen of Heaven."

ICONOGRAPHY

The following description of Lilith is from the Zohar, which is the foundational work in the literature of Jewish Kabbalistic mystical thought that dates back to the thirteenth century AD. You will notice it bears resemblance to Proverbs 7 that was written twenty centuries earlier:

> She adorns herself with many ornaments like a despicable harlot, and takes up her position at the crossroads to seduce the sons of man. When a fool approaches her, she grabs him, kisses him, and pours him wine dregs of viper's gall. As soon as he drinks it, he goes astray after her from the path of truth, she divests herself of all ornaments which she put on for that fool...

> Yon fool goes astray after her and drinks from the cup of wine and commits with her fornications and strays after her. What does she thereupon do? She leaves him asleep on the couch, flies up to heaven, denounces him, takes her leave, and descends.

> That fool awakens and deems he can make sport with her as before, but she removes her ornaments and turns into a menacing figure. She stands before him clothed in garments of flaming fire, inspiring terror and making body and soul tremble, full of frightening eyes, in her hand a drawn sword dripping bitter drops. And she kills that fool and casts him into Gehenna.[3]

Take note of how she flies to heaven and denounces the fool. According to Revelation 12:10, satan accuses men before God. This seems to strengthen the idea that I proposed about the queen of heaven and satan being one just as Jesus and Father God are One.

Figure 9. *Burney Relief* of Lilith (edited)[4]

In his book about Lilith, Siegmund Hurwitz quotes the ancient Labartu texts that clearly show that Lamashtu (Babylonian name for Lilith) has characteristics very specific to satan:

> Her head and her face are those of a fearsome lion
> ...she roars like a lion...A whore is she. Raging,
> furious, fearsome, terrifying, violent, rapacious, ram-

paging, evil, malicious, she overthrows and destroys all that she approaches.[5]

The famous *Burney Relief* (see Figure 9) from Southern Iraq dates back to the Old Babylonian period. It shows Lilith as a bird-woman with wings, dew-claws below the knees, and taloned feet. Bearing the same crown of steppes as Inanna, she is flanked by two owls and stands on the backs of two lions.[6] In another similar relief, she has feathered legs from the knees down, which clearly depicts her as part owl.

Figure 10. Lilith in the Sistine Chapel (edited) [7]

The Jewish Kabbalistic text says she had hundreds of bands of demons under her control. This might be why the Burney Relief also depicts Lilith with the status of the highest demonic order: a rod and ring in each hand. Signifying royalty, the rod is a symbolic meas-uring stick and the ring represents the flat, round earth. The same symbols of royal sovereignty are evident today as a scepter and orb.[8]

Michelangelo painted the most famous and shocking image of Lilith in the Sistine Chapel (see Figure 10). In his disturbing depic-tion of the fall, the tree of life is to the right of Adam and Eve with a being that is half woman and half snake wrapped around its trunk. The revolting, hybrid snake offering Eve an apple has the anatomy of a female from the waist up. The Notre Dame Cathedral also shows Lilith in this form (see Figure 11).

Figure 11. Lilith in the Notre Dame Cathedral (edited)[9]

The idea of Lilith being a snake or bird and associated with the tree of life originated in the tale of *Gilgamesh and The Huluppu Tree,* introduced in the chapter titled, "Inanna." In the story, Inanna tends the huluppu tree that was previously uprooted in a flood from the Euphrates, with plans of using the wood once it matured.

Dashing Inanna's hopes, ten years later a snake, a bird, and the screeching Lilith took up residence in her beloved tree. In the poem, Lilith says to Inanna, "I live in the Tree of Life, with the serpent in the roots and the Thunderbird in its branches. Why are you afraid of me, afraid of the tree?"[10]

Kelley Hunter in *Living Lilith: Four Dimensions of the Cosmic Feminine* says that the tree and animals in the poem are all a part of Lilith:

> They are found in world-wide myths as symbols of life-giving power associated with the goddess [Lilith]. The serpent represents the chthonic wisdom of earth, oracular powers, and the *kundalini*, the subtle life force that awakens consciousness as it courses up the tree of the spinal cord. Winding in the roots of the tree, the serpent also grounds the energy into the earth. (italics added)[11]

I will discuss the kundalini in more detail shortly.

CITIES OF THE SEA

The hybrid snake form of Lilith is known as the Greek Lamia, whose home is in the deep of the sea. Lilith's headquarters was believed to be in the "Cities of the Sea" located in the extreme depths of the ocean where many demons live. The Bible confirms that there are evil spirits and lost human spirits in the sea:

> Woe to the earth and the sea, because the devil has come down to you, having great wrath, knowing that he has only a short time. (Revelation 12:12)

And the sea gave up the dead which were in it, and
death and Hades gave up the dead which were in
them; and they were judged, every one of them
according to their deeds. (Revelation 20:13)

In *Witch Doctor and the Man,* Bishop Kanco shares about his
exploits in the spiritual world of the ocean depths before his
conversion to Christianity.[12] Bishop Kanco recounts, "A person must
have spiritual eyes to tell the differences between demons and the
human being spirits in the sea. Some of the demons in the bottom of
the sea appear in the forms as humans while others proudly sport
their fallen natures and appear as gods and goddesses."[13]

Yoga Kundalini

The quote by Kelly Hunter above and other sources state that
Lilith is the *kundalini* referred to in yoga disciplines. Professor Kurt
Keutzer from UC Berkeley explains, "'Kundalini' literally means
coiling, like a snake. In the classical literature of hatha yoga,
kundalini is a coiled serpent at the base of the spine. The image of
coiling, like a spring, conveys the sense of untapped potential
energy."[14]

In *The Healing Gods: Complementary and Alternative Medicine
in Christian America,* Candy Gunther Brown helps us understand
the purpose of kundalini.

Moving kundalini is the object of many yoga
practices. Kundalini is a force represented as a female
serpent and sometimes envisioned as a goddess, who
lies dormant, coiled at the base of the spine. Her male
counterpart and lover is Shiva, who resides in the

crown of the head or brain. Practicing yoga awakens kundalini so that she uncoils and travels up the spine, opening chakras along the way.

When kundalini reaches the sahasrara chakra, at the crown of the head, kundalini and Shiva unite, and one attains mahasam-adhi (bliss) or moksha (liberation from the cycle of birth and death). Kundalini is closely associated with sexual energy, and physical sex plays a role in certain (especially some Tantra) yoga forms.[15]

There is a lot of contention among Christians concerning the topic of yoga. Many believe there is nothing wrong with doing it purely as a form of exercise. Keutzer says, "There is certainly nothing wrong with trying to improve your health, but there is a tension between awakening an energy that will ultimately burn up the ego and trying to shape that energy to simply fulfill an ego-oriented motive."[16]

The purpose of the movements and positions prescribed in yoga is to use an energy that brings your self-will under control; whether intended or not, that energy will do more than help you maintain a physical stance. That energy is rooted in Eastern Mysticism and worship of the queen of heaven.

RELATIONSHIP WITH ADAM

The supposed relationship between Adam with Lilith has different versions, depending upon what period of Jewish Midrashic literature you read. In *Mythology*, Hamilton explains:

In the Talmudic Erebim (18b), it is said that while Adam was under the curse (before the birth of Seth), he sired demons – both shedim and lilin...There is a similar passage in the Nidda (16b). This was during the time immediately following the death of Abel and the banishment of Cain. For one hundred and thirty years, Adam would not lie with his wife, Eve. Lilith came to him instead and bore all manner of demons (plagues of mankind) by his seed.

Later rabbinical sources identified her as the first wife of Adam, cast from the Garden because she would not submit completely to his rule. Here, again, she fled into the wilderness, where many traditions say she became the mother of demons after coupling with fallen angels like Lucifer and Samael. Jewish folklore, in works like the Haggadah and the Chronicles of Jerahmeel, often presents her as the consort of these fallen angels.[17]

The later story of Lilith being Adam's first wife is based on the idea that the Bible supports two creation accounts, the first in Genesis chapter one and the second in the following chapter. These verses are specifically about Eve:

God created man in His own image, in the image of God He created him; male and female He created them (Genesis 1:27).

The Lord God fashioned into a woman the rib which He had taken from the man, and brought her to the man (Genesis 2:22).

Chapter two also states, "This is the account of the heavens and the earth when they were created" (Genesis 2:4). Therefore, the two Eves rationale would also require two Adams, two sets of heavens, and two earths. Clearly, chapter two is an exposition of chapter one, which means the relationship between Lilith and Adam is not supported in Scripture.

The Babylonian and Assyrian immersion with the queen of heaven is proven throughout this book. Therefore, the Jewish beliefs about Lilith were clearly a result of their captor's influence. Isaiah, which is the only place Lilith is mentioned in the Bible, was written about 1,600 years before the stories of Adam and Lilith were composed. Therefore, we must trust the rest of the biblical record, in which there is no mention of Lilith, let alone her being the spouse of Adam or God.

CHILD KILLER

Many believe that Lilith's mad rampage to destroy the descendant infants of Adam and Eve was her response to being banished from the Garden of Eden. Some think that the Arab phrase, *Lilla Abi*, which literally means "be gone Lilith," is the origin of the word *lullaby*. These songs were meant to quiet a baby in order to not awaken Lilu demons; this explains the disturbing phrases and angelic guards found in so many older lullaby songs.

The fears perpetuated around Lilith and babies are supported archaeologically by the numerous amulets and talismans found with inscribed Jewish incantations. Amulets were hung in the room of a woman in labor in order to fend off Lilith. On one such amulet, Lilith meets with the prophet Elijah on her way to give a mother "the sleep of death, to take her son and drink his blood, to suck the marrow of his bones and to eat his flesh."[18] Sayings like this are most likely what gave rise to Lilith's title as the Mother of Vampires.[19]

Archaeology has also uncovered many similar older amulets with childbirth incantations from the Assyrian and Babylonian Kingdoms, proving that the Jewish ones are a product of Israel's captivity. An amulet found at the archeological site, Arslan Tash in northern Syria, dates back to the seventh century BC has the inscription, "O, Flyer in a dark chamber, Go away at once, O Lili!" [20] These amulets are still popular today.

Lilith's savagery with children is also found in the *Testament of Solomon* (third century BC Greek text) as described by Hurwitz, "As the terrible, devouring mother, she tries to harm pregnant women and to steal their newborn children. She is always poised to kill the child..."[21] Satan did the same in Revelation 12:4, "the dragon stood before the woman who was about to give birth, so that when she gave birth he might devour her child."

While abducting newborn children, Lilith took on many forms including a black cat, which is equated with the Egyptian god, Bastet. Perhaps this is the source of the modern myth that cats can steal the breath of newborns. I will discuss Bastet further in the chapter titled, "Artemis."

$SEDUCTRESS$

The *Alphabet of Ben Sira,* written during the Medieval Age (AD 700-1000) not only made Lilith out to be a baby-eating demon but also a seductress of men, known as a *succubus.* People believed that she died as a virgin and returned as a ghost to prey on men in their sleep, seeking what she was deprived of in life. Men feared this spiritual being because of her fatal embrace.

Strange traditions resulted from these fears. The Jewish Virtual Library states, "Belief in her erotic powers led some Jewish communities to adopt the custom of sons not accompanying their dead father's body to the cemetery because they would be shamed by the hovering presence of their demon step-siblings, born of their father's seduction by Lilith."[22]

Considering the nightly exploits of Lilith, it is not surprising to learn that the word *nightmare* "originated in the 1300s as a nigtmare, a female spirit that attempted to afflict a sleeper with the feeling of suffocating at night."[23] In the book, *How to Interpret Dreams and Visions*, Perry Stone explains, "From a Jewish rabbinical point of view, nightmares and unclean dreams can be the result of a demonic spirit (called a lilin or a night spirit) that is in the room of the person attempting to sleep or in the process of sleep."[24]

FALSE CLAIMS

Besides being the alleged spouse of Adam, she was reported to be the spouse of Lucifer and God at different times. In *The Hebrew Goddess*, Patai explains, "The Zoharic idea that the most terrible outcome of the destruction of the temple and exile of Israel was that because of them God was forced to accept Lilith as his consort."[25] This is no doubt where her title, Queen of Heaven, is from.

Jewish mystical literature and other sources also consider Lilith to be the Queen of Sheba (see Gensis 10:1-10) and one of the two harlots who appeared before Solomon to gain judgement over a disputed child (see 1 Kings 3:16-28). The first is "based on a Jewish and Arab myth that the Queen of Sheba was actually a *jinn*, half human and half demon" who in generations past was known as a "snatcher of children and a demonic witch."[26]

This idea has carried through into German mythology and English folklore from the Ashkenazi Jews. The Bible makes no mention of the harlot nor the Queen of Sheba being anything but human.

LILITH IN THE BIBLE

Hidden in one verse of the Old Testament, Lilith's Hebrew name is spelled Liyliyth. Isaiah 34 contains God's judgment on Edom and resembles a narrative of hell with brimstone, intense heat, and utter desolation. Unclean and demon-possessed animals roam the dismal land. Depending on the Bible version, Liyliyth is translated as either "screech owl" or "night monster" in the Isaiah 34:14:

> The wild beasts of the desert shall also meet with the wild beasts of the island, and the satyr shall cry to his fellow; the *screech owl* also shall rest there, and find for herself a place of rest. (KJV, italics added)

> The desert creatures will meet with the wolves, the hairy goat also will cry to its kind; Yes, the *night monster* will settle there and will find herself a resting place. (NASB, italics added)

LILITH IN ASTROLOGY

Astrology is the "study of the movements and relative positions of celestial bodies interpreted as having an influence on human affairs" according to Google. To base our life on what is happening in the sky is warned about in Deuteronomy 4:19, "beware not to lift up your eyes to heaven and see the sun and the moon and the stars, all the host of heaven, and be drawn away and worship them and serve them." With this in mind, we will look at Lilith in astrology.

Lilith lays claim to the Black Moon, the Dark Moon, the Lilith Star, and the Asteroid Lilith. All of which provide foreboding elements to the Zodiac.

BLACK MOON LILITH

The Black Moon Lilith is an abstract area that is supposedly one of the focus points of the moon's orbit. In the book, *Black Moon Lilith*, Kelley Hunter tells how Lilith can affect zodiac signs: "Persons who have a strong Black Moon signature show different aspects of Lilith's charismatic magic."[27]

This phenomenon is deceptively good: "Its underlying creative live force and spiritual impulse illumines the inner pathway with the most heart for each seeker of Truth and Love."[28] Psychological aspects of the Black Moon include self-centeredness, dwelling in the past, and struggling with fears. Through a relationship with Jesus, who is Truth and Love, these things can be overcome.

DARK MOON LILITH

The Dark Moon Lilith is an unverified dark area circling the earth that appears to absorb light rather than reflect it. Although well documented, this moon remains elusive. The Dark Moon supposedly causes one to desire forbidden fruits, have fears that make no sense, be regretful, and live under compulsions. Doing something as simple as depending on horoscopes to predict the future can cause these sorts of problems in life.

Hunter says both the Dark and Black Moons "can carry heritage from ancestral and/or spiritual lineages, by tradition and by blood."[29] The Bible explains how idol worship spanning generations can occur.

> You shall not make for yourself an idol, or any likeness
> of what is in heaven above or on the earth beneath or
> in the water under the earth. You shall not worship

them or serve them; for I, the Lord your God, am a jealous God, visiting the iniquity of the fathers on the children, and on the third and the fourth generations of those who hate Me. (Deuternomy 5:8-9)

LILITH STAR

The Lilith Star is a name the Hebrews called the Algol star. Also known as "Satan's head" the star's path is connected to violence and catastrophes. In *Living Lilith*, Hunter says, "There is a medical term derived from this star, 'algology' referring to the study of pain. It also gives its name to 'alcohol.'"[30]

The star is three times the size of the sun and twice as hot. This helps to explain why so many believe it to be a raw, intense feminine power, "Algol carries the collective rage for the suppression and repression of this power."[31]

ASTEROID LILITH

The asteroid Lilith #1181 is located between Mars and Jupiter. Character traits of having this asteroid in your Zodiac include resentment, inner rage, independence, repressed anger, and abuse. Hunter says those who are influenced by Lilith refuse to submit to authority or compromise their beliefs.[32]

They are known to stir up discontent around their ideals. This form of Lilith is gaining a stronghold today through the intentional blurring of gender roles and bringing those who were once outcasts into the limelight.

Summarizing the astrological aspects of Lilith, *Living Lilith – Four Dimensions of the Cosmic Feminine* explains, "Lilith confronts us with issues of equality in relationship, and can reflect psychological issues of suppressed rage, resentment, sexual manipulation, and self-exile."[33] This shows that the queen of heaven stirs up unhealthy worship through anger and rage. The apostle Paul said: "Let all bitterness and wrath and anger and clamor...be put away from you, along with all malice" (Ephesians 4:31) and, "Now you also, put them all aside: anger, wrath, malice..." (Colossians 3:8).

ASTROLOGY IN THE BIBLE

Giving heed to astrology accompanies worship of the queen of heaven in the Bible (Asherah and the calves are other aliases of the queen of heaven.):

> They forsook all the commandments of the Lord their God and made for themselves molten images, even two calves, and made an Asherah and worshiped all the host of heaven and served Baal (2 Kings 17:16).

> For he rebuilt the high places which Hezekiah his father had destroyed; and he erected altars for Baal and made an Asherah, as Ahab king of Israel had done, and worshiped all the host of heaven and served them (2 Kings 21:3).

Although God created the stars for important reasons, we must be careful not to allow them to have a defining influence in our lives.

ENCOUNTER WITH LILITH

In coming face to face with Lilith at that quilting convention, I found out firsthand how this demonic principality operates. I share this story with you in order to help you identify the queen of heaven in your sphere of influence, to encourage you not to be fearful, and to show you how to respond to it.

That award winning art quilt, mentioned at the beginning of this chapter, was made by one of my favorite online quilting teachers (I will call her Marie). When I found out that she would be at the convention, I eagerly signed up for her classes.

The quilt now hung, bigger than life, right behind Marie as she taught. I had often tried to duplicate many of its details in my own quilts, using Marie's videos as a guide. Throughout the day, students admired it, taking pictures, and pointing out the amazing quilting designs it contained.

As Marie taught and began to interact with the students, I began to observe something very strange. In the dynamics of a typical quilting class, the students and teacher form a creative environment with no wrong answers due to the versatility of the quilting art. This was not so in her class; it was full of rules, questions that were impossible to answer, and student responses that were never right.

After rudely letting someone know their answer was wrong and revealing the proper answer, Marie would ask the student their birth month and proceed to tell them negative characteristics about their personalities. Despite this, the women seemed to be entranced as they giggled at her antics. Her stories included instances of her superior experience and knowledge compared to the ignorance of others, especially the male engineers who designed the quilting machines that she promoted. All of this made for a very bizarre atmosphere.

Throughout the day, I often stared at that big quilt since it towered directly behind her. During the afternoon session, it seemed to transform. Although the quilt was entirely abstract, I was seeing large owls loom out of each corner. After that moment, they were unmistakable and very disconcerting every time I looked at the quilt.

At the end of class, I purposed to stay until most of the students had left in order to share God's truth with Marie about something she had said at the onset of the class.

When there were just a few women left I kindly told her, "You said earlier, 'God have mercy on me, I'm cursed forever!', and I wanted to let you know that if God has mercy on you, you are certainly not cursed forever." She smiled and replied, "Did I say that? I'm a very spiritual Christian person on the inside. Thank goodness! I can take all of God's mercy I can get!"

After that, the few of us who remained asked her questions about her quilt, curious to know how long it took to make and how she had accomplished the precision and detail that was involved.

Then one lady asked, "What were you thinking when you made it?" Marie's reply put me on guard even more, "I don't remember making any of it. It's like I wasn't around whenever I was working on it."

Then she said, "Since there's just a few of you left, would you like to see something cool about my quilt?" The others eagerly followed her as I lagged behind. As soon as Marie put her hand up in front of the quilt, I became suspicious. She told us to let our hand hover over it without touching it.

"Can you feel that?" she asked. I knew immediately what was going on and refused to participate. I feigned taking pictures and was able to retreat back to my seat. In doing so, I listened to the other women fall prey to an evil scheme.

One said, "I can feel heat over the black sections and it is cooler on the red areas."

To which Marie responded, "That's the energy that I made the quilt with."

At that moment, a woman came in the room and asked me a

question, after which I quickly left. I had the feeling of being spiritually vomited on and had an urgent need to get alone with my heavenly Father. Once in my room, I fell to the floor and prayed.

Crying out, I told the empty room, "That quilt needs to be burned because it's a product of witchcraft." Then God put it on my heart to do a web search for "owls" and "witchcraft." Within seconds, I learned that the owl is associated with the underworld and with the demonic maiden, Lilith.

As I read, tears rolled uncontrollably down my face and I turned to God for strength. I would be completely overwhelmed if it were not for Him holding me up spiritually as I kept reading. The same words that I read countless other times in learning about the queen of heaven jumped off the screen at me.

I prayed in tongues for God's comfort and for Marie's salvation. Then the sobs came pouring out. I felt as if God was sharing His pain with me. The turmoil Marie was in hurt Him deeply! I was heart-broken for this woman because she was unknowingly in the grip of Lilith.

Marie's entanglement with the queen of heaven was unmistakable, not only through her quilt, but also in her domineering feminist attitude and physical ailments she suffered with. In a fit of anger, I called out the demons that were troubling her. I prayed healing for the tremors that were evident as she drew on the whiteboard and for her sleepless nights to end. I cried out for her to know her true identity.

I knew in that moment that God was jealous for her soul. He wanted Marie to receive the generous fullness of His love. God gave me a message to share with her, so I asked Him for an opportunity to talk with her in private the next day.

In the morning, Marie was even more brazen in class,

introducing herself as someone who operates in energy fields. The same disturbing behavior from the day before continued even more strongly. Her manipulation caused me to be in constant prayer, asking God to protect me; I did not want to be part of this game. I praised God her focus never fell on me.

When class was finished, I offered to buy Marie lunch. I brought our food back into her room to find her quietly talking with a distressed student. I sensed she did not want me to hear her telling the young, vulnerable girl that she was an "indigo" and describing to her the energy fields that accompany the color. I knew she was consoling the girl through her knowledge of chakras that are categorized by colors. The young girl was enthralled.

When Marie finished, she and another student sat with me to eat. This did not deter me since I figured this other woman must need to hear what I had to say or else God would not have had her sit with us. I told Marie that God had a message for her.

She was very excited to hear it so I said, "God has a gourmet meal for you and He wants you to quit eating and serving Jack-In-The-Box food. God is jealous for you."

The student started to protest at what I said. Surprisingly, Marie corrected her and said, "She said God is jealous for me, not of me."

I was impressed that she caught hold of God's message. She looked at me and asked if I was speaking this into her life; I assured her I was. She received my words but did not understand what I meant about God being jealous for her. I told her that He wants her all to Himself and does not want her involved in all the other stuff.

Then she informed me that everything is God, even all the evil. I challenged her saying, "Everything is not God." I went on to share that the Bible says we are all sinners. The student then chimed in, telling me that this was my opinion and interpretation.

I said, "No, it is black and white in God's Word. It is not my interpretation." Marie continued her discourse that everything is good and that even Buddhism is good.

Quickly interrupting her, I said, "That's exactly what I mean about God being jealous for you! You can't follow Buddhism and God. He wants you all to Himself."

At that point, both Marie and the student began to argue about what I said, but strangely, they did not include me in their discussion. I knew then that it was time for me to leave. I was obedient and had delivered God's message.

Just then, a lady from the morning class came to the door and waved me over to her. Thankful for God's escape plan, I went to her. In less than five minutes, we discovered we were sisters in Christ. I explained to her what had just transpired. Then she pulled me out into the hallway and began praying a warrior's prayer! God was so good in providing me a partner that would cover the situation in prayer and bring me immediate encouragement.

Just like Jeremiah, if we keep our devotion to God pure and without the defilement of idols, other gods, or any form of ungodly worship, then it will be easy to see the queen of heaven at work. When confronted directly by the queen of heaven, seek out God's plan and obey what He puts in your conscience to do. In this way, the queen of heaven poses absolutely no threat to us and we are able to break the hold of the queen of heaven in other people's lives by sharing God's truth with them.

Isis was the first alias to impose the queen of heaven's presence into people's worship of the One True God. By creating a false Savior, the queen of heaven stole the glory that belonged to God alone.

[1] Spencer, *The Goddess Revival*, 21-22.

[2] Raphael Patai, *The Hebrew Goddess*. (Detroit: Wayne State University Press, 1967) Kindle, Chapter 10, 50%.

[3] Patai, *The Hebrew Goddess*. Kindle, Chapter 10, 52%.

[4] "File:Burney Relief Babylon -1800-1750.JPG" [Online] https://commons. wikimedia.org/wiki/File:Burney_Relief_Babylon_-1800-1750.JPG [2016, Sep]. Edited.

[5] Hurwitz, *Lilith the First Eve*, Kindle, Part I, 10%.

[6] The British Museum, "The 'Queen of the Night' Relief" [Online] http://www.british museum.org/explore/highlights/ highlight_objects/me/t/queen_of_the_night_ relief.aspx [2014, Jul].

[7] "File:Michelangelo Bounarotti - The Fall and Expulsion of Adam and Eve - detail.JPG "[Online]. https://commons.wikimedia.org/wiki/File: Michelangelo _Bounarotti_-_The_Fall_and_Expulsion_of_Adam_and_Eve_-_detail.JPG [2016, Sep].

[8] Rev. Arthur E. Whatham, "The Meaning of the Ring and Rod in Babylonian-Assyrian Sculpture" [Online] http://archive.org/stream/jstor-3141137/3141137 _djvu.txt [2014, Jul].

[9] "Rebecca Kennison , "File:France Paris Notre-Dame-Adam and Eve.jpg "[Onine] https://commons.wikimedia.org/wiki/File:France_Paris_Notre-Dame-Adam_ and_ Eve.jpg [2016, Sep]. Edited.

[10] *The Huluppu Tree*" [Online] http://www.piney.com/BabHulTree.html [2016, Nov].

[11] Hunter, *Living Lilith*, Kindle, Chapter 1, 9%.

[12] Since this book was a stretch for my faith, I sent it to a friend who was a missionary in South Africa. He told me that all it contained was indeed true for the dark spiritual roots of the continent.

[13] Kanco, *Witch Doctor and the Man, Fourth Generation Witch Doctor Finds Christ*, 40 (also see Revelation 20:13, 12:12).

[14] Kurt Keutzer (June 2012), "Kundalini FAQ" [Online] http://www.eecs.berkeley. edu/~keutzer/kundalini /kundalini-faq.html#1a [2015, Aug].

[15] Brown, *The Healing Gods*, 47.

[16] Keutzer, "Kundalini FAQ".

[17] Hamilton, *Mythology*, 189-190.

[18] Jewish Virtual Library, A Division of the American-Israeli Cooperative Enterprise (2008), "Lilith" [Online] https://www.jewishvirtuallibrary.org/jsource/judaica/ ejud_0002_0013_0_12540.html [2015, Aug].

[19] David Kulik, Robyn Reed, Lora Bailey, and Stephanie Brooks (December 27, 2004) "Lilith– Mother of Vampires" [Online] http:/ /homepages.udayton.edu /~farreljp /Vampires/lilith.htm [2016 Apr].

[20] Patai, *The Hebrew Goddess*, Kindle, Chapter 10, 50%.

[21] Hurwitz, *Li0lith, the First Eve*, Kindle, Part I, 8%.

[22] Jewish Virtual Library, "Lilith."

[23] Stone, *How to Interpret Dreams and Vision*,54.

[24] Ibid., 55.

[25] Patai, *The Hebrew Goddess*. Kindle, Chapter 10, 56%.

[26] Jewish Virtual Library, "Lilith."

[27] Hunter, *Black Moon Lilith*, 2.

[28] Ibid.

[29] Hunter, *Living Lilith*, Kindle, Chapter 6, 68%.

[30] Ibid., Chapter 2, 18%.

[31] Ibid., 19%.

[32] M. Kelley Hunter (April/May 1999), The Mountain Astrologer, Editor's Choice Article, "The Dark Goddess Lilith" [Online]http://www.mountainastrologer.com/ standards/editor's%20choice/articles/lilith_hunter/lilith.html [2016 April].

[33] Hunter, *Living Lilith*. Kindle, Chapter 2, 13%.

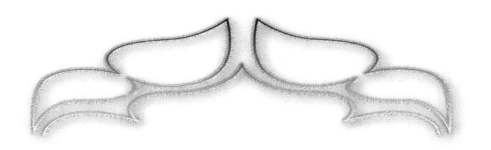

ISIS / HATHOR

IN A HOTEL room in Kansas City, I watched a documentary on my laptop that was previously saved to watch on a rainy day. Little did I know that it would reveal how the queen of heaven, known as Isis, has come between those within a major religious group and the One True God. My heart broke midway through the video. I sobbed as God put in my heart His overwhelming love for those tied up in this lie. Hours later, I forced myself to watch the rest.

TODAY

You may remember Isis as a TV character from the 1970s show *Shazam* or the early 2000s show *Smallville* about Superman. Isis has made many appearances through entertainers like Lady Gaga, Katy Perry, and Rihanna. The "Virgin" Madonna paraded through the 2012 Super Bowl XLVI half-time show as Isis, surrounded by a full Egyptian entourage. I found it interesting that years later she had to defend her son who posted a violent ISIS (Middle East terrorist group) video online. Before the advent of this militant terrorist group, many businesses also carried the Isis name based on the false belief that she represents hospitality and goodness.

ORIGIN AND LOCALE

Figure 12. Map of Roman Empire at its peak (all shaded areas)

Isis was initially an obscure goddess who lacked her own dedicated temples, but she grew in stature becoming one of the most important deities of ancient Egypt. *The Archaeological Study Bible* states:

> From the Eighteenth Dynasty of Egypt has come a stele that contains a hymn celebrating the rule of Osiris over Egypt. In the myth Osiris was slain by his

86

brother, the god Seth, but was restored by his sister/ consort, the goddess Isis...The hymn proclaims how the "Two Lands" (i.e., Upper and Lower Egypt), the Nile and all the beasts of Egypt honor Osiris, Isis and Horus.[1]

The temple of Isis at Medinet-Madi (southwestern Egypt) describes an all-encompassing Isis as "all other goddesses named by the peoples."[2] Her cult was popular throughout Greece and the entire Roman Empire where she was worshiped from modern England to Afghanistan (see Figure 12).

Figure 13 Wings and throne headdress of Isis on a coffin [3]

Archaeological evidence proves that Isis was the principal deity worshiped in and around Philippi. On the Acropolis Hill at Philippi there was a temple complex devoted to Isis that dates back to the early fifth century BC through the third century BC. In *Women and Worship at Philippi*, Abrahamsen says the following about the Isis cult:

> There were daily services at which the shrines were opened and the statue awakened and clothed. Congregational singing and praise, sacred dances and processions and initiations for chosen members were all part of the religious praxis; water was of great significance and was considered to be holy water from the Nile...Both men and women participated in and were officials of the cult, which survived in various parts of the Empire through the mid-sixth century CE.[4]

Worship of Isis continues today throughout the world by an organization called The Fellowship of Isis that began in 1976. Its headquarters is the Clonegal Castle in Ireland that boasts 26,000 members. They proclaim that "Isis of 10,000 names" is the "Divine Mother of all beings." "The Fellowship accepts religious toleration, and is not exclusivist. Members are free to maintain other religious allegiances. Membership is open to all of every religion, tradition and race."[5] Represented religions include Catholic, Protestants, Buddhists, Spiritualists, Hindus, and Pagans.

DESIGNATIONS

Known as the divine mother of ancient Egypt, Isis is the wife of Osiris and is the celestial mother of the sun god, Horus. Worshiped as a funerary goddess, Isis specialized in magic that cured the sick and brought the dead back to life. She was known as: the goddess of ten thousand names; principal of all gods and goddesses; the one who speaks across the river of time; Universal Nature; Eternal Virgin of the World; Mother of All; more powerful than a thousand soldiers; the clever-tongued one whose speech never fails; and Queen Of Heaven, Earth and the Underworld.[6]

ICONOGRAPHY

Isis took on the form of a woman, bird, calf, or a mixture of the three. As you can see in many of the pictures in this chapter, she was often portrayed as a woman with wings. The *ankh* cross that she often held in her left hand represents the "key of the Nile" or the "key of life." It was originally the item used to secure her belt and is a representation of male and female.

Figure 14. *The Virgin with Child* [7]

I took the picture of Isis and her son Horus in Figure 14 at The Nelson-Atkins Museum of Art in Kansas City, Missouri. The figurine dates between 664-632 BC. It is one of many identical statues found around the world that are titled, *The Virgin with Child*. These statues were around long before the famous images of the Catholic Mary with baby Jesus on her lap.

The headdress in Figure 14 is a sun disk between the horns of a bull. It represents the sun rising between the horns of Taurus in the zodiac. Isis also wore a headdress of a throne because that is the meaning of the name, "Isis." She was literally the personification of the throne that Pharaoh sat on. A coronation in Egypt was not effective until a king had literally mounted the throne and sat in the lap of the goddess.[8]

ḤATHOR

Isis was the human form of the much older Egyptian calf deity, Hathor (see Figure 15). Hathor was popular in Canaan (the future land of Israel) in the eleventh century BC in the holy city of Hazor, which at that time was ruled by Egypt. Early stone inscriptions seem to suggest that the Hebrew workers in the mines of Sinai (1500 BC) worshiped Hathor, who they identified with their goddess Astarte.[9]

Isis and Hathor are both related to the sun god, Ra. Hathor is his mother, but it is unclear if Isis is Ra's mother, daughter, or both. Therefore, there is no distinction between the Isis and Hathor, explaining why they are considered the same goddess.

God put me in places where I could not miss His desire for me to include this goddess in my book, but something was missing. Was she in the Bible? I was excited when God showed me that indeed she was. In fact, she had a huge influence on the children of Israel.

ISIS IN THE BIBLE

MOSES

Shortly after leaving Egypt, the people of Israel came to the foot of Mount Sinai. God called Moses up on the mountain in order to show him His plan for His children. After waiting for Moses to come back down from Mount Sinai, the people became agitated. They were ready to leave, but did not want to go alone so they asked Aaron to make them a god.

> Then all the people tore off the gold rings which were in their ears and brought them to Aaron. He took this from their hand, and fashioned it with a graving tool and made it into a molten calf; and they said, "This is your god, O Israel, who brought you up from the land of Egypt." Now when Aaron saw this, he built an altar before it; and Aaron made a proclamation and said, "Tomorrow shall be a feast to the Lord." (Exodus 32:3-5)

This is the first biblical reference of defiling the worship to the One True God with worship to the queen of heaven. The people created a golden Hathor idol with an altar for worship and they worshiped the Lord with a feast. The Hebrew word for Lord is Jehovah, which is the proper name of the One True God. Scripture says that they also played, danced, and sang. Many believe this is a nice way of describing an orgy.

Did the people know they were not to worship as they did in Egypt? Let me take you to earlier in the narrative to find out. Before Moses went up on Mount Sinai, the people spent three days getting

Figure 15. Hathor statue in the Cairo Egyptian Museum [10]

themselves ready to meet with God. On the morning of the third day, God descended on the mountain with fire and spoke as thunder directly to the people.

> I am the Lord your God, who brought you out of the land of Egypt, out of the house of slavery. You shall have no other gods before Me. You shall not make for yourself an idol, or any likeness of what is in heaven above or on the earth beneath or in the water under the earth. You shall not worship them or serve them; for I, the Lord your God, am a jealous God. (Exodus 20:2-5)

The people knew God was speaking to them in the thunder, but were greatly afraid. They insisted that Moses be their mediator. Moses approached God on the mountain. The One True God said,

> Thus you shall say to the sons of Israel, "You yourselves have seen that I have spoken to you from heaven. You shall not make other gods besides Me; gods of silver or gods of gold, you shall not make for yourselves." (Exodus 20:22-23)

After receiving many more ordinances from God, Moses came back to the people and told them everything God had said. They responded with, "All the words which the Lord has spoken we will do!" This was an agreement known as a covenant with God to worship Him alone and to not make any idols of gold.

Moses wrote down God's ordinances in a book and then built an altar at the foot of Mount Sinai with twelve pillars. There were offerings that included sacrificed young bulls. Moses read the book of the covenant to the people and again the people responded, "All the words which the Lord has spoken we will do!" (Exodus 24:3-8).

Then Aaron went with Moses, Nadab, Abihu, and seventy of the elders of Israel to the mountain where "they saw the God of Israel" (Exodus 24:10). At this point God called Moses farther up the mountain in order to give him the stone tablets. It was near the end of this forty day visit with God that the people said to Aaron, "Come, make us a god who will go before us; as for this Moses, the man who brought us up from the land of Egypt, we do not know what has become of him" (Exodus 32:1).

Three times God told them not to worship anything but Him and they had made a covenant with God that included sacrifices of young bulls. They still had the book of the covenant and they still had the altar with twelve pillars. Aaron, the man who saw God with his own eyes less than two months before, made an idol of gold in the shape of a calf for them and said, "This is your god, O Israel, who brought you up from the land of Egypt" (Exodus 32:4). Aaron and the people knew this was wrong, but did it anyway.

Figure 16. Isis protecting King Tut's vital organs vault [11]

Seeing the cloud of the glory of God resting on Mount Sinai was not enough for the people of Israel. They became restless in waiting for Moses. To relieve their anxiety, they determined to have a familiar idol to worship. In creating their own golden version of Hathor, they returned to the comfort of their previous bondage.

Figure 17. Winged Isis at foot of King Tut's coffin[12]

They still believed that God had helped them escape Egypt, but then made His inexpressible image into the likeness of a calf. In worshiping their golden queen of heaven, the people of Israel had lost all self-control. In response, God shared with Moses His intention to destroy all the people. Moses immediately intervened on their behalf:

> I fell down before the Lord, as at the first, forty days and nights; I neither ate bread nor drank water, because of all your sin which you had committed in

doing what was evil in the sight of the Lord to provoke Him to anger. For I was afraid of the anger and hot displeasure with which the Lord was wrathful against you in order to destroy you, but the Lord listened to me that time also.

The Lord was angry enough with Aaron to destroy him; so I also prayed for Aaron at the same time. I took your sinful thing, the calf which you had made, and burned it with fire and crushed it, grinding it very small until it was as fine as dust; and I threw its dust into the brook that came down from the mountain. (Deuteronomy 9:18-21)

As a result of Moses' prayer, only 3,000 people (out of millions) died for their apostasy.

Romans 11:18-32 is a description of exactly what happened at Mount Sinai. A portion of these verses say,

For even though they knew God, they did not honor Him as God or give thanks, but they became futile in their speculations, and their foolish heart was darkened. Professing to be wise, they became fools, and exchanged the glory of the incorruptible God for an image in the form of corruptible...four-footed animals. (Romans 11:21-23)

As a result, God gave them over to the lusts of their own impurity, to degrading passions, to depraved minds, and ultimately to death. God created these people to be pure, passionate, and smart, but through their own desires, they ruined themselves. It is still possible for us to ruin ourselves in the same way. Thankfully, we have a better answer in the covenant of Jesus Christ. We will explore this further in the chapter titled, "Defeat the queen of heaven."

JEROBOAM (ISRAEL)

The next mention of Hathor in the Old Testament is after the nation of Israel had split following Solomon's death. The first king of the northern tribes of Israel, Jeroboam, made calves of gold echoing the sin at Sinai. The queen of heaven most likely influenced him spiritually during the time he spent in Egypt after fleeing from his father, Solomon.

These next verses reveal the mixed worship of the One True God with the queen of heaven. Notice the replication of God's temple rituals and priestly positions used in service of these idols:

> So the king consulted, and made two golden calves, and he said to them [the people], "It is too much for you to go up to Jerusalem; behold your gods, O Israel, that brought you up from the land of Egypt." He set one in Bethel, and the other he put in Dan. Now this thing became a sin, for the people went to worship before the one as far as Dan.
>
> And he made houses on high places, and made priests from among all the people who were not of the sons of Levi. Jeroboam instituted a feast in the eighth month on the fifteenth day of the month, like the feast which is in Judah, and he went up to the altar; thus he did in Bethel, sacrificing to the calves which he had made. And he stationed in Bethel the priests

of the high places which he had made. Then he went up to the altar which he had made in Bethel on the fifteenth day in the eighth month, even in the month which he had devised in his own heart; and he instituted a feast for the sons of Israel and went up to the altar to burn incense. (1 Kings 12:28-33)

He set up priests of his own for the high places, for the satyrs [he-goat demons] and for the calves which he had made. (2 Chronicles 11:15)

Dan is in the northernmost part of Israel and Bethel the southernmost. This helps to understand the significance of God's warnings to Dan and Bethel through His prophets (see Amos 3:14; 5:4-6; 8:14; Hosea 10:13-15; Jeremiah 8:16-17).

God chose the humble herdsman, Amos, as His prophet and revealed to him that He hated the false offerings, solemn assemblies, and songs of Israel. Jeroboam clearly forgot the words of God to his ancestors, "I am the Lord your God, who brought you out of the land of Egypt, out of the house of slavery. You shall have no other gods before Me" (Exodus 20:2). God hated what they were doing because their devotion was not purely to Him alone.

King Jeroboam led Israel to worship the queen of heaven resulting in what the Bible calls a "great slaughter." Half a million men died at the hand of Judah's King Abijah in one of the worst defeats recorded in the Old Testament (see 2 Chronicles 13:17). Jeroboam never fully recovered from this devastation. This event is a clear example of the potential devastation caused when mixing humanity's carnal desires with the worship of God.

Following Jeroboam, there were eighteen successive kings of the northern tribes. Fifteen of those are described as "walking in the way of Jeroboam" or "not departing from the sins of Jeroboam which he made Israel sin." Assyria took the northern tribes of Israel captive, in part, due to their worship of the calves.

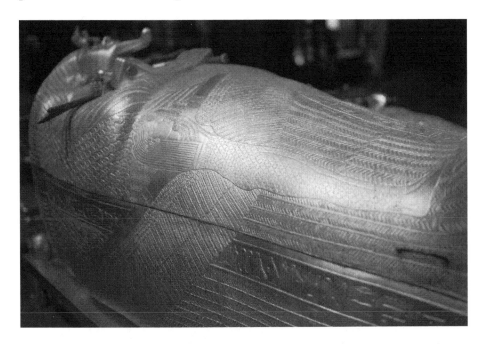

Figure 18. Winged Isis on top of King Tut's coffin [13]

In the battle previously mentioned, the king Abijah of Judah captured Bethel but he did not destroy the golden calf (it was still there much later during Jehu's reign).

JEHORAM (JUDAH)

King Ahab, the sixth king after Jeroboam, encouraged the worship of the calves so much that it extended into the southern kingdom. King Jehoram of Judah married King Ahab's daughter and is described as, walking "in the way of the kings of Israel, just as the house of Ahab did." This means that he introduced the worship of the queen of heaven, through Hathor, to Judah.

First Jehoram's son, Ahaziah, and then his wife, Athaliah, succeeded him on the throne. Both perpetuated the worship of Hathor. Scripture never mentions the destruction of the golden calves located in Bethel and Dan.

ISIS IN MORMONISM

Continuing with the story at the start of this chapter, that evening in Kansas City I watched a documentary titled, *The Lost Book of Abraham, Investigating a Remarkable Mormon Claim*. The video claimed that in November 1842, Joseph Smith, the founder of Mormonism, published *The Lost Book of Abraham* that is also known as *The Pearl of a Great Price*. Joseph described it as

> a translation of some ancient records that have fallen into our hands, from the catacombs of Egypt, purporting to be the writings of Abraham, while he was in Egypt, called the Book of Abraham, written by his own hand, upon papyrus.[14]

The papyrus fell into Joseph's hands by way of a traveling show of Egyptian antiques. Joseph bought a couple of their mummies for a hefty sum of cash and found the papyrus in the breast of one of the mummies. Mormons of the Church of the Latter Day Saints consider *The Pearl of a Great Price* equal in authority to the Bible. This book contains three facsimiles (pictures) that Joseph redrew from the original papyrus.

One of the pictures, known as Facsimile 1 (see Figure 19), is Smith's recreated drawing of a partially torn Egyptian iconograph. It was missing the upper torso and head of the dark-skinned standing figure on the left. Smith took the liberty of filling this in with the head of a man holding a knife. Joseph Smith describes his illustration in *The Book of Abraham*, "And it came to pass that the priests laid violence upon me [Abraham], that they might slay me also, as they did those virgins upon this altar" (1:12).

Figure 19. Mormon Facsimile 1 [15]

Figure 20. Isis with Anubis [16]

The documentary quotes leading Egyptologist, Theodule Devaria from the Louvre:

Smith completely misidentified the character and the scene. In Facsimile 1, Smith identified the figure on the left as a priest, knife in hand, attempting to slay Abraham. In reality, this is the Egyptian god Anubis assisting the resurrection of a deceased Egyptian. Anubis was also drawn incorrectly. He should have been drawn with the head of a jackal, not the head of a man.[17]

Figure 20 is a photograph of an original papyrus that I took at the *Discovering King Tut* exhibit in Kansas City that clearly shows the same scene described by Devaria. The liberty that Joseph Smith took with filling in the torn segment is obvious. Although not included in Smith's drawing, the kneeling figure on the left wearing the throne crown is Isis.

Figure 21. Mormon Facsimile 3 [18]

In 1912, the first opposition to the work of Joseph Smith was published as *An Inquiry Conducted* by Rt. Rev. F.S. Spaulding, D.D., Bishop of Utah. Egyptologists today confirm Spaulding's proof that these documents were Egyptian burial letters.

Isis is on Mormon Facsimile 3 (see Figure 21). In Spaulding's pamphlet, he describes Smith's faulty translation of this illustration and explains that the deity crowned with a sun disk and bull's horns is Isis, not the king of Egypt.

> It is difficult to deal seriously with Joseph Smith's impudent fraud...Facsimile Number 3 is a representation of the Goddess Maat leading the Pharaoh before Osiris, behind whom stands the Goddess Isis. Smith has turned the Goddess [Isis] into a king and Osiris into Abraham. The hieroglyphics, again, have been transformed into unintellible lines. Hardly one of them is copied correctly.[19]

This discovery was disturbing to me because I have family and friends who are Mormon, but what I found out about Isis in Freemasonry hit even closer to home for me.

ENCOUNTER WITH ISIS IN FREEMASONRY

In my teen years, I was a member of the International Order of the Rainbow for Girls of the Freemasons. The formality, secrecy, and mystery of the Masonic rituals enthralled me. Being entrusted with information that I could not even tell my parents was exciting.

Dressing up in a white gown, performing ceremonial rituals, and reciting memorized passages for the meetings drew me right into the organization. The dances with the Masonic DeMolay boys were always a highlight for me too. My parents were proud of my participation, especially since the Masonic Society tradition went back a few generations on my father's side.

Figure 22. Isis on King Tut's sarcophagus [20]

It is a common misconception, even by those involved in the organization, that Freemasonry is based on the Christian religion. A pamphlet put out by the Grand Lodge of New Jersey lists the requirements for membership into the Masonic Fraternity. The very last item is, "He must be a believer in a Supreme Being, called by Masons the Great Architect of the Universe."[21]

Although a very religious organization, individual members are the ones who define who their own "Supreme Being" is. The One True God is certainly an acceptable candidate and is often mistaken as the alias behind the use of the word "god" in many of their materials. It is not until high levels of masonry are achieved that one discovers the truth.

Albert Pike, one of the Freemason's founding fathers in the United States said, "The first Masonic teacher was Buddha...She [Masonry] invites all men of all religions to enlist under her banner."[22] A mason's "religion must be universal: Christ, Buddha, or Mohammed, the name means little, for he recognizes only the light and not the bearer."[23]

The Journal of Masonic Research & Letters reveals who the true "Supreme Being" is. *The Origin of Free-Masonry by Thomas Paine,* quoted in the journal says:

> In 1783, Captain George Smith, inspector of the Royal Artillery Academy at Woolwich, in England, and Provincial Grand Master of Masonry for the county of Kent, published a treatise entitled, *The Use and Abuse of Free-Masonry...*

> "Egypt," says Smith, "from whence we derive many of our mysteries, has always borne a distinguished rank in history, and was once celebrated above all others for its antiquities, learning, opulence, and fertility. In their system, their principal hero-gods, Osiris and Isis, theologically represent the Supreme Being and universal Nature; and physically the two great celestial luminaries, the Sun and the Moon, by whose influence all nature was actuated...The experienced brethren of the Society are well informed what affinity these symbols bear to Masonry, and why they are used in all Masonic Lodges."[24]

Jahbulon is the secret name of the "Supreme Being" of Masonry, which is a conflation of the names of Jehovah, Baal, and a phrase used in the "Babylonian mysteries to call upon the deity Osiris." (Osiris and Isis are inseparable in Egyptian mythology.)[25]

Figure 23. Albert Pike statue with Minerva [26]

Albert Pike was a Scottish Rite Masons Grand Commander and a Confederate Brigadier General. Honored by the federal government in 1898, he was the recipient of federal land where his statue (see Figure 23) is now located between the Department of Labor and Municipal buildings in Washington, DC.

At the base of this granite-stepped statue is the female Roman goddess of wisdom, Minerva, who is the equivalent of the Egyptian Isis. Freemasons usually display Minerva in their lodges with an owl by her side.[27]

My childhood deception with the Freemasons did not become clear to me until later in life. The masonic culture of keeping secrets and withholding information fed my sinful habit of lying as a child. Unfortunately, this harmful childhood behavior perpetuated into my adulthood and caused many of those I love a lot of pain. The sin of agreement with this demonic force gave the devil a legal right to inflict harm in my life.

I repented to God and renounced my involvement with the Freemasons in order to break the subtle hold the queen of heaven had on my life. I also determined to never lie again, which is something that I have held to ever since.

Today prostitution is finally called by what it truly is: human trafficking. Those who were once arrested as criminals are now seen as victims. Have you ever wondered how the idea of money for sex ever came about to begin with?

---

[1] *Archaeological Study Bible*, 827.

[2] Budin, "A Reconsideration of the Aphrodite-Ashtart Syncretism."

[3] Taken by the author at The Nelson-Atkins Museum of Art.

[4] Abrahamsen, *Women and Worship at Philippi*, 34.

[5] "The Fellowship of Isis" [Online] http://www.fellowshipofisis.com/manifesto.html [2016, Oct].

[6] Carl Teichrib, "Isis: queen of heaven" [Online] http://www.crossroad.to/articles2/2002/ carl-teichrib/5isis.htm [2014, Aug].

[7] Taken by the author at The Nelson-Atkins Museum of Art, Kansas City, MO.

[8] Johnson, *Lady of the Beasts*, 250.

[9] New World Encyclopedia, "Hathor" [Online] http://www.newworldencyclopedia. org/entry/hathor [2015, Jan].

[10] Gérard Ducher , "File:GD-EG-Caire-Musee091.JPG" [Online] https://commons. wikimedia.org/wiki/File:GD-EG-Caire-Mus%C3%A9e091.JPG [2016, Nov].

[11] Taken by the author at the *Discovering of King Tut* exhibit at Union Station in Kansas City, MO.

[12] Ibid.

[13] Ibid.

[14] "The Lost Book of Abraham" video [Online] https://www.youtube.com/?v= hcyzkd_m6KE [2016, April].

[15] "File:Abraham Facsimilie 1.png" [Online] https://commons.wikimedia.org/wiki/ File: Abraham_Facsimile_1.png [2016, Nov].

[16] Taken by the author at the *Discovering of King Tut* exhibit at Union Station.

[17] Ibid.

[18] "File:Abraham Facsimili 3.png" [Online] https://commons.wikimedia.org/wiki/ File:Abraham_Facsimile_3.png [2016, Oct].

[19] Spaulding, *Joseph Smith, Jr.*, 23.

[20] Ibid.

[21] *Grand Lodge of the Most Ancient and Honorable Society of Free and Accepted Masons for the State of New Jersey. n.d.* (booklet) "On the Threshold" 10.

[22] Carlson, *Fast Facts on False Teachings*, 81.

[23] Ibid., 83.

[24] Philalethes, *The Journal of Masonic Research & Letters, Bonus Supplement for Fall 2010*, "The Origin of Free-Masonry by Thomas Paine" [Online] http://free masonry.org/pdf/2010_04_supplement_paine.pdf [2014, Nov].

[25] Carlson, *Fast Facts on False Teachings*, 86.

[26] "File:Albert Pike memorial.jpg" [Online] https://commons.wikimedia.org/wiki /File:Albert_Pike_memorial.jpg [2016, Sep].

[27] Macoy, *Illustrated History and Cyclopedia of Freemasonry*, 587.

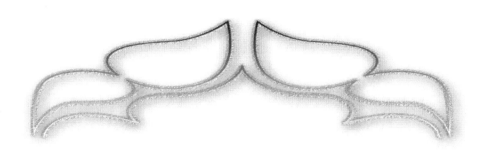

ASHTORETH

IN THE MIDST of my studies of the queen of heaven, my dad sent me a box full of old books for my birthday. I often receive the fruits of his antiquing adventures that include timeworn biblical references. This time one of the treasures was a Bible dictionary copyrighted in 1884. I immediately looked up the definition for queen of heaven, which said, "the moon, worshiped as Ashtoreth or Astarte, to whom the Hebrew women offered cakes in the streets of Jerusalem."[1]

TODAY

Unlike the rest of the queen of heaven aliases, Ashtoreth is true to form in today's culture and is portrayed outright as the demonic principality that she is. Well-liked by dark heavy metal bands, they bear her name, have her seal on their album covers, and devote songs to her. The popular 1971 movie *Bedknobs and Broomsticks* included an artifact called 'The Star of Asteroth.' Comic book readers may recognize the name Ashtaroth as a character from *Hellboy*. Christian and secular fiction authors write about her, such as the *Left Behind* series, the *Trinity Blood* series, and books by Stephen King. Her TV appearances include *Batman, Friday the 13th: The Series, Twin Peaks,* and *Supernatural. Final Fantasy 2* and *Dungeon and Dragons* are only a few of the many games that have a dark character by her name.

ORIGIN AND LOCALE

Ashtoreth was worshiped in Aram, Moab, and Ammon. The Philistines, who are mentioned throughout the Old Testament, and the Phoenicians also revered Ashtaroth. She was one of the gods that was to be purged from the land God promised to Israel.

DESIGNATIONS AND GENDER

The Theological Wordbook of the Old Testament says Ashtoreth is "a vivid representation of paganism in its most corrupt manifestations."[2] Worshiped as a goddess of fertility, sex, love, and war, Ashtoreth is known as: the moon goddess; the goddess of Venus; the Virgin Mother; the Holy Virgin; and the consort of Baal. Thought to be the productive power of nature, she may very well be the original Mother Nature.

Other name variations are Ashteroth, Astareth, Astaroth, and Astaro. Ashtaroth, the plural form of the goddess's name in Hebrew, became a general term denoting fabricated idols, goddesses, and paganism.[3] Hebrew scholars believe that the name, Ashtoreth, is a deliberate conflation of the Greek name Astarte and the Hebrew word *boshet,* meaning "shame." This indicates the Hebrews' contempt for her cult.

The *Dictionary of the Holy Bible* explains why Ashtoreth maybe the same as Venus (I address Venus in more detail in the chapter titled, "Aphrodite/Venus"):

> The word Ashtoreth, for which an etymology has long been sought, is equivalent to the Syriac ashteruth and estero, and to the Persian sitarch, which all signify star; and it therefore denotes by way of eminence the Star, ie: Venus.[4]

Ashtoreth is female in the Bible but in all other literature appears as a high-ranking male demon known as Astaroth.

ICONOGRAPHY

Some describe Astaroth as a loathsome angel, appearing as a naked man with wings riding a dragon. With the title, Duke of Hell, he supposedly commands many legions of lesser spirits including all the evil spirits in the Americas. Listed in some references as the Prince of the Demonic Order of Accusers, we are reminded of satan who is the chief accuser of the brethren, furthering the evidence that the queen of heaven is one with the devil as his daughter.

If you ever thought demons were dumb and powerless spirits, the famous historian Edith Hamilton begs to differ by revealing the intellectual abilities of Ashtoreth in her book, *Mythology:*

> Astaroth is said to teach the liberal sciences and, like many of the Goetic spirits, he will also discourse on matters of the past, present and future, as well as the secrets of occult knowledge. In addition to this, Astaroth can confer heavenly knowledge as well: he is said to speak freely about the creator of spirits, the fall

of the spirits, and the various sins they committed that inspired their fall...He has the power to discover minds and transmute metals...He has impressive powers of destruction, causing tempests and demolishing buildings. He can also transform men and animals.[5]

Demons have many capabilities that are meant to annihilate the human race. Remember, that by having a relationship with the One True God we are already victorious against the devil's plans.

Although most of the other queen of heaven aliases promoted worship through cult prostitution, the Bible has specific accounts of temple prostitution participation by Ashtoreth's worshipers. Therefore, I am providing an in-depth look about this topic in the next section.

CULT PROSTITUTION

On a warm spring morning at 6:00 am, I joined a group of twelve people in my church's parking lot. Laden down with twenty-five gallons of paint, beds, furniture, cleaning supplies, and many prayers we headed out on a mission trip. Our destination was an old hotel in eastern South Dakota that was soon to be a safe house for people rescued from human trafficking.

South Dakota may not strike you as a hot spot for prostitution, but as a world famous destination for pheasant hunting and home of the Sturgis motorcycle rally, it is no stranger to human trafficking. Sixteen hours later we pulled back into that same parking lot exhausted, but very satisfied that the three rooms we transformed would benefit a lot of hurting people.

Just like the other queen of heaven aliases we have looked at so far, temple prostitution was a form of worship to Ashtoreth. The Biblical Archeological Society states:

> Archaeology has shown that Ashtoreth worship and associated rites of sacred prostitution were common throughout the ancient Mediterranean. At the Etruscan site of Pyrgi, excavators identified a temple dedicated to Ashtoreth that featured at least 17 small rooms that may have served as quarters for temple prostitutes.[6]

It seems certain that prostitution originated in temples where devotees were impersonating a god or goddess during the sexual act. The payment for sex went to the temple. Cult prostitution mentioned throughout the Old Testament was usually specific to the worship of the queen of heaven.

JOB

The term *cult prostitution* appears first in Job, "The godless in heart layup anger, they do not cry for help when He binds them. They die in youth, and their life perishes among the cult prostitutes" (Job 36:13-14). The Hebrew word for prostitutes, *qades,* is a masculine noun, indicating male prostitutes that were most likely bisexual. Job accounts for some of the earliest histories of the world, giving us an idea of how old cult prostitution is.

ISAIAH

The book of Isaiah makes it clear that cult prostitution was the same as sorcery (see Isaiah 57:3). The Mosaic Law states that -

none of the daughters of Israel shall be a cult prostitute, nor shall any of the sons of Israel be a cult prostitute. You shall not bring the hire of a harlot or the wages of a dog into the house of the Lord your God for any votive offering, for both of these are an abomination to the Lord your God. (Deuteronomy 23:17-18)

JUDAH

Israel was not to take part in temple prostitution in any way. However, in Genesis 38 Judah assumed he was hiring a temple harlot when he had sex with his disguised daughter-in-law, Tamar.

REHOBOAM (JUDAH)

When Rehoboam took the throne from his father Solomon, the Bible says, "There were also sodomites in the land: and they did according to all the abominations of the nations which the Lord cast out before the children of Israel" (1 Kings 14:24). Scripture is not clear if this first occurred under King Solomon's reign, but since he had many foreign wives who defiled his worship of God, it is probable.

King Rehoboam's grandson, King Asa, removed many of the male cult prostitutes (see 1 Kings 15:11-12) while his son, King Jehoshaphat removed the remaining ones (see 1 Kings 22:46).

Some Bible translations use the word *sodomite* in place of *cult prostitute* in 1 Kings 22:46. The term sodomite is derived from Latin in reference to the sin of Sodom. Although I have found nothing in Scripture that clearly links sodomy with temple prostitution, we cannot rule it out, especially since there were male cult prostitutes.

The *Theological Wordbook of the Old Testament* says that acts of worship "included male and female cultic prostitutes in hetero- and homo-sexual liaisons."[7]

JOSIAH (JUDAH)

The next mention of cult prostitution is during Josiah's reign. It is disturbing to discover that he removed houses of male cult prostitutes that were in Solomon's Temple (see 2 Kings 23:7). This is extremely troubling evidence of the children of Israel polluting their worship of God with homage to the queen of heaven.

HOSEA

The prophet Hosea makes it clear that worshiping the queen of heaven is a form of spiritual prostitution. In the following verses, we see references to harlotry through idol worship, apostasy, immorality, and temple prostitution. (Note: queen of heaven worship is directly related to the italicized phrases.)

> Harlotry, wine and new wine take away the under-standing. My people consult their *wooden idol, and their diviner's wand* informs them; for a *spirit of harlotry* has led them astray, and they have played the harlot, departing from their God. They offer sacrifices on the *tops of the mountains and burn incense on the hills, under oak, poplar and terebinth,* because their shade is pleasant. Therefore your daughters play the harlot and your brides commit adultery. I will not punish your daughters when they play the harlot or your brides when they commit adultery, for the men themselves go apart with harlots and offer sacrifices

with temple prostitutes; so the people without understanding are ruined. (Hosea 4:11-14, italics added)

Having sex with a temple prostitute was a sacrifice to the queen of heaven, but notice in the verses above that spiritual prostitution occurred by turning away from God. The spirit of harlotry (queen of heaven) promotes this by leading people astray to their own destruction as we saw in Proverbs seven. Hosea makes it clear that it is impossible to maintain pure worship to God while relenting to the queen of heaven.

God rejects those with a lack of knowledge. The purpose of this book is to give you knowledge about things no one wants to talk about. Many Christians think that talking or learning about the devil's schemes somehow empowers him. Others do not even acknowledge that satan exists. This type of thinking is exactly what "without understanding" means.

God does not punish women and brides in the verses above. I would like to suggest that this is because they were victims. Today, law enforcement has finally understood this reality and do not usually arrest women who are caught up in prostitution. Instead, they are going after the leaders of the prostitution rings, pimps, and customers.

ASHTORETH IN THE BIBLE

CITY OF ASHTEROTH- KARNAIM

The first mention of Ashtoreth in the Bible is as the name of a city in Bashan called Ashteroth-karnaim that was located east of the

Sea of Galilee. The word, *karnaim,* signifies "horns." Therefore, the literal meaning of Ashteroth-karnaim is "Ashtoreth of the two horns or peaks" or "the horned Astartes."[8] The Rephaim (giants) worshiped Ashtoreth in this city. Although the king of Elam conquered Ashteroth-karnaim, the giants continued to live there (see Genesis 14:5).

While the children of God were wandering in the wilderness for forty years, they did a fair amount of fighting and conquering in the land east of the Promised Land of Canaan. During that time, the city of Ashteroth-karnaim was called by the plural form of the name, Ashtaroth, and was ruled by King Og. Moses and the children of God destroyed King Og, his family, and his people (including the giants) until there was not even a remnant left (see Numbers 21:35; Deuteronomy 1:4).[9]

King Og did absolutely nothing to provoke Israel. Requesting safe passage through his land never occurred as it did for the King of Sihon in the preceding days. (Sihon refused to let God's people on his land and did not live to tell about it). Concerning Og, God told Moses, "Do not fear him, for I have delivered him and all his people and his land into your hand; and you shall do to him just as you did to Sihon king of the Amorites" (Deuteronomy 3:2).

Moses and God's people annihilated the city of Ashtaroth due to their worship of the queen of heaven. If only future generations of Israel had remembered this incident, it would have served as a deterrent for many of the hard times they would face as a result of their worship of the queen of heaven.

JUDGES

Ashtoreth shows up next in the book of Judges, where Israel is in a cycle of sin, repentance, and obedience. The nation was repeatedly falling into the trap of worshiping foreign gods, including Ashtaroth. Their impure devotion roused the jealousy of God. As a result, they were robbed and became slaves of their enemies (see Judges 2:11-15).

The same is still true today. People can cause toxicity in their own life when their worship to God is not purely to Him alone. The desires of their hearts contaminate their godly devotion and that is when He will allow those desires to overtake them. This is the ultimate answer to the question, "Why does God let bad things happen?" It is through the freedom of our own desires that evil can prevail.

PHILISTINES

During the rule of the judges of Israel, Ashtoreth was a goddess of the Philistines. In the Bible, the "land of the Philistines" was one of the many nations God commanded Israel to destroy (see Joshua 13:1-2) that was located directly west of Jerusalem on the Mediterranean. The books of Samuel and Kings reveal how troubled Israel was by the Philistines. It is quite ironic that Israel worshiped the deity of their enemies.

In 1 Samuel 7, God promises Israel that if they stop worshiping Ashtoreth, then He will deliver the Philistines into their hands. In response, Israel purified their worship to God by eliminating all connections with the queen of heaven. Then, "the Lord thundered with a great thunder on that day against the Philistines and confused them, so that they were routed before Israel" (1 Samuel 7:1-11). This event is significant: it should cause us to pause and realize that purifying our devotion to God will ensure His protection, even today. Many years later, the Philistines killed Israel's first king, Saul, and put his weapons in their temple of Ashtaroth as war trophies (see 1 Samuel 31:10).

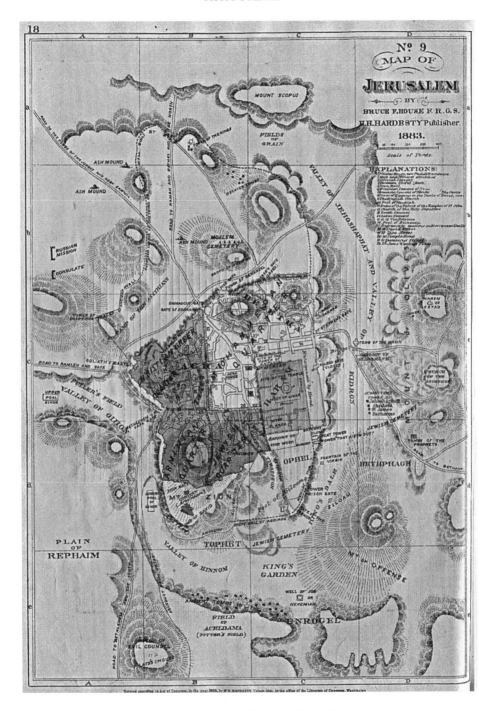

Figure 24. Map of Israel AD 1883

Solomon

Solomon, who built the first temple of God, also created a high place devoted to Ashtoreth near Jerusalem. In his later years, he placed this abomination on the eastern side of the Mount of Offense, also known as the Mount of Destruction, the Mount of Corruption, or the Mount of False Council (see 2 Kings 23:13). This hill is one of three peaks that form a mountain ridge about two miles north and east of Old Jerusalem.

The northern-most peak, highest in elevation, is Mount Scopus; the middle peak is the Mount of Olives; and the southern-most peak, lowest in elevation, is the Mount of Offense (see Figure 24). According to a friend of mine who visits Israel often, the Mount of Offense is the site of the United Nations complex.

The Ashtoreth Solomon put in place had a view of the Judean Desert sunrise.[10] How menacing it must have looked to travelers. I was saddened to learn that this Ashtoreth existed through the reign of eighteen Judean kings, lasting more than 300 years. Some of these kings tried to do good, but their people still worshiped the queen of heaven in the high places, including the Ashtoreth on the Mount of Offense.

Solomon's worship of Ashtoreth caused the Israel to split. In 1 Kings 11, God's jealous anger is evident when King Solomon, who was the wisest of men, corrupted his heart with the queen of heaven. Scripture says that God appeared to him twice, directing him to stay away from Ashtoreth. Astonishingly, these personal visitations did nothing to rekindle Solomon's love for God. In following his own desires, Solomon removed himself from God's divine favor and protection. This caused God to divide Israel into the northern and southern tribes (see 1 Kings 11:4-5; 9-13).

TOWN OF ASHTAROTH

The last mention of Ashtoreth in the Bible is when the town of Ashtaroth is given to the half-tribe of Manasseh. The mention of its pastures makes it sound innocent enough, but it makes me wonder if retaining the name was for historical purposes or for the stronghold it still may have contained.

Through this study of Ashtoreth we were able to understand that the jealousy of God is a serious matter. Devoting worship to God alone ensures His blessing and favor; whereas, mixing worship to God with other entities will cause us to stray from God's divine protection.

Jesus said, "Woe to you...For if the miracles had been performed in Tyre and Sidon which occurred in you, they would have repented long ago." Learning about Astarte will expose the sin of these cities.

---

[1] Smith, *Dictionary of the Bible*, 563.
[2] Harris, *Theological Wordbook of the Old Testament*, 707.
[3] Ibid.
[4] Calmet, *Dictionary of the Holy Bible*, 115.
[5] Hamilton, *Mythology*, 48-49.
[6] Edward Lipiński (01/24/2014), Bible History Daily, Biblical Archaeology Society, "Sacred Prostitution in the Story of Judah and Tamar?" [Online] http://www. biblicalarchaeology.org/daily/ancient-cultures/ancient-israel/sacred-prostitution-in-the-story-of-judah-and-tamar/ [2014 Jun]. Other sources claim this Ancient Italian temple was for Astarte.
[7] Harris, *Theological Wordbook of the Old Testament*, Vol 2, 707.
[8] Blue Letter Bible, "Lexicon :: Strong's H6252 - ʿAshtarowth" [Online] http://v3 .blueletterBible.org/lang/lexicon/ lexicon.cfm?Strongs= H6252&t= KJV [2014, Jan] and "Lexicon :: Strong's H6255 - ʿAshtĕroth Qarnayim" [Online] http:// www.blue

letterBible.org/lang/lexicon /lexicon.cfm?strongs=H6255&t=KJV [2014, Jan]. I was unable to find out why there are discrepancies in the spelling for the town – Ashteroth-karnaim as opposed to Ashtoreth.

[9] It would be interesting to know the difference between the giants that the spies faced in the Promised Land compared with the ones Israel later destroyed in Og.

[10] Wikipedia. "Mount of Olives" [Online] http://en.wikipedia.org/wiki/Mount_ of_Olives [2014, Jan].

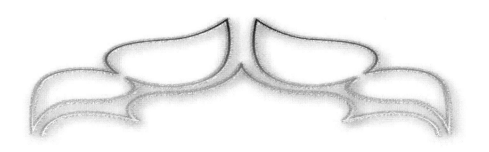

ASTARTE

TODAY

JOFFREY BALLET'S PRODUCTION of *Astarte* ran for nine years. The ballet was a popular psychedelic dance about a mortal man having sex with a goddess. Considered consequential in the dawning of a new age for both for its shock value and the creative use of film with moving screens, it premiered in 1967.

ORIGIN AND LOCALE

Astarte has many of the same characteristics as Inanna, who took on the very same identities as Christ. Some think this goddess emerged out of the combination of the Semitic masculine god Athtar and the Sumerian Inanna. Others believe Astarte is another name for Ashtoreth. Due to their uniqueness, I chose to separate these aliases.

In *A Reconsideration of the Aphrodite-Ashtart Syncretism*, Stephanie Budin states, "When the early Semites came into contact with the Sumerians in Mesopotamia, they adjusted some of their deities to have them align with the Sumerian pantheon."[1] Later, when Astarte showed up in the Ugarit texts, she was distinctly feminine, proving that this queen of heaven alias also changed genders.

In Egyptian mythology Seth is Astarte's spouse, but it is unclear if the Ptah (supreme creator) or Ra is her father.[2] Depending on which literature you read she was either a consort of, relative of, or just a strong supporter of Baal.

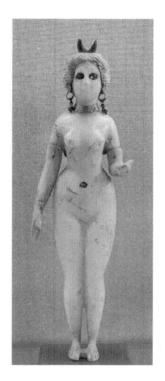

Figure 25. Astarte idol figurine [3]

Many royal families honored Astarte's priesthood. Sixth and fifth century BC funerary inscriptions from the royal family of Sidon along with a seventh century peace treaty signed between King

Esarhaddon of Assyria and King Ba'al of Tyre show that Astarte was the Queen of all Phoenicia (during the time that Manasseh was king of Judah). She was later the Holy Queen in Kition, Cyprus due to the influence of Phoenician settlers from Tyre and Sidon.[4]

Depicted with at least five different pharaohs and several other gods including Hathor and the Syro-Palestinian Baal, Egyptian relief fragments bear inscriptions of Astarte as a menacing goddess. Astarte was popular in Asia Minor, Tyre, Sidon, Elat, Canaan, and Akkad. The ancient Hittites also revered her. Astarte is mentioned on the *Sphinx Stela,* which is perhaps her first appearance in Egyptian texts. She is said to be delighted with the young prince's equestrian skill and was believed to protect the pharaoh's chariot in battle.[5]

DESIGNATIONS

Astarte was worshiped as a goddess of love, fertility, and war. Connected with the sea, she was believed to be a beautiful, strong warrior, and hunter.

Variants of her name include Ashtart, Athtart, Atirat, Dastartu, Astartu, Uni-Astre, Ashtart, and Asarte. Summoning Astarte-Name-of-Baal to kill the sea god Yam occurs in the story of *Astarte and The Sea.* She was known as the deified evening star, face of Baal, and Queen of Heaven.

In the Egyptian pantheon she was known as Astarte of Battle, Goddess of Horse Riders, and Mistress of the Animals. By the title, Astarte of Battle, she was incited to "break the bow in the treaty of the Neo-Assyrian king Esarhaddon with Baal of Tyre."[6] The remains of some ancient Egyptian hieroglyphics show the title, Lady of Heaven, along with signs '-z-t-r-t' that stood for Asarte.

Ba'alat Gebal (Lady of Byblos) was another name for Astarte in Byblos, Phoenicia (Lebanon). Her circa 2700 BC Byblos temple overlooked the Mediterranean Sea where she was the patroness of shipmasters. In this capacity she was a protective force as the figurehead leaning forward at the bow of ships. The sacred pool near this temple was in use for 2000 years. Egyptian kings sent gifts to this temple, equating her with their goddess Hathor.[7]

ICONOGRAPHY

The Dictionary of the Holy Bible states that Astarte also took on the form of a cow just like Isis and Ishtar.

> A part of the Phoenician mythus respecting Astarte is given by Sanchonianthon, Euseb. De Preaep. Evang. I 10. "Astarte the most high, and Jupiter Demarous, and Adodus king of the gods, reigned over the country, with the assent of Saturn. And Astarte placed the head of a bull upon her own head, as an emblem of sovereignty. As she was journeying about the world, she found a star wandering in the air, and having taken possession of it, she consecrated it in the sacred island of Tyre. The Phoenicians say that Astarte is Venus.[8]

Figure 25 is a white naked figurine of Astarte from the Louvre museum. It has her wearing earrings with her left hand lifted and horns on her head. An *atef crown* of a sun disk with horns was also common for her to wear (identical to the headdress of Isis). She is usually either standing or riding a horse naked with a bow raised, which is her weapon of choice.

ASTARTE AND KINGS IN THE BIBLE

The famous Jewish historian, Josephus Flavius, wrote about King Hiram I of Tyre and his devotion to Astarte in the following quote. This king provided cedar trees, carpenters, and stonemasons for constructing God's temple that King Solomon built (see 2 Samuel 5:11).

> Upon the death of Abibalus, his son Hirom [Hiram] took the kingdom; he lived fifty-three years, and reigned thirty-four... he also cut down timber from the mountain called Libanus, and got timber of cedar for the roofs of the temples. He also pulled down the old temples, and built new ones: besides this, he consecrated the temples of Hercules and Astarte. He built that of Astarte when he made his expedition against the Tityans, who would not pay him their tribute.[9]

It is highly possible that King Hiram also provided Solomon with a few wives who worshiped Astarte.

> King Solomon loved many foreign women...from the nations concerning which the Lord had said to the sons of Israel, "You shall not associate with them, nor shall they associate with you, for they will surely turn your heart away after their gods." Solomon held fast to these in love. He had seven hundred wives, princesses, and three hundred concubines, and his wives turned his heart away. For when Solomon was old, his wives

turned his heart away after other gods; and his heart was not wholly devoted to the Lord his God, as the heart of David his father had been. (1 Kings 11:1-4)

The cult of Astarte continued in Tyre with King Ethbaal, who was Astarte's high priest before his kingship.[10] He established her divine supremacy during his reign, which included the land of Sidon (Lebanon). Known as the king of Sidon in the Bible, this man was also the father of the Phoenician Princess of Sidon. We know her as King Ahab's wife, Jezebel (see 1 Kings 16:31), who was also loyal to Asherah.

Not a day goes by that the Islamic State of Iraq and Syria (ISIS) is not in the news. Not only is this acronym, ISIS, telling in this book's context, it may surprise you what spiritually fuels this evil organization.

---

[1] Budin, *A Reconsideration of the Aphrodite-Ashtart Syncretism*, 104.

[2] Cornelius, *The Many Faces of the Goddess*, 23, 75, 85.

[3] Marie-Lan Nguyen, "File:Statuette Goddess Louvre AO20127.jpg" [Online] https://commons.wikimedia.org/wiki/File:Statuette_Goddess_Louvre_AO20127.jpg [2016, Sep].

[4] Cornelius, *The Many Faces of the Goddess*, 108, 115, 121.

[5] Wilkinson, *The Complete Gods and Goddesses of Ancient Egypt*, 138.

[6] Budin, *A Reconsideration of the Aphrodite-Ashtart Syncretism*, 104.

[7] Neferuhethert (1999-2007) "Byblos" [Online] http://www.hethert.org/byblos.htm [2014, Aug].

[8] Calmet, *Dictionary of the Holy Bible*, 115.

[9] Whiston, *Josephus The Complete Works*, "Against Apion" 1.18.

[10] Budin, *A Reconsideration of the Aphrodite-Ashtart Syncretism*, 116.

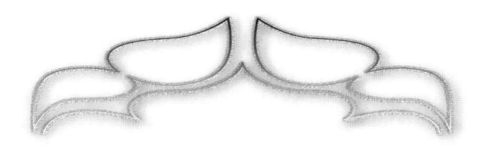

APHRODITE / VENUS

TODAY

FRAGRANCES, MAKEUP, AND clothing bear Aphrodite's name.
Pop artists sing about her and moviegoers have enjoyed her on the
big screen. The name Aphrodite gave rise to the term *aphrodisiac*,
while the term *venereal* is derived from the name Venus. The herbal
concoction *Aphrodite* will leave you high for hours. Her name is
prevalent in our culture; I even remember learning about her in
grade school.

ORIGIN AND LOCALE

Aphrodite held a prestigious rank in the Greek mythology
pantheon as one of the Twelve Olympians. Hephaestus was her
spouse and Cupid, god of erotic love, was her son. There is
confusion as to whether she was the daughter of Zeus, as mentioned
in the *Iliad*, or came from the foam of the sea, as written by the
Greek poet, Hesoid. In the latter version she first stepped on land in

Cyprus of Phoenicia as Cytherea the Cyprian.

Aphrodite was worshiped as a great goddess of the ancient Middle East, being the chief deity of the biblical cities of Tyre, Sidon, and Elat, all major Mediterranean seaports. She was also popular in: Eryx (western Sicily), Sparta (Greece), Tarnto (southern Italy), Syria, and Corinth.

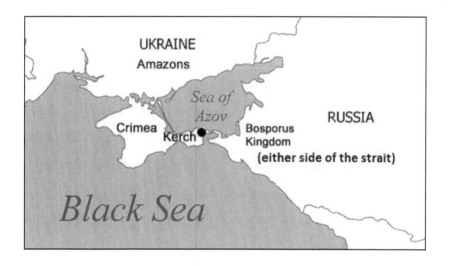

Figure 26. Map of the Bosporus Kingdom[1]

In the seventh century BC, the Greeks colonized the Kingdom of the Bosporus, located along the Kerch Strait that is in between the Black Sea and Sea of Azov (see Figure 26). This resulted in Aphrodite Ourania to be their Great Goddess until the kingdom's demise.

Lucian (AD 125) wrote about Aphrodite temples that he visited. One was in Byblos and another built by Cinyras was in the Libanus region of Syria. He stated the following about the Libanus temple:

> The statues [asssociated with the temple] sweat, and move, and utter oracles, and a shout has often been

raised when the temple was closed; it has been heard by many. And more: this temple is the principal source of their wealth, as I can vouch. For much money comes to them from Arabia, and from the Phœnicians and the Babylonians: the Cilicians, too, and the Assyrians bring their tribute. I saw with my own eyes treasures stored away privately in the temple; many garments, and other valuables, which are exchanged for silver or gold. Nowhere among mankind are so many festivals and sacred assemblies instituted as among them.[2]

DESIGNATIONS

Venus was originally an Italian deity who later merged with Aphrodite by the Romans. *Goddesses Who Rule* explains how Venus changed into Aphrodite.

In Latin the word Venus was originally the neuter noun from which the verb uenerari was derived. In ancient times, uenerari was restricted to religious contexts and referred to an attitude of hospitality means of which humans sought to attract the benevolence of the gods. The noun expressed this quality as an abstraction: graciousness or charm. Eventually the term was personified as a goddess: Venus…the Romans simply gave the name and attributes of the Italian Venus to the complex figure of Aphrodite.[3]

The seemingly innocent and calm Venus portrayed in Botticelli's famous painting of her birth from the foam of the sea, does not reveal her true character (see Figure 27) as we will soon discover.

Figure 27. Botticelli's *Birth of Venus* (edited) [4]

Worshiped as a goddess of love, fertility, and war, Aphrodite was known as: grace of physical charm and beauty incarnate; Lady of the Wild Things; Enchantress; guardian of kings; protectress of the dead; Queen of Heaven; supreme heavenly deity of earth; the mother of men and gods; and guide of souls to the underworld.

According to Stephanie Budin, "Assyrians call Aphrodite Mylitta; the Arabs call her Alilat, and the Persians Mitran." [5] The Persians learned from the Assyrians and Arabs how to worship Aphrodite.

GENDER

Aphrodite's gender was not exclusive since another name for her was Bearded Aphrodite of Cyprus. Zeus Aphrodisios, may have been the male manifestation of Aphrodite. Her son, Hermaphrotidus, was female from the waist up and male from there down. These physical characteristics are evident on a statue at the National Museum in Stockholm Sweden that is titled *Herm of Aphroditus*.[6]

ICONOGRAPHY

With thrones, crowns, and lions by her side, Aphrodite appeared in art and on coins. These items were signs of her divinity and royal standing. In her iconography, she shares the same symbol as Inanna, which is an eight-pointed star.

Lady of the Beasts reveals Aphrodite's original physical form and her effect on those who worshiped her:

> The earliest images of the deity were often in animal form and only later assumed anthropomorphic [human] shape. At times the actual process of trans-formation is recorded on tablets from the ancient Near East, the goddess is described as part fish, part maiden – the fabulous mermaid of more recent times.

> As Aphrodite Pandemos, she stands on a dolphin. The terra cotta from eastern Greece (6th Century BC) is less the image of a gentle deity born in foam than the expression of the goddess who rules what has been called the irresistible and harrowing domain of love. She is an alluring and seductive figure of fatal enchantment leading others to doom.

> Many of Aphrodite's temples and shrines have been described as haunting and terrible, expressing a nature that appears to be beyond the reach of reason or control.[7]

You can get an idea of what a fatally enchanting Aphrodite might be like in the movie, *Pirates of the Caribbean: Stranger Tides*. The mermaid creatures in the movie appear sweet, sexy, and desirable while they lure the sailors into the sea. Once the enchanted seamen leave the safety of their boat, they are violently attacked and tortured. These mermaids fit the mold of the queen of heaven perfectly, agreeing with the ancient legends and myths about Aphrodite.

JESUS CHRIST IMPOSTER

As seen in previous chapters, many of the other queen of heaven aliases have a connection with the planet Venus. Venus is known physically and spiritually as both the morning and evening stars.

The Bible translates the Greek word *phosphoros* as the term "morning star" only once in a chapter that is entirely about Jesus. "So we have the prophetic word made more sure, to which you do well to pay attention as to a lamp shining in a dark place, until the day dawns and the *morning star* arises in your hearts" (2 Peter 1:19, italics added).

The verses preceding this refer to the second coming of Jesus Christ. In staying with the context of the chapter, "the day that dawns" and the "rising of the morning star" are symbolic ways to describe Jesus' return to the earth. The book of Revelation states that when Jesus returns He will have the title King of kings. This reveals the queen of heaven's alias Venus as a counterfeit of the true morning star, King Jesus Himself.

CULT STONE

Kouklia, Cyprus holds the ruins of the Palaepaphos Aphrodite temple, which dates back to the twelfth century BC.[8] Today this temple displays a cult stone where worshipers revere it as a literal form of Aphrodite. They believe that she was a star that fell from heaven in the form of this stone.

Worshiping Aphrodite as a fallen star is more evidence that the queen of heaven is one with the devil as his daughter. Isaiah said this about the devil, "How you have fallen from heaven, O star of the morning, son of the dawn!" (Isaiah 14:12). The angels that fell with satan are also referred to as fallen stars in Revelation, "His tail swept away a third of the stars of heaven and threw them to the earth" (Revelation 12:4).

A similar cult stone, made smooth from the touch and kisses of thousands of Muslims, is in the sacred Muslim Kaaba in Mecca. Muhammed placed it in the Kaaba years before his visions. Muslims worshiped Alitta or Alilat, otherwise known as Aphrodite, right up until the advent of Islam.

Lennard James quotes author Rufus C. Camphausen from his article titled, *The Ka'bah at Mecca* (Bres (Holland) No.139, 1989), saying, "Allah is a revamped version of the ancient goddess Al'Lat, and it was her shrine, which has since continued with little change, as the Kaaba."[9]

PROSTITUTION

The pattern of temple prostitution is carried on with this queen of heaven alias also. An article from the University of Houston explains how it was a common form of worship in Aphrodite's temples:

> Women, often of good birth, voluntarily served in her temples, where they had intercourse with men who paid in the form of offerings to the goddess. Such

service guaranteed the favor of the goddess and ensured large families to the devotee, once she married. The sometimes prissy Greeks did not like the practice, but it did occur in temples to Aphrodite at Corinth and Cythera.[10]

SPLIT PERSONALITY

Aphrodite, like Ishtar, was also split into two deities: Aphrodite Ourania (literally means "queen of heaven") and Aphrodite Pandemos. An article from the University of Houston explains how the wholesome identity of Aphrodite is separated from the sexually immoral one:

> In the fourth century [BC] we find Aphrodite sep-
> arated into two aspects: higher, celestial love,
> Aphrodite Ourania, and the love of the whole people,
> Aphrodite Pandemos, who is responsible for lower
> sexual life and in particular for prostitution.[11]

This split personality is a common phenomenon in the world of modern prostitution. The film *Nefarious, Merchant of Souls* is a documentary uncovering the worldwide tragedy of human slavery as encountered in many different countries. In it, psychologist Dr. Melissa Farley explains how pimps use emotional abuse on young girls in order to get them to comply:

> Other techniques of mind control include the creation
> of a part of the personality that prostitutes. So that
> there might be Genie who is the young woman who
> has girlfriends in high school and then Veronica is the
> prostituting part. Because you can't prostitute without

splitting part of the self psychologically, Veronica is deliberately created by pimps. The child slips off that part of the self that has to prostitute for 6-10 hours.[12]

There is no doubt that Aphrodite represents and perpetuates the polar opposite of love. Only the true love of God can heal those caught in the prostituting snare of the queen of heaven. The following quote is from *Nefarious* from a person who was rescued from prostitution by the Lover of her soul:

[I said] "Jesus, I just want to see You. I want to talk to You." He granted my request. I had a dream one night and He came to me. He was the most handsome man I had ever seen. Beautiful! He came close to me and read me, from when I was a baby until the age that I was. Everything I'd done.

He didn't say a word to me. He looked at me with love in His eyes and was like "I love you." He took me. I was nothing. When He found me I hadn't had a bath in a year. I was covered in abscesses. I cut myself. I was stinky. I was rotten and He made me into something beautiful.

That is so wonderful and so worth giving myself to. I don't want to stop talking about Him. My heart is so full of joy. I just want everyone to know about Him. I know He loves me and He's real.

Aphrodite had great influence on some of the major people groups mentioned in Scripture.

APHRODITE IN THE BIBLE

ASHKELON

The Bible refers to a city called Ashkelon throughout the Old Testament. This city had a temple devoted to Aphrodite that employed the office of eunuch. Stephanie Budin quotes *Herodotus* Book I, sections 103 and 133:

> And when the Skythians appeared in Syro-Palestine, Psammetikhos, the King of Egypt, entreating them with gifts and prayers dissuaded them from proceeding further. Then they, heading back again, appeared in the city Ashkalon [Ashkelon] of Syria; the majority of the Skythians passed by unharmed, but some of them, seizing the sanctuary of Aphrodite Ourania, plundered it. This is the sanctuary, as I discovered through inquiry, which is the oldest of all the sanctuaries of this goddess; for the sanctuary of Cyrpus originated there (Ashkalon). [13]

ROMAN EMPIRE

The man who was the Roman Emperor at the time of Jesus' birth, described himself as "the descendant of Aphrodite, the Divine Augustus Caesar."[14] When Jesus walked the earth, it was common belief that Aphrodite established the Roman Empire (see map at Figure 12).

Goddesses Who Rule explains this phenomenon:

> In her oldest known myth, her [Aphrodite's] descendants ruled in Asia Minor, while the later development of this myth brings her son Aeneas and his

family to Italy to found the Roman civilization. This ancient tradition was revitalized by the rulers of the Roman Empire, above all, Julius Caesar.

Believing that their divine right to rule rested on an ancestral bond to the queen of heaven – known to the Romans both as Aphrodite and as Venus – they continued to build of this foundation of sacred kingship.[15]

(Note – Julius Caesar ruled in the period between the demise of the Roman Republic and the rise of the Roman Empire.)

This is why all Roman emperors believed Venus was their ancestor, patron, and source of kingship. They also identified her as their war deity, Venus Bringer of Victory. The Roman poet and philosopher, Lucretius, claimed that Venus alone ruled the world and through her, "each living thing takes life and birth, and sees the light of the sun."[16]

In the Gospel of Matthew, the Pharisees questioned Jesus about paying taxes. He responded to them by saying, "Show Me the coin used for the poll tax." His disciples brought Him a denarius. Jesus asked the Pharisees, showing them one side of the coin bearing the bust of Caesar, "Whose likeness and inscription is this?" It is highly probable that the other side of the coin bore an image of Venus.

HEAD COVERING

Practices of Aphrodite worship are present in Scripture, although her actual name is not. In 1 Corinthians 11, Paul gives some rather obscure instructions about women covering their heads while praying or prophesying. He says that if they leave their head uncovered, they are no different from a woman who shaves her head. Unless you are familiar with the culture Paul lived in, this makes little sense. At that time, there were certain women who shaved their heads in Corinth. *The Goddess Revival* explains who they were:

> Near Eastern goddesses were frequently served by sacred prostitutes who lived in the temples and offered worshipers a mystic union with the goddess herself. Their position was one of honor and power. Indeed, the cult prostitutes attached to the great temple of Aphrodite at Corinth were said by their prayers to have stopped the Persian fleet as it advanced upon mainland Greece.
>
> During the period of temple service, the woman – even if she was married – was considered a "virgin." Women in the cult of the Syrian Goddess would serve one day a year as a prostitute or else cut off their hair as a sacrifice.[17]

The Syrian Goddess describes that a woman who refused to shave her head in worship to Adonis, would be required to offer herself for sale for a single day, to foreigners only. Her payment was given as an offering to Aphrodite.[18]

The *AMG Complete Word Study Dictionary New Testament* explains why the head covering that Paul mentions was needed, "What happened when one of these prostitute priestesses was saved in Corinth? Since she could not grow her hair immediately, she used a veil to cover her head to show that she no longer belonged to the prostitute caste."[19]

Nearly every king of Israel came under the dark mindset of the queen of heaven through Asherah. I believe that out of all the aliases, this one has the strongest presence in the Christian culture.

---

[1] Location of cities and regions are author's estimation.

[2] Lucian translated by Herbert A. Strong and John Garstang (1913), *The Syrian Goddess*, 49 [Online] http://www.sacred-texts.com/cla/luc/tsg/tsg07.htm [2014, Jul].

[3] Benard, *Goddesses Who Rule*, 18. Kindle, Chapter 1, 8%.

[4] "File:Sandro Botticelli - La nascita di Venere - Google Art Project - edited.jpg" [Online] https://commons.wikimedia.org/wiki/File:Sandro_Botticelli_-_La_nascita_di_Venere_-_Google_Art_Project_-_edited.jpg [2016, Sep].

[5] Budin, *A Reconsideration of the Aphrodite-Ashtart Syncretism*, 125, 126.

[6] Wikimedia Commons, "File:Hermaphroditus(herma).jpg" [Online] http://commons.wikimedia.org/wiki/File:Hermaphroditus_(herma).jpg [2015, May].

[7] Johnson, *Lady of the Beasts*, 239-240.

[8] Philip Mozel (2006), *The Journal of the Royal Astronomical Society of Canada 100.4*, "The Cult Statue of Aphrodite at Palaepaphos: A Meteorite?" 149-155.

[9] Lennard James (26 May 2009), "Islam's Sacred Stone of Mecca" [Online] http://www.islam-watch.org/Lennard/Islam-Sacred-Stone-of-Mecca.htm [2015, May].

[10] University of Houston, "Class 3308: Myths And The Cult Of Ancient Gods Notes On Aphrodite (Topic 8)" [Online] http://www.class.uh.edu/mcl/classics/Aphr/Aphr.html [2014 Jun].

[11] Ibid.

[12] *Nefarious, Merchant of Souls*, Dir. Benjamin Nolot, Nefarious LLC, 2011. DVD.

[13] Budin, *A Reconsideration of the Aphrodite-Ashtart Syncretism*, 125, 126.

[14] Braund, *Augustus to Nero*, Google eBook.

[15] Benard, *Goddesses Who Rule*, 18. Kindle Chapter 1, 7%.

[16] Harrison, *Myths of Greece and Rome*, 21.

[17] Spencer, *The Goddess Revival*, 57.

[18] Lucian, *The Syrian Goddess*, 46.

[19] Zodhiates, *Complete Word Study Dictionary*, #2619.

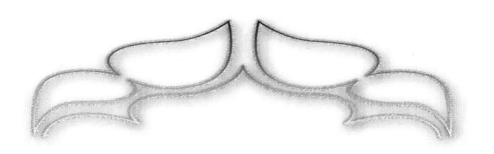

ASHERAH

MANY MONTHS AFTER completing this chapter, and much to my disgust, Asherah symbols were uncovered in my own life. Up until then, they were priceless to me because some were childhood gifts, while others were connected to events and people precious to me.

This personal revelation was intensified by the effort it took to sort through all the kings of Israel. As I researched the reign of each king, he seemed to take on life for me, as I learned how a particular aspect of the queen of heaven's influence had deprived him of the fullness of God's love.

My heart broke for many of them, especially King Josiah who did everything right, yet died an unnecessary death and whose sons were horribly tortured. It was due to this powerful learning experience that I reacted so passionately when God showed me my own defilement.

TODAY

After walking into a Mexican restaurant in Woodland Park, Colorado, I nearly lost my appetite when a modern painting of an Asherah greeted me. It was a tree in the form of a woman with branches for the hair and the trunk was her body and legs.

Figure 28. Latter Day Saints sacred grove in Palmyra, NY [1]

Famous wood carver and sculptor, David Hostetler, has his commissioned work that takes the same form of a female as a tree in prominent places like the Trump International Hotel and Tower in New York City and in many museums. His website states:

Among all goddesses, Asherah is my inspiration, for it
is she who was carved from living trees as well as the
image of the tree of life. This goddess is the
embodiment of my passion for wood and all that is
woman. I want to resurrect the Goddess Asherah and
the goddess within all of us through my art.[2]

The popular and highly violent HBO Series, *Game of Thrones*,
has a sacred grove with carved trees called Wierwood. If you play the
video game Morrowind, you are most likely puzzled over the odd,
useless Ash statue. I cannot promise any clues to master the game,
but maybe this chapter will make you wonder about the game's
intent.

ORIGIN AND LOCALE

Asherah was the goddess wife of the Sumerian (Iraq) god Anu
who was known as the King of Gods and the God of Heaven.
However, in the Syrian Ugaritic culture, her spouse was El, the
supreme god of the Canaanite religion and Father of All Gods. Their
son was Baal. The Amorite culture was also steeped in Asherah
worship. According to *The Hebrew Goddess*, one of the Amorite
kings, Abdu-Ashirta, had a name that meant, "Slave of Asherah."[3]

Asherah is found in many ancient texts, the oldest being
Gilgamesh and The Huluppu Tree, which we have already looked at
with Inanna and Lilith. In the remainder of the story, Gilgamesh
gives Inanna part of the chopped down huluppu tree for her throne
and bed, but "of the remainder of the tree, Gilgamesh makes for
himself the pukku and mikku, two wooden objects of magic
significance."[4] These might have been Asherah idols.

Ancient cities were named in tribute to Asherah, such as

Atharath in southern Arabia and Elath of Sidon (east of Sinai). She was also a chief deity known as the "Asherah of Tyre."

DESIGNATIONS

Reference to this queen of heaven alias takes on different names in the Bible, depending on the translation used. These include Asherah, asherim (plural form), Asherah pole, carved image, grove, horrid image, and luxuriant tree. It is used over fifty times in the Old Testament as both the formal name of the goddess and as a reference to a cult object of worship.

Ancient texts use different forms of her name that include:[5]

- Ashratum and Ashratu in Akkadian writings
- Asherdu, Ashertu, Aserdu, or Asertu in Hittite texts
- Elat, Lady Athirat of the Sea, and the Creatrix of the gods in the Ugaritic language
- Qudshu in Egypt
- Ashira of Tema in Arabia that was written in the Aramaic language
- Goddess Par Excellence in the most ancient works of the Phoenician religion authored by Sanchuniathon

In the Canaanite pantheon she was the chief goddess as Lady Asherah of the Sea. The Canaanites also believed the One True God was the same as their pagan god, El. Since Asherah's spouse was El, she was considered Yahweh's partner as well.

William Dever, an expert in ancient Near East archeology, discovered an inscription in a cemetery west of Hebron from the eighth century BC that says, "Blessed may he be by Yahweh and his Asherah." This same Hebrew inscription was in a small desert fort in the Sinai. *The Archaeological Study Bible* gives more details:

> A cache of inscriptions [were] found at a site called
> Kuntillet Ajrud, located 31 miles south of Kadesh-
> barnea in the northern Sinai. Especially enlightening
> are three texts from this site that say, "I bless you by
> Yahweh of Samaria and by his Asherah," "I bless you
> by Yahweh of Teman and by his Asherah" and "to
> Yahweh of Teman and to his Asherah."[6]

These discoveries are hard evidence of people defiling their worship
of the One True God with that of the queen of heaven.

ICONOGRAPHY

An Asherah idol took on the form of a living tree, a pillar, a
grove of trees, a woodcarving, and possibly a clay figurine. Created
from oak, cedar, poplar, terebinth, cypress, and fig (sycamore) trees,
asherim were worshiped on "every high hill and under every green
tree."

High areas of worship were "at the top of every street" and "in
every square" (Ezekiel 16: 25, 31) where sacrifices were offered and
drink offerings were poured out (see Ezekiel 20:28). This practice
was a replication of worshiping God on the high places (see 1 Samuel
9:12-25).

The sacred pillars God mentioned when He told Moses of His
plans for Canaan were asherim:

> For My angel will go before you and bring you in to
> the land of the Amorites, the Hittites, the Perizzites,
> the Canaanites, the Hivites and the Jebusites; and I
> will destroy them. You shall not worship their gods,

nor serve them, nor do according to their deeds; but you shall utterly overthrow them and break their *sacred pillars* in pieces. (Exodus 23:23-24, italics added)

Religious wooden sacred pillars used today that are known as the Great Goddess, the Tree of Life, or the Axis of Mundi fit the spiritual profile of Asherah. The sites of these sacred pillars are significant since they represent the center of the earth, the connection between heaven and earth, and/or the point where all four compass directions meet.

HOUSEHOLD IDOLS

Abundant archeological evidence in the form of small clay figurines (see Figure 29) may indicate that Asherah was a household idol. William Dever, Professor Emeritus at the University of Arizona, says the following about these household idols:

> For a hundred years now we have known of little terracotta female figurines. They show a nude female; the sexual organs are not represented but the breasts are. They are found in tombs, they are found in households, they are found everywhere. There are thousands of them. They date all the way from the 10th century to the early 6th century [BC]. They have long been connected with one goddess or another, but many scholars are still hesitant to come to a conclusion.

> I think they are representations of Asherah. We found molds for making Asherah figurines, mass-producing

Figure 29. Judean Asherah clay idol figurines [7]

them, in village shrines. So probably almost everybody had one of these figurines, and they surely have something to do with fertility. They were no doubt used to pray for conceiving a child and bearing the child safely and nursing it. It's interesting to me that the Israelite and Judean ones are rather more modest than the Canaanite ones, which are right in your face. The Israelite and Judean ones mostly show a nursing mother.[8]

In the book of Genesis, Jacob dealt with these household idols.

> So Jacob said to his household and to all who were with him, "Put away the foreign gods which are among you, and purify yourselves and change your garments; and let us arise and go up to Bethel, and I will make an altar there to God, who answered me in the day of my distress and has been with me wherever I have gone." (Genesis 35:2-3)

Figurines that are used to represent God, a religious deity, or person that is ascribed spiritual power can be just as dangerous today as it was during biblical times. I address this further in the Chapter titled, "Defeat the Queen of Heaven."

SACRED TREE

Tree worship has come down through the ages beginning with Adam and Eve who believed the fruit of a tree would give them supernatural powers. We see the same today in religions and cultures around the world that either worship or place great value on trees.

Vividly represented in the popular movie, *Avatar*, The World Tree of Shamanism was called the Hometree. I will cover the sacred fig trees that are worshiped all over the world by Buddhists in the chapter titled "Bonus Chapter / The Fig Tree."

The British Museum has a stone relief from the throne room of an Assyrian king that has a prominent sacred tree in the center of the image.[9] The comparison of Assyria to a mighty cedar in Ezekiel 31 is no doubt in reference to the Assyrian's worship of trees. In response to this foolish worship, God sees them as a mighty tree that He will cut down.

> Because it is high in stature and has set its top among the clouds, and its heart is haughty in its loftiness, therefore I will give it into the hand of a despot of the nations; he will thoroughly deal with it. According to its wickedness I have driven it away. Alien tyrants of the nations have cut it down and left it; on the mountains and in all the valleys its branches have fallen and its boughs have been broken in all the ravines of the land. And all the peoples of the earth

have gone down from its shade and left it. On its ruin all the birds of the heavens will dwell, and all the beasts of the field will be on its fallen branches so that all the trees by the waters may not be exalted in their stature, nor set their top among the clouds, nor their well-watered mighty ones stand erect in their height. For they have all been given over to death, to the earth beneath, among the sons of men, with those who go down to the pit. (Ezekiel 31:10-14)

LAKOTA SUNDANCE

Native American ceremonies across the United States and Canada use sacred trees or poles. In the Lakota Sioux Sundance ceremony a mature cottonwood tree represents

a vertical connection (axis mundi) to the sun and the cosmos...The tree is adorned with flags and artefacts of six colors, representing the six cardinal directions (east, west, north, south, above, below.) The dancing ground is surrounded by an arbor covered with boughs with an opening to the east, where the dancers and the Sun enter each day.[10]

The *National Geographic* magazine explains how this honored tree is both physically and spiritually the center of the ritual. "With the reverence afforded a sacred being, Oglala men fell a specially chosen cottonwood tree and carry it to the center of a Sun Dance circle. Erected in the earth, the tree will become the focus of a days-long spiritual ceremony."[11]

The ceremony includes piercing two hooks into the chests of

each chosen male participant. Those hooks are then attached to the sacred tree with cords. In his book, *The Blue Road, Jesus Fulfilled the Old Way*, Pastor Quincy Good Star, of the Cheyenne River Sioux Tribe, describes it as "a man hanging from a tree, pierced, and looking toward the sun."[12] The men dance around the tree for days until the hooks tear free. Good Star further explains,

> Jesus hung on a tree so we wouldn't have to. Jesus was pierced so we no longer have to pierce ourselves or offer up our flesh as offerings. Jesus, the sinless God-Man, hung on the tree, was pierced in the sight of God – one perfect sacrifice that never needs to be repeated. My relatives, Jesus finished the work. Now we have the real substance, and peace with God through Jesus; let us not go back to the shadow.[13]

In South Dakota I had the honor of participating in a prayer meeting that coincided with a Sundance ceremony. We set out a meal in an old abandoned church that was located near the entrance to the Sundance grounds. Ceremonial participants were welcomed to come in and join us or to take a meal with them to the ritual.

When the Sundance began, our group interceded in the Spirit on behalf of the Lakota dancers. Two Lakota men who were part of our group played the traditional drum while singing to God in their native tongue. I will never forget the worshipful atmosphere that they created. It was a privilege for me to worship God in the company of Christian Lakota tribal members.

JESUS CHRIST IMPOSTER

To be clear, the tree of life from the Garden of Eden represents the New Covenant, which is Jesus Christ. God said that anyone who eats of the tree of life would live forever. Jesus said the same of anyone who eats His flesh (see John 6:51).

It is God who is the good tree, "I am like a fresh, green cypress tree; your fruitfulness comes from me" (Hosea 14:9). Asherah is a deadly, fake imposter whose only power is to curse and bring death.

ASHERAH IN THE BIBLE

This queen of heaven alias is the most popular in the Bible; appearing throughout the entire Old Testament. Asherah caused the downfall of many of God's people.

MOUNT SINAI

The first place in the Bible that the name Asherah occurs is when God spoke on Mount Sinai. God told Moses to cut two new stone tablets to replace the ones he had smashed when he saw the golden calf (Hathor) that Aaron made.

Moses took the tablets up on the mountain and God told him He was going to make a covenant in which He would perform miracles they had never seen before. God then said,

> Be sure to observe what I am commanding you this day...Watch yourself that you make no covenant with the inhabitants of the land into which you are going, or it will become a snare in your midst. But rather, you are to tear down their altars and smash their sacred pillars and cut down their asherim — for you shall not worship any other god, for the Lord, *whose name is Jealous*, is a jealous God — otherwise you

might make a covenant with the inhabitants of the land and they would play the harlot with their gods and sacrifice to their gods, and someone might invite you to eat of his sacrifice, and you might take some of his daughters for your sons, and his daughters might play the harlot with their gods and cause your sons also to play the harlot with their gods. (Exodus 34:11-17, italics added)

This is the first use of God's name, Jealous, which is a direct response to the worship of Asherah in Canaan. This idol existed in the land designated as God's promise to Abraham long before the children of Israel lived there (see Genesis 12:6-7).

NEW GENERATION

Moses repeats God's command concerning Asherah three times in the book of Deuteronomy when he was teaching the Mosaic Law to a new generation who was about to enter the Promised Land. Scriptures that repeat the same idea are cause for us to pay close attention.

In these verses, Moses shares what seems like step-by-step instructions about how to avoid coming under the influence of the queen of heaven:

When the Lord your God brings you into the land where you are entering to possess it, and clears away many nations before you…You shall make no covenant with them and show no favor to them. Furthermore, you shall not intermarry with them…For they will turn your sons away from following Me to serve other gods;

then the anger of the Lord will be kindled against you and He will quickly destroy you. But thus you shall do to them: you shall tear down their altars, and smash their *sacred pillars*, and hew down their asherim, and burn their *graven images* with fire. (Deuteronomy 7:1-5, italics added)

These are the statutes and the judgments which you shall carefully observe in the land which the Lord, the God of your fathers, has given you to possess as long as you live on the earth. You shall utterly destroy all the places where the nations whom you shall dispossess serve their gods, on the high mountains and on the hills and under *every green tree*. You shall tear down their altars and smash their *sacred pillars* and burn their asherim with fire, and you shall cut down the *engraved images* of their gods and obliterate their name from that place. (Deuteronomy 12:1-3, italics added)

You shall not plant for yourself an Asherah of *any kind of tree* beside the altar of the Lord your God, which you shall make for yourself. You shall not set up for yourself a *sacred pillar* which the Lord your God hates." (Deuteronomy 16:22-23, italics added)

Of all the gods that were worshiped in the land, the name of Asherah is specifically mentioned along with her many forms (see italics in above verses). This means that every nation who occupied the land before Israel worshiped the queen of heaven. This is why God wanted those nations destroyed. Asherim were to be cut down, burned, and never replanted. Obliterating the name, Asherah, from the land was a part of God's purification plan.

GIDEON

You might be familiar with the mention of Asherah in the book of Judges concerning Gideon (see Judges 6:11-32). This passage reveals the enormous size of the Asherah tree, since it was big enough to burn the entire bull that was used for the burnt offering. This Asherah idol had an intoxicating influence on God's people because Gideon obeyed God under the cover of night and nearly died in doing so. The fact that Gideon, his entire family, and city worshiped Asherah makes it clear that Israel did not obey God's commands nor take heed of Moses' warnings.

Gideon's words to the angel who came to visit him in the winepress reflect the same outcry of many people today. "If there is a God then why has all this bad stuff happened to us? I've read about all His miracles, but that was for people in the Bible, not for me." How ironic that the very ones who claimed God was no longer a miracle worker were the ones with an Asherah in the town square.

Besides the city of Ophrah, where Gideon lived, large asherim were located in other prominent cities; including the capital city of the northern tribes of Israel, Samaria, and the capital city of the southern tribes, Jerusalem. This brings new understanding to Ezekiel 23 and the book of Micah that refer to both Samaria and Jerusalem. In Micah 5:13-14, God says,

> I will cut off your carved images and your sacred pillars from among you, so that you will no longer bow down to the work of your hands. I will root out your asherim from among you and destroy your cities.

FOREIGN WIVES

The kings of Israel struggled greatly because they intermarried with women they were supposed to destroy. Those wives turned their hearts and their sons away from God. These foreign women slaughtered their children and gave drink and grain offerings to their asherim.

Isaiah 57 calls them sorceresses and prostitutes whose sons are children of rebellion, offspring of deceit, and those who inflame themselves among the oaks and under every luxuriant tree. Hosea calls them adulterers (idol worshipers). Many of these sons became kings of Israel.

The prophet Amos, further shows the character of these women who worshiped Asherah on the mountain of Samaria by calling them "cows of Bashan." The fact that Amos refers to these women as such says quite a bit about their character, but he elaborates about their domineering attitude.

> Hear this word, you cows of Bashan who are on the mountain of Samaria, who oppress the poor, who crush the needy, who say to your husbands, "Bring now, that we may drink!" (Amos 4:1-3)

This domineering attitude is a form of worship to the queen of heaven. Jesus encourages women who worship Him to give to the poor, feed the needy, and respect their husbands.

CAPTIVITY

The last mention of Asherah in the Old Testament is found in Micah, whose prophecy was fulfilled when Judah was taken captive to Babylon.

It will be in that day," declares the Lord, "I will cut off your *carved images* and your *sacred pillars* from among you, so that you will no longer bow down to the work of your hands. I will root out your *asherim* from among you and destroy your cities." (Micah 5:10, 13-14, italics added)

God called His people to worship only Him. Serving the asherim of the native people was of the utmost evil. God describes the people of Israel who worshiped Asherah as "selling themselves to do evil."

They made themselves slaves to the very entities over whom God had given them full authority to destroy. Instead of entering into God's rest in their Promised Land, they fell headlong into the treachery that they had the power to destroy. Spiritually, it was no different from their physical enslavement in Egypt.

God's people did not heed the words of Moses in Deuteronomy: they did not destroy all the nations, they made covenants with the people of the land, they intermarried, they turned away from God, they served other gods, they neither cut down nor burned the asherim, and they planted Asherah next to God's altar.

Their worship to God was not pure but defiled through their devotion and attention to the queen of heaven. As a result, God allowed their nation to be destroyed and for the people to be led away to exile in foreign lands. In essence, God was giving them over to their desires to worship the queen of heaven since she was a deity of those foreign nations.

Now we will discover how Asherah worship affected Israel after it split. First, we will look at the history of the kings of the northern tribes of Israel, and then we will turn to the kings of Judah. Please use the Kings Chart at Appendix B as you go through these sections.

ASHERAH AND THE NORTHERN TRIBES

JEROBOAM

Recall that Israel split in two due to Solomon's worship of Ashtoreth. Jeroboam, son of one of Solomon's servants, was the first king of Israel's northern tribes. He made the two Hathor calves as mentioned in the chapter about Isis.

Jeroboam also planted an Asherah in Bethel that stood in place for the next 300 years. This northern king put his own priests in office to serve the asherim, satyrs (he-goat demons), and calves; in response, all the godly priests fled to Judah.

> Have you not driven out the priests of the Lord, the sons of Aaron and the Levites, and made for yourselves priests like the peoples of other lands? Whoever comes to consecrate himself with a young bull and seven rams, even he may become a priest of what are no gods. (2 Chronicles 13:9)

God sent Jeroboam warnings through His prophets, but these messengers did not sway his heart. One prophet said that God was provoked to anger and promised to uproot Israel and scatter them because of the asherim the people had made (see 1 Kings 14:15-16).

Of the eighteen kings that followed Jeroboam, fifteen are described as "walking in the way of Jeroboam" or "not departing from the sins of Jeroboam which he made Israel sin." Since the asherim of the land still existed, all the kings of the northern tribes allowed God's children to mix their worship of God with the queen of heaven.

AHAB

King Ahab married the famously evil, Jezebel. In Sidon, where Jezebel was from, Asherah was the chief deity known as the "Elath of Sidon." Sidon was the capital city of the king who was Jezebel's father. No doubt, Jezebel grew up worshiping Asherah. This strong influence of the queen of heaven on Jezebel explains why she had Ahab plant an Asherah tree in his capital city of Samaria (in the land belonging to the tribe of Manasseh, west of the Jordan river). This was not just a new tree put in the square on Main Street for people to admire as they walked by. It was a sacred demonic object that demanded reverence and worship.

The appointing of priests and priestesses who served the idol occurred as the cult of Asherah grew. By the time Elijah confronted them, there were 950 people who were employed by the cult. The influence of the queen of heaven on the people of Israel is clearly seen in the story of Elijah's spiritual clash with the prophets of Baal and Asherah. Elijah demanded that the people choose between their idols and God. The prophets of Baal and Asherah mutilated themselves in the process of trying to get a response from their gods.

The prophets "cut themselves according to their custom with swords and lances until the blood gushed out of them" (1 Kings 18:28). Satan accomplished his goal to kill, steal, and destroy through this queen of heaven worship. She takes pleasure in causing people to hurt themselves. The priests cut themselves because of their lack of self-worth, in hopes of moving an evil entity into action.

This practice is still common today for both religious purposes and among precious young people who can only get satisfaction in the pain felt by cutting themselves. No other god but Jesus Christ can satisfy that depth of emptiness and heal that kind of pain. I share a personal story about this in the chapter titled, "Defeat the Queen of Heaven."

Neither Baal nor Asherah could bring down fire from heaven, but God could, and did. In response, the people turned from their false gods to the One True God. Elijah ordered the killing of all the false prophets who had misled them; thus purifying the people and their land. Despite this purging of the false prophets, the Asherah in Samaria remained due to Jezebel's protection.

Tossed about by both his own desires and those of his wife, King Ahab was a double-minded man. While at home he succumbed to defiling his worship of God because of Jezebel. Yet, when on the battlefield he would repent and give his full devotion to God allowing God's power to win his battles. Scripture is clear about the effect that Asherah had on Ahab:

> Surely there was no one like Ahab who sold himself to do evil in the sight of the Lord, because Jezebel his wife incited him. He acted very abominably in following idols, according to all that the Amorites had done, whom the Lord cast out before the sons of Israel. (1 Kings 21:25-26)

Today it is common to hear the phrase "the spirit of Jezebel" in reference to sexually immoral practices, but I think this is an incorrect expression. Although her influence was great, Jezebel was only a vessel to the one controlling the people and the prophets. She was a human being who was driven by the dark power of the queen of heaven.

Two of Ahab's sons succeeded him on the throne, both of which were dedicated to their mother, Jezebel. It is in this generation that intermarriage occurred between Israel and Judah's royal families.

We will look at this in more detail in the next section titled, "Asherah and Judah."

JEHU

While Ahab's second son, Jehoram was on the throne, God gave a word to one of his army captains named Jehu. The prophet Elisha told him,

> I have anointed you king over the people of the Lord, even over Israel. You shall strike the house of Ahab your master, that I may avenge the blood of My servants the prophets, and the blood of all the servants of the Lord, at the hand of Jezebel. (2 Kings 9:6-7)

Jehu slaughtered Ahab's house, killing royalty from both Israel and Judah. He killed the remaining prophets of Baal and completely desecrated the temple of Baal. However, the Asherah in Samaria escaped the attention of this new king. Scripture says that King Jehu walked in the ways of Jeroboam, meaning he too worshiped Asherah.

JEHOAHAZ

Jehu's son was the next king of Israel. Jehoahaz followed in the sins of Jeroboam causing Israel to sin. In response God gave them over to their enemy, the king of Aram. Jehoahaz finally entreated God, but Israel did not turn from their ways and the Asherah remained standing in Samaria.

REMAINING KINGS OF ISRAEL

Beginning with Omri, Ahab's father, fourteen kings of Israel ruled from Samaria. These kings were fully aware and supported the Asherah tree of Jezebel that stood tall in the city. Amos prophesied about this city, "As for those who swear by the guilt of Samaria, who say, 'As your god lives, O Dan,' and, 'As the way of Beersheba lives,' they will fall and not rise again" (Amos 7:14).

The Asherah remained in Samaria even until the Assyrian exile around 722 BC, which means Israel worshiped this queen of heaven idol for about 140 years. The Assyrian exile occurred because the sons of Israel walked in the customs of the nations whom the Lord had driven out before them.

The legacy of the northern tribes of Israel was this:

> The sons of Israel did things secretly which were not right against the Lord their God. Moreover, they built for themselves high places in all their towns, from watchtower to fortified city. They set for themselves sacred pillars and asherim on every high hill and under every green tree, and there they burned incense on all the high places as the nations did which the Lord had carried away to exile before them; and they did evil things provoking the Lord. (2 Kings 17:9-11)

JESUS IN SAMARIA

Jesus met a woman in Samaria who possibly embodied the culture of the area. She was away from home alone, had multiple ex-husbands, was a fornicator, and was comfortable approaching all the men in her town. Although doing these things today are quite common, they were unheard of during the New Testament era. This behavior is a reflection of generations who worshiped Asherah.

Once realizing that Jesus was a prophet, the woman informed Jesus that her fathers "worshiped in this mountain." She did not say what they worshiped, but Jesus gives a clue in His response. "You worship what you do not know" (John 4:22a). Jeremiah claimed the very same thing of those who worshiped the queen of heaven (see Jeremiah 7:9). We have clearly seen that this woman's ancestors, beginning with King Ahab, worshiped Asherah in Samaria.

Jesus goes on to tell the woman, "an hour is coming, and now is, when the *true worshipers* will worship the Father in spirit and truth; for such people the Father seeks to be His worshipers" (John 4:23, italic added). Here Jesus, Himself, encourages people to have a pure devotion to God alone. True worshipers are those who only worship the One True God.

ASHERAH AND JUDAH

REHOBOAM

Solomon's son, Rehoboam, initially led the southern tribes of Judah and Benjamin after Israel split. During the first three years of his reign, he received many Levitical priests who fled south to get away from King Jeroboam and his idols. This was a blessed time for Judah as they obeyed the statutes of God and took in the northern refugees.

Unfortunately, King Rehoboam fell away from the Lord just as his father had done. He had eighteen wives, two of whom were from the tribe of Judah. It is most likely that the rest were foreign women who drew his heart away from God in drastic measure. Under Rehoboam's reign, Judah "built for themselves high places and sacred pillars and asherim on every high hill and beneath every luxuriant tree. There were also male cult prostitutes in the land. They did according to all the abominations of the nations which the Lord dispossessed before the sons of Israel" (1 Kings 14:23-24).

This verse reveals the abundance of asherim idols and the link of male prostitution with the queen of heaven. Due to their impurity,

God sent the king of Egypt to attack Judah. In response, Rehoboam obeyed the prophet of God who told him to repent.

ABIJAH

Micaiah, one of the women King Rehoboam married, was a great granddaughter of King David. Her name means, "Who is like Jehovah." The first-born male to the king was her son, Abijah. I wonder how often she brought this future king to Solomon's temple as a young boy and taught him about God.

King Abijah's upbringing by this godly woman is echoed loud and clear on Mount Zemaraim as he addressed King Jeroboam of Israel, upon succeeding his father as king of Judah. Recall from the section titled, "Isis in the Bible," that Jeroboam was responsible for defiling Israel's worship of God long after his reign ended.

> The Lord is our God, and we have not forsaken Him; and the sons of Aaron are ministering to the Lord as priests, and the Levites attend to their work. Every morning and evening they burn to the Lord burnt offerings and fragrant incense, and the showbread is set on the clean table, and the golden lampstand with its lamps is ready to light every evening; for we keep the charge of the Lord our God, but you have forsaken Him. Now behold, God is with us at our head and His priests with the signal trumpets to sound the alarm against you. O sons of Israel, do not fight against the Lord God of your fathers, for you will not succeed. (2 Chronicles 13:10-12)

The battle that ensued between Israel and Judah resulted in the largest amount of casualties recorded in the Old Testament of half a million men. The king of Israel never recovered.

King Abijah became powerful and married many wives after this battle. Unfortunately, he married Maacah who was known to have "horrid image" of Asherah. She obviously turned him away from the One True God because the asherim and male prostitution re-appeared in Judah later in his reign. This might explain his name change from Abijah in the book of Chronicles, which means "Jehovah is my father," to Abijam in the book of Kings which means "my father is the sea."

ASA

Maacah's son, Asa, was unusual because he was not fooled by his mother's infatuation with the queen of heaven. Beginning his reign faced with the largest Old Testament battle, Judah stood against a million Ethiopians. Asa, united together with Israel, sought God in the midst of overwhelming odds. Victory resulted along with a great plunder.

King Asa then heeded the words of the prophet Azariah by removing the high places and all the abominable idols, including the multitude of asherim from Judah, Benjamin, and Ephraim. Scripture says he followed Mosaic Law by cutting down, crushing, and burning his mother's Asherah. God gave Judah undisturbed rest in the land for the next thirty-six years, until the king's heart turned away from God. Asa ended his reign in disobedience that included reestablishing the high places and placing asherim throughout Judah. In doing so, he removed himself from the presence of God's peace. This brought on wars and disease until his death.

JEHOSHAPHAT

Asa's first wife was a strong godly woman. Credit goes to her for the king turning to God during the battle that ushered in the years of rest. When her son, Jehoshaphat, succeeded his father, he cleansed the southern lands of asherim, removed the high places, and humbled himself in the ways of the Lord. However, neither Asa nor his son removed Solomon's Ashtoreth and asherim that were still on the Mount of Destruction.

Jehoshaphat sent his officials and priests throughout all the land, teaching the people from the book of the Law of the Lord. As a result, other kings brought him gifts instead of war. He was highly respected by the prophets of God. He made peace with Israel's King Ahab and both of Ahab's sons, who were to be future kings of Israel.

The alliance of these two royal families was further established when Jehoshaphat married a woman from Ahab's family; this is the royal family intermarriage I made mention of in the previous section about the northern tribes. It is not clear if this woman was of Jewish descent, but she did not sway Jehoshaphat's desire away from God.

The tight-knit relationship between the royal families was obvious since one son of each king shared the same name, Jehoram. This was also true of another son of Ahab and grandson of Jehoshaphat who shared the same name, Ahaziah. Unfortunately, Jehoshaphat's alliance with King Ahab proved to be devastating to his descendants. Although Jehoshaphat was a man who "sought the Lord with all his heart," he followed in his father's footsteps by allowing the high places to be reestablished.

JEHORAM

After becoming king, Jehoshaphat's son, Jehoram, strengthened the alliance with the north further by marrying Ahab and Jezebel's daughter, Athaliah. Ironically this would result in the downfall of

Judah. Jehoram was an evil king and no doubt, because of his wife, was the first king of Judah to "walk in the ways of the kings of Israel."

This meant that he worshiped Asherah and "made high places in the mountains of Judah, and caused the inhabitants of Jerusalem to play the harlot and led Judah astray" (2 Chronicles 21:11). As a result, provinces revolted against him, he lost his family, and he died in great pain.

AHAZIAH

Ahaziah, Jehoram's son, became the next king of Judah. During his rule, the wicked counsel of both his grandfather, King Ahab, and his mother, Athaliah, heavily influenced him. At this time, King Ahaziah's uncle, Jehoram (Ahab's son) was Israel's king. This is when God anointed the captain of Israel's army, Jehu, to be the next king of Israel and commissioned him to destroy the house of Ahab. Due to the intermarriage of the royal families, this commission included King Ahaziah of Judah, King Jehoram of Israel, and everyone in both royal families.

In the previous section, we learned of the bloody slaughter Jehu inflicted on the king of Israel. The very same thing occurred in Judah where King Ahaziah and all his descendants died, except for his youngest son, Joash. God preserved Joash as a baby through his aunt who was the wife of the godly priest, Jehoiada. She hid him safely for six years during Queen Athaliah's reign in Judah.

JOASH

Brought out from hiding at the age of seven, Joash became king under the close counsel of Jehoiada. The priest tried to ensure their devotion to God, but the people rebelled. While continuing with their rituals for the Law of Moses, they were also making sacrifices and burning incense on the high places to their asherim. This defilement nullified their obedience to the One True God.

King Joash married a woman whose name means, "Jehovah is her ornament." This woman reared the king's successor.

Jehoiada died more than half way into the king's forty-year reign, at which time Joash turned to the counsel of his officials and "they abandoned the house of the Lord, the God of their fathers, and served the asherim and the idols" (2 Chronicles 24:18). The queen of heaven influenced Joash to the extent that he murdered Jehoiada's son after he entreated the king to return to God. Eventually Judah underwent attack and the king was murdered.

AMAZIAH, AZARIAH, AND JOTHAM

The next three kings of Judah did right in the sight of the Lord, but the people still sacrificed and burned incense to the asherim on high places. The Ashtoreth and asherim that Solomon erected on the Mount of Destruction were still in place.

It is important to understand that these kings did not worship on the high places themselves, but they did allow their people to do so. Although God prospered them, their lives did not end well.

AHAZ

Unlike the preceding three kings, Ahaz himself worshiped Asherah by burning incense and making sacrifices "on the hills and under every green tree" (2 Chronicles 28:4). Neither his mother nor his wives are mentioned in Scripture, but we can only surmise that they were the reason for his grand departure from the three generations that preceded him.

King Ahaz married Abijah whose name means, "my father is Jehovah." Her son, Hezekiah, became the next king.[14]

HEZEKIAH

King Hezekiah was a very godly man who "removed the high places and broke down the sacred pillars and cut down the Asherah" (2 Kings 18:4). Most likely put in place by his father, the Asherah he cut down was presumably worshiped corporately in a prominent place, like Jerusalem. Hezekiah told his people, "our fathers have been unfaithful and have done evil in the sight of the Lord our God, and have forsaken Him and turned their faces away from the dwelling place of the Lord, and have turned their backs" (2 Chronicles 29:6).

King Hezekiah reestablished the rituals in Solomon's temple and sent couriers to the tribes of Ephraim and Manasseh with a message requesting the people to join in a Passover celebration. Everyone enjoyed interacting with God so much that the event was extended for seven days. During that time, the people's hearts returned to God and they purified their devotion to Him.

> All Israel who were present went out to the cities of Judah, broke the pillars in pieces, cut down the asherim and pulled down the high places and the altars throughout all Judah and Benjamin, as well as in Ephraim and Manasseh, until they had destroyed them all. (2 Chronicles 31:1)

It is clear that obeying God's command to destroy the queen of heaven idols was due to the joyful celebration and enjoyment of God's presence. Allowing God to change their hearts brought about a desire to purify their devotion to Him. It did not happen as a result of legalism or fear of their spiritual enemy. This is an important lesson for us today.

Even the king of Assyria had something to say about Hezekiah's devotion when he taunted the people in Jerusalem about their God, "Has not the same Hezekiah taken away *His* high places and *His* altars, and said to Judah and Jerusalem, 'You shall worship before one altar, and on it you shall burn incense?'" (2 Chronicles 32:12, italics added). This Assyrian king reveals that Asherah and God were worshiped together in these places (see italics). Hezekiah's pure devotion and obedience to God gained him immense riches and honor.

PATTERN OF WORSHIP

Are you seeing a pattern emerge? None of the kings who worshiped Asherah thrived and all came to a bad end. Even the kings who did not personally worship Asherah suffered because they did not cleanse the land of the mixed worship of Asherah and God. The only kings who flourished were those who were fully devoted to a pure worship of God. It is extremely important to realize that God never changes and always desires our complete affection. Without this pure devotion to Him alone, we rob ourselves of all that God is willing to give us. Pay close attention to this next king. Scripture reveals a depth of God's wrath that was yet to be experienced with any of the previous kings of Israel or Judah.

MANASSEH

Manasseh, Hezekiah's son, was nothing like his godly father. His first wife, Meshullemeth, was a foreigner whose idolatrous influence on Judah was far worse than Jezebel's earlier manipulation of Israel. Under Meshullemeth's direction, Manasseh rebuilt all the high places of asherim that his father had destroyed.

Manasseh's hardcore worship revolved around his deep devotion to the queen of heaven. He instituted many forbidden practices such as witchcraft, divination, sorcery; even killing his own son in the fires of Molech. He worshiped the sun, moon, and stars which no doubt included the astrology of Lilith. Mediums and spiritists were his guides. Aside from all the evil that Manasseh practiced, there was one thing he did that no king had ever done before him. This one thing provoked our God, whose name is Jealous, to a holy and righteous eruption of wrath.

Other kings of God's people had defiled their worship with the queen of heaven. Other kings led God's people astray. Kings of Israel had even torn away the precious metals from the temple as payment to foreign kings who worshiped the queen of heaven. None of this compared to what Manasseh did.

He defiled Solomon's temple that was a sacred place for the presence of the One True God to meet with the people of Israel. The temple was a copy and foreshadow of Jesus Christ. In this hallowed place of the One True God, Manasseh "set the carved image of Asherah that he had made, in the house of which the Lord said to David and to his son Solomon, "In this house and in Jerusalem, which I have chosen from all the tribes of Israel, I will put My name forever" (2 Kings 21:7). He directly disobeyed God, who had said, "You shall not plant for yourself an Asherah of any kind of tree beside the altar of the Lord your God" (Deuteronomy 16:21).

Ezekiel, who was a prophet nearly fifty years after Manasseh's death, helps us to understand the gravity of this horrible mistake. In a vision, he is in the temple where he saw the glory of God. Ezekiel was shown the exact location of this Asherah, described as the "idol of jealousy" (see Ezekiel 8:3; Jeremiah 7:30).

Imagine God as the dishonored husband, giving His prophet a good long look at the adulteress in His holy marriage bed. Scripture uses the phrase "provokes to jealousy" to describe this adulteress Asherah. The world has hundreds of names for the queen of heaven, but none of those names comes close to her only true name, Provokes God to Jealousy.

Many servants of God spoke and wrote about the full extent of God's wrath toward Manessah. In 2 Kings, God declares that He will destroy Jerusalem just as He did Samaria, the capital city of Israel, and the lineage of Ahab. Who can forget Jehu's bloody rampage against both royal families of Israel? The following verses contain strong language describing the future of Judah:

> I will abandon the remnant of My inheritance and deliver them into the hand of their enemies, and they will become as plunder and spoil to all their enemies. (2 Kings 21:14-15)

> So I will hurl you out of this land into the land which you have not known, neither you nor your fathers; and there you will serve other gods day and night, for I will grant you no favor. (Jeremiah 16:30)

> "So as I live," declares the Lord God, "surely, because you have defiled My sanctuary with all your detestable idols and with all your abominations, therefore I will also withdraw, and My eye will have no pity and I will not spare." (Ezekiel 5:11)

> I will make them an object of horror among all the kingdoms of the earth because of Manasseh, the son of

Hezekiah, the king of Judah, for what he did in
Jerusalem. (Jeremiah 15:4)

King Mannaseh was taken captive with hooks and bronze chains
to Babylon, after which he repented upon realizing his grave error.
In response, God returned him as king to Jerusalem where he threw
the asherim outside the city. The heat of God's wrath lasted long
after Mannaseh died and the Israelites were scattered away from
their Promised Land.

Why did this one act of disobedience bring on such a strong
response from God? Why was God's wrath not satisfied with this
king's repentance? The abominable act of placing an Asherah tree in
God's temple is what caused His presence to leave and never be able
to meet with His people in that place again.

More devastating than that, because the temple was an
embodiment of Jesus Christ, I believe that the intrusion of this
Asherah idol in temple of the One True God is what gave the devil a
legal right to curse Jesus by hanging Him on an Asherah tree. I will
explore this more deeply in the next section titled, "My Asherim."

AMON

Unfortunately, when Mannaseh's son, Amon, became king, he
salvaged the asherim his father threw away and put them back into
service. King Amon clearly demonstrated his mother's influence by
re-erecting the Asherah in Solomon's temple. He also instituted male
cult prostitution in Solomon's temple. *Yes, you read that right, there
was cult prostitution occurring in the temple of God* just like it was
in all the other temples devoted to the queen of heaven.

During this time, women wove tapestries for Asherah in God's
temple that were most likely also hung in the temple.

JOSIAH

Amon married Jedidah, whose name means "darling of Jehovah" whose son, Josiah, succeeded his father after he was killed. Josiah was only eight years old when he became king. The first mention of Josiah's name in Scripture is during the reign of Jeroboam, first king of the northern tribes. A man of God came to Bethel, to the altar where Jeroboam was burning incense. This altar was next to an Asherah tree. The prophet said,

> O altar, altar, thus says the Lord, 'Behold, a son shall be born to the house of David, Josiah by name; and on you he shall sacrifice the priests of the high places who burn incense on you, and human bones shall be burned on you. (1 Kings 13:2)

Roughly 300 years later, Josiah fulfilled that prophecy by using the Asherah to fuel the fire of his sacrifice to the One True God. He completely eradicated the queen of heaven from Judah, Samaria, and Bethel. He demolished all the high places, obliterated all the asherim, and destroyed Topheth (where children were sacrificed).

Josiah destroyed the 300-year-old Ashtoreth and the asherim on the Mount of Destruction in Jerusalem, put in place by Solomon. He purified the temple of God by eradicating and burning everything that was unholy, including all items devoted to the queen of heaven. Although not specifically mentioned, this included the Asherah his father planted in Solomon's temple. The asherim were chopped down, broken into pieces, burned, and then beaten into powder. The destruction of these idols followed the Old Covenant Law and could not have been more complete. Josiah's entire reign was devoted to purifying the Promised Land, its people, and the temple.[15]

> Josiah removed all the abominations from all the lands belonging to the sons of Israel, and made all who were present in Israel to serve the Lord their God. Throughout his lifetime they did not turn from following the Lord God of their fathers. (2 Chronicles 31:33)

> Before him there was no king like him who turned to the Lord with all his heart and with all his soul and with all his might, according to all the law of Moses; nor did any like him arise after him. (2 Kings 23:24-25)

Even the devotion of such an obedient king could not change the mind of God concerning the future of Judah: "The Lord did not turn from the fierceness of His great wrath with which His anger burned against Judah, because of all the provocations with which Manasseh had provoked Him" (2 Kings 22:26).

JEHOAHAZ II, ELIAKIM, JEHOIACHIN, MATTANIAH

Three of Josiah's sons and one of his grandsons, were successive kings of Judah over the next 23 years. His youngest reigning son was carried off to Egypt while the other three were later taken captive to Babylon. Although their mothers were from Israel, they were all evil.

The only explanation of this can be God's plan of purification from what Manasseh had done. After Josiah purged the land of the asherim, nothing is ever said about these idols again in the history of the kings. Once all of God's people were in captivity, the land had to rest for seventy years in order to be cleansed from the mixed worship and to honor the Sabbath.

Notice in these verses from Exodus that the restriction from worshiping other gods immediately follows the command for a Sabbath rest.

> Six days you are to do your work, but on the seventh day you shall cease from labor...Now concerning everything which I have said to you, be on your guard; and do not mention the name of other gods, nor let them be heard from your mouth. (Exodus 23:12-13)

This rest was not required when Joshua initially cleansed the Promised Land of pagan worship nearly 800 years earlier. However, during the years of the kings, the land became "a desolation and a horror" (Jeremiah 25:11) due to the defiled worship of God with the queen of heaven.

God said, "I poured out My wrath on them for the blood which they had shed on the land, because they had defiled it with their idols" (Ezekiel 36:18).

ENCOUNTER WITH ASHERAH

Although I was finished with my initial research for Asherah, I pulled a book off my shelf that previously escaped my attention in order to look up Asherah. In it I read,

> Bible scholars who have studied ancient East artwork have said that some figures in drawings could be representations of Asherah. Drawings of plain and carved poles, staffs, a *cross*,...could be illustrations of an Asherah (italics added).[16]

In that moment, my mind reeled at what God showed me. My precious Jesus, My Lord and King, sacrificed Himself on the very abomination with which Israel had played the harlot. I sobbed. The thought of Jesus' hands and feet being nailed, not just to a piece of wood, but nailed to an Asherah pounded in my head.

All of a sudden, the Scripture that says, "everyone who hangs on a tree is cursed" made a lot more sense to me (see Galatians 3:13). I always wondered in the past, "Why a tree?" I then remembered a blog post I wrote the previous month about the adulteress that the Pharisees expected Jesus to condemn. Here is a portion of the post:

> As Jesus stooped to write on the ground, I wonder if He wrote the names of all the nations Israel forfeited her livelihood to. God was unable to write His law upon their hearts, so did He write their sin in the sand? Did the woman wonder about what was written and why it caused such a reaction from her accusers? Especially the older ones who were the first to leave? Were they the first to remember the words written in the scrolls of how Asherahs were erected and worshiped in God's temple?
>
> The idolatry of feminine Asherah trees was a form of adultery (idolatry and adultery are synonymous in the Hebrew language). It's interesting that those accusers didn't hang around - Jesus never told them to leave. Maybe in realizing how much more of a magnitude their adultery was than the woman at their feet, the shame was too much to remain in His presence.[17]

Now I thought to myself, "If those men considered the magnitude of their nation's adultery, would they really have hung Jesus on an Asherah?"

An hour later, I got up off the floor, wiped my tears, and became disgusted with the fact that I had crosses hanging in my jewelry box. To me these were no longer a sign of the sacrifice that Jesus had made for me, but an abominable symbol of the queen of heaven and defiled worship. I could not get them into the trash soon enough.

The popularity of the cross today, as an icon of Jesus, can be compared to the fiery bronze serpent that Moses held up in the wilderness. Those who were dying received immediate healing when they lifted their eyes to it (see Numbers 21:9). That serpent became an object of worship for next 700 years.[18]

King Hezekiah destroyed the bronze serpent along with the Asherah, "He removed the high places and broke down the sacred pillars and cut down the Asherah. He also broke in pieces the bronze serpent that Moses had made, for until those days the sons of Israel burned incense to it" (2 Kings 18:4). Hezekiah destroyed it because it had become an idol. Just like the cross, the serpent represented the Messiah.

Many may argue that Jesus Himself talked about the cross. When He told His disciples to take up their cross daily, they did not know that Jesus would be hung on one (see Luke 9:23). To them, a wooden cross was a means to provide a horrible death to those who broke Roman laws. Jesus was referring to a cross as a device that death was achieved on, not the holy thing we have turned it into.

The cross was a torturous way that the Romans dealt with sin. "Take up your cross," means to die to your sin. I have heard too many songs and too many sermons about the cross that seem to forget about Jesus. The cross has done nothing for us, Jesus has done everything for us. To apply the work of Jesus to a cross is to turn that cross into an object of worship no different than the bronze serpent.

The queen of heaven literally tried to cut off my voice. Without knowing about Artemis' ability to afflict physical harm, finishing this book may not have happened.

---

[1] George Edward Anderson, "File:Sacred Grove (1907).jpg" (circa 1907) [Online] https://commons.wikimedia.org/wiki/File:Sacred_Grove_(1907).jpg [2016, Dec].

[2] "About David Hostetler" [Online] http://www.hostetlersculpture.com/artist [2015, May].

[3] Patai, *The Hebrew Goddess,* Kindle, Chapter 1, 6%.

[4] Wolkstein, *Inanna,* 9.

[5] Wikipedia, "Asherah" [Online] http://en.wikipedia.org/wiki/Asherah [2015, Mar] and Harris, *Theological Wordbook of the Old Testament,* 81.

[6] Harris, *Theological Wordbook of the Old Testament* ,1043.

[7] Chamberi, "File:Judaean female figurines - Israel Museum, Jerusalem.jpg" [Online] https://commons.wikimedia.org/wiki/File:Judaean_female_figurines_-_Israel_Museum,_Jerusalem.jpg{2016, Dec}.

[8] NOVA (11.18.08), "Archeology of the Hebrew Bible" [Online] http://www.pbs.org/wgbh/nova/ancient/archeology-hebrew-bible.html [2014, Oct].

[9] J.E. Reade, Assyrian sculpture (London, The British Museum Press, 1983), "Stone panel from the North-West Palace of Ashurnasirpal II (Room I) Nimrud (ancient Kalhu), northern Iraq Neo-Assyrian, 883-859 BC, Supernatural spirits and a sacred tree" [Online] http://www.saylor.org/site/wp-content/uploads/2011/09 /Related-Highlight-Objects_1.pdf [2016, Sep].

[10] Florida International University, Steven Mizrach, "Lakota Ethnoastronomy" [Online] http://www2.fiu.edu/~mizrachs/lakota.htm [2016, Oct].

[11] I recommend going to this site in order to see a picture of the tree being carried. *National Geographic,* "In the Shadow of Wounded Knee" 2012 [Online} http://ngm.nationalgeographic.com/2012/08/pine-ridge/huey-photography#/20-sacred-cottonwood-tree-carried-670.jpg [2015 Sep].

[12] Good-Star, *The Blue Road, Jesus Fulfilled the Old Way,* 12.

[13] Ibid., 15.

[14] Six years into Hezekiah's reign in Judah, Israel was taken captive by Assyria.

[15] The Ark of the Covenant was placed back in the temple of God by Josiah 2 Chronicles 35:3. Josiah died in a battle he was not meant to be in. Just like David was a man of war and was not allowed to build God's temple, I believe the same was

true of Josiah. He was not meant to be a man of war because of the work he did to purify the land and the temple.

[16] Freeman, *The New Manners & Customs of the Bible*, 191.

[17] Kelly Whitaker (September, 2013), "Who is the Adultress?" [Online] http:// kwinrc. blogspot.com/2013/09/who-is-adulteress.html [2016, Sep].

[18] Rough estimate for time frame between Moses and Hezekiah.

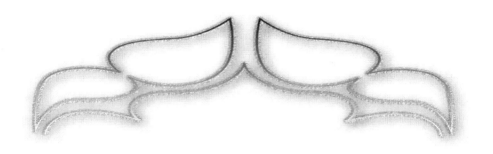

ARTEMIS / DIANA

MY CHURCH HOSTED Robert Henderson, who taught us about how to operate in the courts of heaven. The following Sunday my pastor gave a follow up message about Robert's teaching. As I sat listening to him, I felt a constriction grow stronger and tighter around my throat.

This feeling had come over me a few times before, but never so strong. As my pastor's message continued, the feeling of strangulation became more intense. Later that same day I was a bit surprised to find out that this painful experience was due to the queen of heaven.

TODAY

You may think you have never heard of Artemis except in the Bible, but think again if you enjoyed the super heroes of the mid-1990s. In the comic book, *Artemis of Bana-Mighdall*, she became Wonder Woman. One of my favorite books as a teenager was the

Mists of Avalon, which was the retelling of King Arthur through the famous women in the story. Little did I know back then who the Lady of the Lake really was in the novel.

In Acts 19, the idol maker named Demetrius said Artemis was worshiped in "all of Asia and the world." Unfortunately, this is still true today. Search an online map of the world and you will find the name Artemis splattered all over the place.

A Google search on "Artemis business" will get over a half a million hits. Artemis is one of the best-documented and widely spread idols of all the ones addressed in this book. In this chapter, I will attempt to give you a comprehensive overview of her ubiquitous presence.

ORIGIN AND LOCALE

There is a wide range in beliefs concerning her origin, ranging from prehistoric existence, to Minoan roots, to her mythical birthplace in Delos-Ortygie, Italy. The 1832 *Dictionary of the Holy Bible* says Artemis was "one of the twelve superior deities" in reference to the famous Greek Twelve Olympians where she was the daughter of Zeus and twin sister of Apollo.

Callimachus, a third century BC Greek poet, wrote *Hymn 3 to Artemis* in which she asks her father to make her into a Bringer of Light.[1] She also asks him for all the mountains so that she may dwell there. This sounds like the worship of Asherah occurring on "every high hill."

Archaeological evidence of many Artemis statues excavated from various regions, prove her worship was spread widely throughout the ancient world. Artemis worshipers included the ancient Thracians, Byzantines, Lydians, Egyptians, and the Amazons. The Romans knew her as Diana.

184

Pia Guldager Bilde, in his article titled *Quantifying Black Sea Artemis*, conducted a global search in a database containing Greek inscriptions that gave over 5,000 hits for Artemis.[2] Almost half of those were from Asia Minor (Turkey), the region where Colossae, Ephesus, Galatia, and many other countries and cites of the New Testament are located.

This so-called deity also ruled in ancient countries known today as Jordan, Syria, Bulgaria, Romania, France, Spain, and Italy. Artemis was syncretized with Ishtar, Aphrodite, the Iranian Anahita, the Egyptian Bastet, and the Celtic bear goddess Artio.

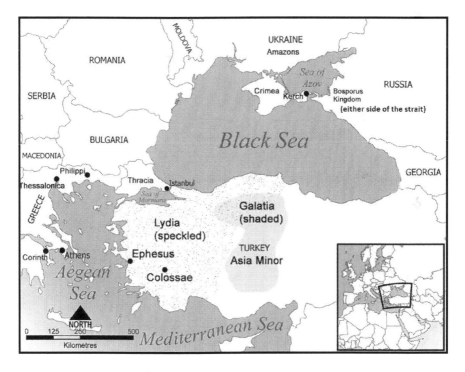

Figure 30. Map of Black Sea area[3]

Worshiped at the Philippi Acropolis Hill during the second century BC, Artemis appeared at this site a century earlier than Isis. Although there was no temple on the hill devoted to Artemis, ninety of her reliefs were discovered at this location. Unlike the other deities on the hill, there were no males associated with Artemis. There were less than twenty male depictions compared to 138 female images in this location.[4]

Like Aphrodite, the Roman Diana was popular in the Kerch strait between the Northern Black Sea and the Sea of Azov (see Figure 30). Southwest of this strait lies the Peninsula of Crimea where sacred groves were devoted to her and the Tauri people worshiped her.

DESIGNATIONS

Artemis was the deity of the sun, moon, childbirth, and war among many other things. As a mother goddess, people believed she had control over earth's environment and was the source of life from which humans and animals came forth. Although she supposedly caused birth, she also inflicted disease or death on those who displeased her, including children.

Artemis' worshipers considered her as their savior, healer, huntress, warrior, guarantor of immorality, keeper of the dead, and helper in childbirth to both women and dogs. In her book *Artemis*, d'Este defines 114 names used for Artemis, all which were dependent on either the location of an Artemis temple or a particular story about her. Some of those names are: Queen of Heaven; Queen of the World; Bearer of the White-Rayed Torch; Savior of Ships; Protectress of Sailors; Bringer of Light; Phoebe (Light); Potnia Theron (Lady of the Beasts); and First Among Thrones.

In 2000 BC in Crete during the Minoan times, Artemis was worshiped as the Divine Virgin. Unlike the other queen of heaven aliases, Artemis was a revered virgin because she never participated in sexual activity. In fact, she was maliciously severe on her attendants and god-friends who had lost their virginity. *From Artemis to Diana: The Goddess of Man and Beast* gives the reason for her abstinence: "When Artemis continued as a virgin, she also continued to be her own master, and thereby more powerful."[5] This is more evidence of the queen of heaven's aversion toward men.

ICONOGRAPHY

The worshipers in Acts 19 describe Artemis as "the image which fell down from heaven." Of course, this reminds us of Aphrodite who was worshiped as a literal rock that fell from heaven, but I have found nothing of the kind that refers to the same for Artemis.

Figure 31. Funeral vase with Artemis [6]

Portrayed as a woman, Artemis at times had wings similar to Isis. Most often, you will see her surrounded by woodland animals, holding her bow. The legend of her weapons stated that, "her bow and quiver of arrows had been given to her as a young girl by the Cyclops, the one-eyed giants who specialized in making weapons."[7] At times, her beloved nymphs accompanied her.

187

Figure 32. Artemis of Ephesus idol statue in the Vatican museum [8]

"Romans cared deeply about their household gods…and worshiped them daily at in-home shrines."[9] These household idols included Diana due to her popularity in Rome. This was also a common practice in Ephesus.

Figure 31 is a *Boeotian Amphora* funeral vase from 680 BC that bears an image of Artemis. This vase shows her as a deity of lakes, marshes, and streams. Hence, she was known as, Lady of the Lake. The vase has a central image of Artemis with a fish on her skirt surrounded by birds, swastikas, and aggressive four-legged beasts.

The Lady of the Beasts describes the images on this two-handled vase: "Every animal and symbol represents the 'Life-Giver's' descent to the underworld and rebirth thereafter."[10] Clearly, this is evidence of the original story of Inanna that was an account of a counterfeit resurrection.

One of her stone idol statues, excavated from the temple near Ephesus, was an ivory figurine crowned with a hawk on top of a pole.[11] This is reminiscent of Isis who sometimes wore a crown of a kite bird.

The Archaeological Study Bible has an excellent description of the Ephesian Artemis cult statutes one of which was found in Corinth (see a similar statue at Figure 32):

> Her cult idol was unusual – a stiff, elongated body with legs bound together in mummy-like fashion. The upper half of the front torso was covered with protuberances resembling human breasts, so that she was sometimes called the "many-breasted Artemis."
>
> She wore a necklace of acorns, for the oak tree was sacred to her, and on her breastplate appeared the signs of the zodiac. On her head rose a high crown, often topped with the turrets of the city of Ephesus. This crown may have concealed a meteorite "which fell down from Jupiter" (Acts 19:35).
>
> Frequently her skirt was decorated with rows of animals, an indicator of fertility, and along the sides were bees, depicted as both actual insects and as priestesses ("honey bees"), adorned with crowns and wings. Artemis herself was known as the queen bee, and her castrated priests were called "drones." Her image, said to possess particular sanctity, appears on

coins, papyri, wall paintings, reliefs, statuettes and in larger statuary.[12]

Surprisingly, an identical reconditioned cult statue that was made for Pope Urban VIII is in the Candelabra Gallery of the Vatican Museum. In *Confronting the Queen of Heaven*, Peter Wagner states, "When I took a guided tour of the Vatican in Rome a few years ago, we had a hard time trying to understand why a life-sized statue of Diana of the Ephesians should be located in a room in the Vatican along with statues of Christian saints."[13]

The Vatican also holds a less offensive version of one of the many existing *Artemis of Versailles* Roman statues (see Figure 33), given by Pope Paul IV to Henry II of France, showing her as a woodland goddess.[14]

WORSHIP RITUALS

Goddesses Who Rule describes Artemis' drone priests:

> Male devotees, in cults such as those of Artemis of Ephesus, castrated themselves in the service of the goddess...these men were thereafter identified as women and served the goddess as the 'she priests.' These officiants also practiced self-mutilation and cross dressing.[15]

Worship rituals of the goddess included sacrificing goats, wearing grotesque masks, and dressing up like bears. God gave me a few dreams that exposed a modern version of this practice.

In the first dream I heard the word "kippel" and saw an arrow that could not go through chainmail. It gave me the distinct impression that the word meant impenetrable. The following night, I dreamt I was in a cathedral on a tour. It was very upsetting because everywhere Jesus was supposed to be (statues and paintings) there were goats in His place. The priest giving the tour was part goat too. The priest proudly told us this was a very popular sect. I woke up very disturbed.

To my surprise, a Google search revealed that Kippel is a town in Switzerland known as "Catholic Country." Their Tschaggatta Carnival celebration occurs during the dark nights preceding Ash Wednesday. Poor souls that are walking the streets at night can expect an extremely frightening experience if they are found by grotesque goat-looking beasts.

Donning horrid horned masks and shaggy animal skins makes for a fun evening by many of Kippel's residents. The ritual dates back hundreds of years, which would explain the impenetrable chainmail of my dream.[16] This festival certainly fits the ancient worship practices of Artemis.

A more disturbing worship ritual occurred in the southern region of Crimea (see map at Figure 30), that was home to the savage Tauri people. They provided the goddess with cannibalized human sacrifices. The Roman historian, Ammianus Marcellinus, recorded the activities of the tribes that made up the Tauri.

> For they propitiated the gods with human victims, sacrificing strangers to Diana, whom they call Oreiloche, and fix the heads of the slain on the walls of their temples, as perpetual monuments of their deeds.[17]

Cannibalism is a mark of the queen of heaven. The Bible mentions this horrid act in the context of Israel's apostasy as it occurred in Samaria:

As the king of Israel was passing by on the wall a woman cried out to him, saying, "Help, my lord, O king!" He said, "If the Lord does not help you, from where shall I help you? From the threshing floor, or from the wine press?" And the king said to her, "What is the matter with you?"

And she answered, "This woman said to me, 'Give your son that we may eat him today, and we will eat my son tomorrow.' So we boiled my son and ate him; and I said to her on the next day, 'Give your son, that we may eat him'; but she has hidden her son." (2 Kings 6:26-29)

The king of Israel in this verse was Ahab's son, which means that at this time Samaria was engrossed in worship to the queen of heaven as outlined in the chapter titled, "Asherah."

Apostasy always removes people from God's protection, allowing the dominion of darkness free reign.

ARTEMIS AS ASHERAH

Known as the Queen of Groves or Guardian of the Oak, Artemis seems to be a shadow of Asherah with idols of wooden images, trees, and sacred groves. The Greek philosopher, Strabo, said Artemis' birthplace was in a sacred grove of trees. Describing one of the names of Artemis, d'Este says, "The term Caryatid, for [wood] pillars shaped like female figures, is derived from the Greek [word] *karyatides*."[18]

The old city of Orkhomenos used the name Artemis Kedreatis that meant Lady of the Cedar. Antique vases from Athens show women bowed down to an altar by a palm tree representing Artemis.

Coins from 43 BC bear the triple cult statue of Diana Nemorensis (Nemi) showing three women supporting a beam that holds cypress trees.[19]

Figure 33. *Artemis of Versailles* idol statue in the Vatican[20]

The Festival of Burning Torches took place in the sacred forests around Lake Nemi, known as Diana's Mirror, near one of her oldest and largest temples in Italy. During this full-moon festival in August, girls would write prayers and tie them to the trees.

The *Vitruvius's De Architectura* (On Architecture) from the late first century BC says that a statue of Diana made of imported cedar stood in her temple at Ephesus.[21] Prior to this famous temple's construction, the supposed man-slaying female Amazons conquered the area and erected a tree shrine devoted to Artemis in Ephesus.

Honoring the Amazons was a part of the worship ceremonies to Diana. This temple will be discussed in more detail in the section titled, "Artemision."

Ammianus Marcellinus, an AD fourth century Roman historian, refers to a grove of pine and cypress trees in western Crimea that were sacred to Diana worshipers.[22]

OFFERINGS

Just like Ishtar, honoring Artemis with cakes was common, bringing to mind the Jewish women in Jeremiah who said they made sacrificial cakes to the queen of heaven. Women would make bread cakes in the form of infirmed body parts as offerings to Artemis in hopes of healing. This was a rather ironic offering for a deity that struck people with sickness.

Sweet sesame honey *elaphos cakes*, shaped as deer, were offered to her during the ancient Greek festival called Elaphebolia that was devoted to Artemis, the deer slayer. One such celebration, recorded by Herodotus, took place on the Greek Island of Samos.[23] In Athens, round cakes called *selenia* representing the moon, were made for Artemis.

Keeping in mind that Diana was a torchbearer, the *Virgin Goddess of the Sun, Moon & Hunt* describes a tradition that may surprise you.

> The festival of Mounykhia was celebrated on 16th Mounykhion to Artemis at Piraeus. This was a full moon ceremony and was sacred to Artemis-Hekate, as small cakes called amphiphontes meaning, shining on both sides, were offered to the goddess...Reference is made to dadiai (little torches) decorating the cakes,

much in the style of birthday cakes with small candles on them today. Some writers have even speculated that the dadiai may provide clues to the origins of our own modern birthday cake.[24]

BRUTALITY

Artemis' horrifying behavior are found in Homer's *Iliad* and *Odyssey*, along with the work of Euripides, a Greek playwright and Ovid, a Roman poet. Her arrows killed giants, men, gods, and beasts. Her battle skills were prominent among the Amazons and in the ancient Greek city-state of Sparta.

Also in Sparta, at the Sanctuary of Artemis Orthia, there are documented accounts of devotional rituals that involved assaults on children. Initiation into manhood required boys to endure cruel whippings while their taskmaster held a wooden idol of Artemis.

Artemis' warrior achievements included many victories such as the slaying of the giant Aigaion in the battle between the giants and the Olympians. Her killing sprees were not however, limited to war. *The Goddess Revival* states, "Tatian (AD 72-110) announced that after he had been initiated into the mysteries and studied the various rites, he discovered that near Rome Artemis was worshiped with the slaughter of men."[25] Her deadly wrath also extended to children and the elderly.

MOLESTATION

Ironically, chaste behavior was not a part of the worship rituals held to honor Artemis, the Divine Virgin. During festivals honoring Artemis, mothers would present their girls to the goddess for their initiation into womanhood:

It is often when they dance for her [Artemis] that the virgins (parthenoi) are raped, underlining their change of status. Artemis and parthenoi are often associated in myths, in reference to the girls' initiation.[26]

Saturated with devotion to Artemis, Herodotus recorded the following about the area of Lydia (see map in Figure 30) in his first book of histories written in the fourth century BC:

Of marvels to be recorded the land of Lydia has no great store as compared with other lands...but one work it has to show which is larger far than any other except only those in Egypt and Babylon: for there is the sepulchral monument of Alyattes the father of *Croesus*, of which the base is made of larger stones and the rest of the monument is of earth piled up.

This was built by contributions of those who practised trade and of the artisans and the girls who plied their traffic there; and still there existed to my own time boundary-stones five in number erected upon the monument above, on which were carved inscriptions telling how much of the work was done by each class; and upon measurement it was found that the work of the girls was the greatest in amount. For the daughters of the common people in Lydia practice prostitution one and all, to gather for themselves dowries, continuing this until the time when they marry; and the girls give themselves away in marriage (italics added).[27]

Here again we see worship in the form of prostitution offered to the queen of heaven, but this time coupled with child molestation. Child trafficking was clearly a cultural norm for the people who revered Artemis in this region. It is unfortunate that Herodotus was convinced that it was the will of the young girls to trade their bodies for sex. Unfortunately, the same belief still hold true today by many.

Figure 34. Artemis Temple in Jaresh (Jordan) [28]

Other ancient writings record Croesus' (see italics in the quote above) respect for Artemis when he refused to attack Corinth during what appeared to be a time of worship for Artemis. Therefore, it is safe to say that these horrid practices occurred in Corinth too.

BUBASTIS TEMPLE

Herodotus went into detail in explaining the Artemis temple in

Bubastis. He visited this temple in the fifth century BC. He said there were "none larger, more costly, or more pleasant to the eyes."

> Except the entrance, it is completely surrounded by water; for channels come in from the Nile, not joining one another, but each extending as far as the entrance of the temple, one flowing round on the one side and the other on the other side, each a hundred feet broad and shaded over with trees; and the gateway has a height of ten fathoms [sixty feet], and it is adorned with figures six cubits [nine feet] high, very noteworthy.

> This temple is in the middle of the city and is looked down upon from all sides as one goes round, for since the city has been banked up to a height, while the temple has not been moved from the place where it was at the first built, it is possible to look down into it: and round it runs a stone wall with figures carved upon it, while within it there is a grove of very large trees planted round a large temple-house, within which is the image of the goddess: and the breadth and length of the temple is a furlong [one eighth of a mile] every way.

> Opposite the entrance there is a road paved with stone for about three furlongs, which leads through the market-place towards the East, with a breadth of about four hundred feet; and on this side and on that grow trees of height reaching to heaven.[29]

ARTEMISION (ARTEMIS TEMPLE IN EPHESUS)

In the eighth century BC, a primitive tree shrine sanctuary was erected by the Amazons where the future grand temple of Artemis would stand in Ephesus. *The Archaeological Study Bible* explains the progression of this site.

> The sanctuary was soon surrounded by a village as it became a site of pilgrimage. On the site one temple succeeded another in size and splendor, until the final shrine was considered one of the wonders of the ancient world. Thousands of personnel served within the immense confines of the sanctuary, and huge sums of money were entrusted to the keeping of Artemis. As a result the temple complex became the major banking center of Asia.[30]

The Artemision was one of the Seven Wonders of the Ancient World. In the *Greek Anthology*, Antipater (third century BC), who devised this list, describes its beauty.

> I set eyes on the wall of lofty Babylon on which is a road for chariots, and the statue of Zeus by the Alpheus, and the hanging gardens, and the colossus of the Sun, and the huge labour of the high pyramids, and the vast tomb of Mausolus; but when I saw the house of Artemis that mounted to the clouds, those other marvels lost their brilliancy, and I said, "Apart from Olympus, the Sun never looked on aught so grand."[31]

The Goddess Revival explains the activities of the Artemision.

During the classical age, four enormous statues of Amazons stood in the temple of Artemis of Ephesus; and for centuries after Christ, the Amazons were commemorated yearly in a marvelous dance at Ephesus. In Ephesus women also assumed the role of the man-slaying Amazons who had founded the cult of Artemis of Ephesus...Evidence of actual human sacrifice has been discovered at the lowest level of the great Artemisium.

An ancient record of martyrs preserves a curious tradition about the cult of Artemis of Ephesus. It is contained in the work of a famous Byzantine scholar (Symeon Mataphrastes) who flourished in the last half of the tenth century...His account of St Timothy describes a festival of Artemis of Ephesus that was known as the katagogion or bringing home of the goddess. It seems to refer to a yearly procession in which the cult statue was carried through the streets and back to her temple.

Mataphrastes described the procession in which people walked through the streets with idols in their hands and masks on their faces. They were also said to carry rhopala, understood by later martyrologists to mean clubs...the instruments with which Timothy was to meet his fate...The next part of the description grows more curious. These citizens were said to walk around the more prominent parts of the city as they chanted hymns, apparently in honor of the goddess.

This too, accords well with what we know of such celebrations, but here the tale takes a strange turn: "In the manner of brigands they fell upon both men and women and worked a great slaughter among them. The wretches believed that in this way they honored their goddess, so that they might appear as the sort whose greatest religious service was the death of worshipers."

There may well be a grain of truth in the concept that Artemis was most honored by an action that secured death to her worshipers.[32]

Rebuilt many times due to fires and disrepair, the Artemision was used for about three hundred years after the book of Ephesians was written. The temple's ruins still stand today. It spawned many other temples in Asia Minor, Greece, and the islands in the Agean Sea. Artemis temples and sacred groves were established in eighty-five Grecian islands and towns, including Corinth.

When the apostle Paul walked the streets of Ephesus, he most certainly saw the Artemision nearly every day.

ARTEMIS IN THE BIBLE

Acts 19 takes place in Ephesus where the Apostle Paul was enjoying the work of God (see map at Figure 30). His daily life included healing, baptizing in the Holy Spirit, speaking boldly about God's Kingdom, setting people free from demons, and allowing God to do extraordinary miracles through him. "The word of the Lord was growing mightily and prevailing" (Acts 19:20).

In the span of two years Ephesus was transforming into a

righteous city. Prior to that, it was known as the city of Artemis. The uproar this caused in the dominion of darkness literally spilled out into the physical realm.

> There occurred no small disturbance concerning the Way. For a man named Demetrius, a silversmith, who made silver shrines of Artemis, was bringing no little business to the craftsmen; these he gathered together with the workmen of similar trades, and said, "Men, you know that our prosperity depends upon this business. You see and hear that not only in Ephesus, but in almost all of Asia, this Paul has persuaded and turned away a considerable number of people, saying that gods made with hands are no gods at all."

> "Not only is there danger that this trade of ours fall into disrepute, but also that the temple of the great goddess Artemis be regarded as worthless and that she whom all of Asia and the world worship will even be dethroned from her magnificence." When they heard this and were filled with rage, they began crying out, saying, "Great is Artemis of the Ephesians!" The city was filled with the confusion. (Acts 19:23-29a)

Then a chaotic crowd filled an auditorium where, for the next two hours, a riot took place. The majority of people simply joined in, clueless about what was going on. The riled throng of people yelled repeatedly, "Great is Artemis of the Ephesians!" Paul wanted to talk to the people, but his friends encouraged him not to. The Jews who were forcefully dragged in were fortunate they were not killed. The town clerk was finally able to quiet the crowd, convincing them that the best plan of action was to use the legal system.

In this situation anger, confusion, ignorance, and group rage allowed the dark dominion of the queen of heaven to spread rapidly. Just as the good works of the saints clothe the Bride of Christ, I believe these works of the flesh clothe the queen of heaven because she imitates Jesus Christ.

MAGIC

The *Handbook of Today's Religions* defines magic as "the practice which seeks to use or manifest occult powers."[33] This is different from the sleight of hand tricks used in the entertainment industry. However, it is the same as what you will find in the *Harry Potter* book series and Disney's blockbuster movies, *Frozen* and *Moana*.

Induction into Artemis's cult required devotees to participate in secret rituals. Magical papyri contained the incantations they needed to memorize. Before Paul came to Ephesus, magic was a common practice. After turning from Artemis to the One True God, "those who practiced magic brought their books [papyri] together and began burning them in the sight of everyone; and they counted up the price of them and found it fifty thousand pieces of silver [a day's wage]" (Acts 19:19). These same people were putting Demetrius out of business.

The magic of Artemis included shapeshifting herself and others into various animals. She turned the queen of the Amazon into a horse when the queen refused to dance around Artemis' altar in Ephesus, and the prince of Thebes into a stag when he saw her naked. She also turned a few of her nymphs into springs of water in order to save them. Cult devotees most assuredly practiced shapeshifting also.

One of the animals Artemis herself would change into was a cat, otherwise known as the Egyptian Bastet (see the chapter titled, "Isis"). Ezekiel 30:17 refers to a city called Pi-beseth, located in Lower Egypt, which is included in the prophet's list of cities whose idols and people were to be destroyed. The Egyptian name for Pi-beseth was Bubastis. The *Hebrew-Chaldee Lexicon* states that Bubastis was "regarded as the proper name of a deity, which was worshiped in the form of a cat." Herodotus said that the greatest zeal and devotion for an Egyptian deity was the worship of Artemis in the city of Bubastis. He also stated, "Bubastis in the Hellenic tongue is Artemis."[34] Therefore, Artemis was the main deity of Pi-beseth.

ARTEMISIA WORMWOOD

Named after Artemis, the genus of plants called Artemisia, have psychoactive properties and taste bitter. Wormwood is a part of this genus. The *Herbarium,* written by Apuleius around AD 1000, says Artemisia is named after the goddess because she discovered the plant and delivered its powers. The modern day liquor, Absinthe, contains wormwood. It has an extremely high alcoholic content and is very addictive because of its hallucinogenic effect. Historically known as the Green Fairy, those drunk on Absinthe might see fairies; or are they Diana's nymphs?

With what we know about this bitter herb, the use of torches to worship Artemis, the murder of her worshipers, and what Acts 19 says about her image that "fell down from heaven," you may understand the following passage a little better:

> The third angel sounded, and a great star fell from heaven, burning like a torch, and it fell on a third of

the rivers and on the springs of waters. The name of the star is called Wormwood; and a third of the waters became wormwood, and many men died from the waters, because they were made bitter. (Revelation 8:10-11)

This verse is not about a future event. It has occurred from the ancient times right up to today. It is about those who die a bitter death because they worship the queen of heaven. The fresh spring water of Holy Spirit is not meant to be mixed with worship to the queen of heaven.

ENCOUNTER WITH HEALING

While sitting in church listening to my pastor's message about the courts of heaven, I could have assumed the feeling of being strangled was just some sort of inflammation and taken a pill for relief. That is what I would have done before learning about the queen of heaven. I did not know that evil entities like Artemis could inflict pain and sickness on people. In this case, taking a pill would not have helped me. How many times have you taken medication that did absolutely nothing?

With a bit more wisdom under my belt, I now know that some sicknesses and some instances of pain are due to the devil trying to destroy me. That morning in church, I sensed my pain was due to something demonic since it seemed proportional to what I was hearing about the courts of heaven.

Later at home, I got alone with God and asked Him to reveal to me what was going on. The word "tarot" came to mind. Therefore, I did an online search for "tarot queen of heaven." I should not have been shocked when the *Empress* tarot card sprang up on my screen, showing a queenly-looking woman dressed in long robes with a crown on her head. The description for the card included the names Venus, Queen of Heaven, Great Goddess, Isis, and Ishtar. As you know, that covers many of the chapters in this book. Knowing I was on to something, I continued to pray and ask God what this meant.

I then remembered having a conversation with my mom, in the distant past, about a relative who did fortune telling. I immediately texted her to find out exactly who this relative was, not revealing why I wanted to know. She identified the fortuneteller as my grandfather's sister who used tarot cards.

I realized that it was most likely possible that I was present during those demonic sessions as a child. With a mixture of deep sorrow and anger, I got on the floor before God and repented on behalf of my great aunt and the many relatives who naively participated in her dark deeds. I forgave them and thanked God for the truth.

Robert Henderson taught us that unrepentant sin gives the devil a legal right to inflict harm. Due to my great aunt's sin, the devil knew he could rightfully silence me concerning anything to do with the queen of heaven. Better yet, my Father God also knew and wanted me free from that strangle hold. I sincerely believe this feeling of strangulation was a manifestation of what was happening to me spiritually. The devil was trying to cut off my voice so that I would be unable to expose his queen of heaven.

I believe God revealed this to me in a safe place while giving me the key to walk in complete freedom. The feeling of strangulation stopped and I have been pain free ever since.

Although I attended Catholic school for kindergarten and first grade, I had no idea that the Catholic Mary's title is Queen of Heaven. Days after my vision, I read a Christian newsletter in which a reader wrote in and asked if the Mary of the Bible was the queen of heaven in Jeremiah 44. I nearly fell off my chair in shock, but that was not the biggest reveal God had for me with this alias.

---

[1] "Artemis Myths 1" [Online] http://www.theoi.com/Olympios/ArtemisMyths.html #Childhood [2016, May].

[2] Fischer-Hansen, *From Artemis to Diana*, 307.

[3] Location of cities and regions are author's estimation.

[4] Abrahamsen, *Women and Worship at Philippi*, 26.

[5] Fischer-Hansen, *From Artemis to Diana*, 43.

[6] Johnson, *Lady of the Beasts*, 237.

[7] D'Este, *Artemis*, Kindle, Chapter 1, 4%.

[8] Pvasiliadis ,"File:Artemis Efes Museum.JPG" [Online] https://commons.wikimedia .org/wiki/File:Artemis_Efes_Museum.JPG [2016, Sep].

[9] National Geographic Partners, LLC. "The Most Influential Figures of Ancient History." *National Geographic Time Inc. Specials (2016): 112.* Magazine. 97.

[10] Ibid., 236-237.

[11] Ibid., 51, 54.

[12] *Archaeological Study Bible*, 1573.

[13] Wagner, *Confronting the Queen of Heaven.* 31.

[14] "File:Vatican Museum Diana statue.jpg" [Online] http://commons.wikimedia.org/ wiki/ File:Vatican_Museum_Diana_statue.jpg [2013, Mar].

[15] Spencer, *The Goddess Revival*, 58.

[16] Swiss Vistas Experience Switzerland Your Way!, "Swiss Carnival Tschäggättä in the Lötschental Valley (VS)" [Online] http://www.swissvistas.com/tschaggatta.html [2016, Oct].

[17] Lexundria, *The Roman History of Ammianus Marcellinus*.

[18] d'Este, *Artemis*, Kindle, Chapter 6, 24%.

[19] Wikipedia, "Two examples of the denarius (RRC 486/1) depicting the head of Diana Nemorensis and her triple cult statue." [Online] https://en.wikipedia.org/ wiki/Diana_Nemorensis#/media/File:Diana_Nemorensis_denarius2.jpg [2015, Jun].

[20] Sting, "File:Diane de Versailles Leochares 2.jpg" [Online] https://en.wikipedia.org/wiki /File:Diane_de_Versailles_Leochares_2.jpg [2016, Sep].

[21] Lexundria, *The Ten Books on Architecture*, 2.9 translated by Morris Hicky Morgan [Online] http://lexundria.com/vitr/2.9/mg [2015, Jun].

[22] Lexundria, *The Roman History of Ammianus Marcellinus fourth century*, 22.8.39, translated by C. D. Yonge (1862), [Online] http://lexundria.com/go?q=Amm. %2022.8.39&v=y [2015, Jun].

[23] Herodotus, *The History of Herodotus*, 1:48.

[24] D'Este, *Artemis* 634-646.

[25] Spencer, *The Goddess Revival*, 61.

[26] Bron, *The Sword Dance for Artemis*, 73.

[27] Herodotus, *The History of Herodotus*, 1:93, 94.

[28] Jamin Hubner, "Photo Journalism: 2013 Middle-Eastern Tour-Part 2" [Online] https://blackhillsphoto.files.wordpress.com/2013/04/25-temple-of-artemis.jpg [2015, Oct]. Used with permission.

[29] Ibid., 1:137, 138.

[30] *Archaeological Study Bible*, 1573.

[31] *Full text of "The Greek anthology"* Book IX 58 [Online] http://archive.org/stream/greekanthology03newyuoft/ reekanthology03newyuoft_djvu.txt [2015, Jun].

[32] Spencer, *The Goddess Revival*, 60-62.

[33] McDowell, *Handbook of Today's Religions*, 545.

[34] Herodotus, *The History of Herodotus*,1:59, 137.

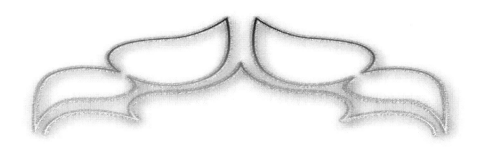

CATHOLIC MARY

A FEW MONTHS after my vision, God gave me the desire to go on a short-term mission trip to Brazil. He told me before I was even certain of going that I would learn much about the queen of heaven there. Midway through that trip, I was moved by Holy Spirit to share my vision with a group of Brazilian believers. Then one of my new friends from São Paulo told me of a city not far from where we were, called Aparecida do Norte, which was dedicated to the queen of heaven.

This is a hard chapter for me to include because I have so many good friends who are Catholic. When asked by one of these friends if I was including the Mary of the Bible as the queen of heaven in my book, I could honestly tell her "no" because after this journey it is clear to me that what Catholics believe about Mary is not in the Bible. This is explained further in the section titled, "The Biblical Mary is Not the Queen of Heaven."

In complete respect and love for my Catholic friends, and you, if you are Catholic, I encourage you to notice the similarities between the Catholic Mary and the queen of heaven aliases presented in prior chapters. The history of the Catholic Mary did not begin in Scripture, but rather through a culture that was steeped in Rome's history of devotion to the queen of heaven.

APARECIDA DO NORTE

Unfortunately, there was no way for me to personally go to the city of Aparecida do Norte on my trip, but my friend told me everything she knew about it. The city is famous for the Basilica of Our Lady of Aparecida (Our Lady who Appeared). The Basilica is devoted to a small black Madonna statue made of clay. You may recall that Inanna was known as the Black Madonna and that clay idols are a common form for the queen of heaven.

Figure 35. Aparecida do Norte Basilica [1]

Today the black figurine (see Figure 36) is covered in the same way as idols of Ezekiel's day were, with embroidered cloth (see Ezekiel 16:18). Originally crowned in 1904, the figurine was honored as the patron saint of Brazil in 1930 by Pope Pius XII. I watched a video of a priest parading this idol he held high down the main aisle of the basilica. Before putting it down, he kissed its feet. These displays of devotion to the black madonna bear resemblance to the cult of Isis.

Our Lady of Aparecida Basilica became what it is today because of the idol statue. It was found in 1717 by three fishermen in the Paraíba River, between Rio de Marieiro and São Paulo.[2] The story says that some fishermen, who were short on catching fish, landed a headless black female statue in their nets; later they found the head. Immediately after bringing up the statue, they started catching many fish and attributed their good fortune to the statue they presumed to be Mary.[3]

A Carioca monk from São Paulo, Frei Agostino de Jesus, originally made the statue in 1650. Once brought home by the fishermen, the statue seemed to bring about miracles. Moved many times to larger and larger buildings, the black madonna's devotees kept growing. This is how the city of Aparecida do Norte came into being. This may sound familiar since the same held true for the Artemision in Ephesus. I shared the following quote in the chapter titled, "Artemis," but I am sharing it again because of the striking similarities between that temple and the basilica of Aparecida do Norte.

The sanctuary was soon surrounded by a village as it became a site of pilgrimage. On the site one temple succeeded another in size and splendor, until the final

shrine was considered one of the wonders of the
ancient world. Thousands of personnel served within
the immense confines of the sanctuary and huge sums
of money were entrusted to the keeping of Artemis.[4]

The history of Aparecida do Norte is identical, and it too is a
hub of commerce due to religious activities. The entire city exists
only because of the basilica. My Brazilian friend told me that only
people who support the basilica in one form or another are allowed
to live in the city.

Figure 36. Our Lady of Aparecida idol figurine[5]

Just as the Artemision ranked as an ancient wonder of the world,
Our Lady of Aparecida Basilica also ranks as one of the wonders of
the world today with over 12 million visitors per year. It is the largest
Marian shrine, and the second largest church in the world; second

only to Saint Peter's Basilica in Vatican City. Aparecida is one of thousands of Catholic Marian shrines found throughout the world today.

One of those Marian shrines is in Ephesus very close to the ruins of the Artemision. In *Confronting the Queen of Heaven*, Wagner describes the Ephesian Shrine of the Virgin Mary:

> While there may be relatively little overt worship at the altar of Diana of the Ephesians, Mary's idol is actively worshiped 365 days a year with candles, gifts of flowers and other things. Paul VI was the first pope to visit this place in the 1960s. Later, in the 1980s, during his visit, Pope John-Paul II declared the Shrine of Virgin Mary as a pilgrimage place for Christians. It is also visited by Muslims who recognize Mary as the mother of one of their prophets.[6]

CIRIO DE NAZARE

Brazil is also home to the Cirio de Nazare, which is the country's largest religious event of the year. In October 2014, *The National Catholic Reporter* website stated:

> ore than 2 million worshipers, pilgrims and on-lookers poured around an 11-inch wooden figure of the Virgin Mary as it made its way through the streets. A crush of the faithful heaved and hauled away at a rope that stretched over a thousand feet from the cart that bore the beloved statue, dragging it inch by inch through the sweat-soaked crowd. Bursts of fireworks marked its passage.[7]

This appears to be a scene straight from the city of ancient Babylon where a wooden cult idol of Ishtar "was paraded through the Ishtar gate and down the Processional Way each year." Many such processionals are held in honor of the Catholic Mary all over the world.

The article quoted above goes on to relay another familiar story.

> Cirio has been celebrated for 222 years, first inspired by a local man named Placido Jose de Souza, who stumbled across a long-lost carved statue of Virgin Mary by the side of a creek. According to legend, every time he brought the figure away with him, she would stubbornly return to the place where he had discovered her - the spot where the basilica now stands.[8]

DESIGNATIONS

The Catholic Mary is called Mother of God, Mother of the Church, and Mother of Men. The Catholic Church also believes that Mary is the mother of all people (see Catholic Church 489 and 501). These are similar to the titles of:

- Ishtar, who was the Mother of Creation
- Isis, who was the Mother of All
- Aphrodite, who was the Mother of Men and Gods

The Catholic Mary is also known as the Queen of Heaven, New Eve, Protectress, and Miracle Worker. New Eve reminds us of Lilith who was called the First Eve. Ishtar, Isis, Astarte, Aphrodite, and Artemis were all considered protectors too.

Believed to be a liaison between Jesus and men, she carries the titles of Advocate, Helper, Benefactress, and Mediatrix (see Catholic Church 969). Many of these attributes and titles originated from the words spoken by apparitions assumed to be Mary.

Figure 37. *Star of the Sea* idol statue with orb and anchor

Although the majority of the queen of heaven aliases discussed in this book were classified as virgins, the Catholic Virgin Mary shares the same eternal abstinence quality with Artemis (see Catholic Church 499). Coming short of being made into a deity, it is believed that she kept her virginity throughout life and into eternity.

ICONOGRAPHY

The most common depictions of the Catholic Mary show her with the baby Jesus on her lap. We discovered with Isis that this imagery originated in Rome long before Mary gave birth to Jesus. Like Lilith, the Catholic Mary can also be pictured with an orb (see Figure 37) or scepter that represents sovereignty over the earth. Only our One True God has this supreme power.

Figure 38. *Coronation of the Virgin* as the Queen of Heaven [9]

Often with a crown of stars on her head, sunrays emanating behind her, and the moon under her feet, she appears to be a celestial queen. We will discover the significance of this symbolism in the section titled, "The Catholic Mary is not the Biblical Mary."

JESUS CHRIST IMPOSTER

Just like the other queen of heaven aliases, the Catholic Mary proclaims many of the attributes that belong to Jesus Christ alone. The Catholic faith is not solely based on the Bible, but also on traditions of the church fathers. It has never been clear to me how church traditions can be instituted that contradict the Bible.

Below are quotes from the *Catechism of the Catholic Church*

216

that describe the Catholic Mary. Each are followed by Scripture that apply to Jesus Christ.

"preserved free from all stain of original sin" (966)

He made Him who *knew no sin* to be sin on our behalf, so that we might become the righteousness of God in Him. (2 Corinthians 5:21, italics added)

"exalted by the Lord...over all things" (966)

He [Jesus] is the image of the invisible God, the firstborn of *all creation*. For by Him *all things* were created, both in the heavens and on earth, visible and invisible, whether thrones or dominions or rulers or authorities—*all things have been created through Him and for Him*. He is before *all things*, and in Him *all things* hold together. (Colosians 1:15-17, italics added)

"deliverer our souls from death" (966)

Death has been swallowed up in victory...He gives us the victory *through our Lord Jesus Christ*. (1 Corinthians 15:54, 57, italics added)

"the image and beginning of the Church" (972)

He is also *head of the body, the church*; and *He is the beginning*, the firstborn from the dead, so that He Himself will come to have *first place in everything*. (Colossians 1:18, italics added) "by her manifold intercession [she] continues to bring us the *gifts of eternal salvation*...Therefore, the Blessed Virgin is invoked in the Church under the titles of *Advocate, Helper,* Benefactress, and *Mediatrix*" (italics added)

He [Jesus] became to all those who obey Him the source of *eternal salvation,* being designated by God. (Hebrew 5:8b, italics added)

If anyone sins, we have an *Advocate* with the Father, Jesus Christ the righteous. (1 John 2:1b, italics added)

So we say with confidence, "The Lord is my *helper.*" (Hebrews 13:6, italics added)

For there is one God, and *one mediator* also between God and men, the man Christ Jesus. (1 Timothy 2:5, italics added)

The following is a quote from Pope Pius XII followed by the truth about Jesus:

We are taught that Mary, the Virgin Mother of God, *reigns...over the entire world* (italics added). [10]

Let the heavens rejoice, let the earth be glad; let them say among the nations, *"The Lord reigns!"* (1 Chronicles 16:31, italics added)

The famous Brigittine Convent of Syon near London based their worship on *The Myroure of Oure Ladye* (The Mirror of Our Lady) which outlined their Marian beliefs. It stated that God ordained Mary "without beginning to be queen of heaven."[11] However, Jesus Christ is the One without beginning:

> Without father or mother, without genealogy, *without beginning* of days or end of life, resembling the Son of God, he remains a priest forever. (Hebrews 7:3, italics added)

God is also the only One who is worthy of our praise, but it seems Pope Pius XII disagreed with this also,

> From the earliest ages of the Catholic Church a Christian people, whether in time of triumph or more especially in time of crisis, has addressed prayers of petition and hymns of *praise and veneration to the queen of heaven* (italics added). [12]

As we have discovered, Scripture proves beyond a reasonable doubt, that mixing praise to God with "praise and veneration to the queen of heaven" will always result in removing oneself from the presence and protection of God (see Hosea 8:3). God alone reigns over the entire world and our prayers, praise, and adoration needs to be purely to Him alone, "For great is the Lord and most worthy of praise; He is to be feared above all gods. For all the gods of the nations are idols" (Psalm 96:4-5).

STAR AND SEA

Like Inanna, Ishtar, Lilith, Isis, Ashtoreth, Astarte, and Aphrodite, the Catholic Mary is also connected to the sea and is referred to as a star. Her ancient title, Star of the Sea, relates to her as a guiding star for worshipers. It is in this capacity that the Catholic Mary is considered a protector of those on the sea, which is why many coastal churches bear the same name.

Figure 37 is a picture of a famous statue of the Catholic Mary found in the Basilica of Our Lady Maastricht, Netherlands. It is called, "Our Lady, Star of the Sea." The oldest known hymn about Mary, *Ave Maris Stella,* is Latin for "Hail Star of the Sea." *Hail, Queen of Heaven, the Ocean Star* hymn was written by a Catholic priest in the late 1700s. In his Encyclical, *Doctor Mellifluus,* Pope Pius XII says the following about Mary as a star:

> Oh, whosoever thou art that perceiveth thyself during this mortal existence to be rather drifting in treacherous waters, at the mercy of the winds and the waves, than walking on firm ground, turn not away thine eyes from the splendor of this guiding star, unless thou wish to be submerged by the storm! When the storms to temptation burst upon thee, when thou seest thyself driven upon the rocks of tribulation, look at the star, call upon Mary. When buffeted by the billows of pride, or ambition, or hatred, or jealousy, look at the star, call upon Mary. Should anger, or avarice, or fleshly desire violently assail the frail vessel of thy soul, look at the star, call upon Mary.[13]

Whether on the wild waters of the Sea of Galilee or in the storm of temptations given by the devil, Jesus never turned to Mary for help.

QUEEN OF HELL

Medieval Catholic theologians generally concurred that Mary's power extended beyond heaven to both earth and hell through her co-rulership with Christ. Inanna and Ishtar also had claimed powers in these realms. The Catholic Mary's rulership over heaven and hell is evident in artwork dating back to the eleventh century and many literary works as well.

One such story about her dealings with the devil was written in AD sixth century and reappeared 900 years later in fifty manuscripts. This story also exhibits the false doctrine of seeking repentance with Christ through an idol that represents the Catholic Mary. Elisabeth Benard shares it in *Goddesses Who Rule:*

> In most versions of this tale, Theophilus, a well-respected archdeacon, refuses the role of bishop when it is offered to him. The new bishop, resenting Theophilus's popularity demotes him. Grieved by the loss of his position, Theophilus signs a pact with the devil in which he renounces his belief in Christ; however, he soon repents and prostrates himself before an image of the Virgin, pleading with her to intercede with Christ on his behalf.
>
> Although she lets him know in no uncertain terms that her son is very angry with him, Mary manages to obtain mercy for Theophilus. In addition, she retrieves the contract he's signed with the Devil. In this tale, Mary establishes herself as Queen of Hell as well as queen of heaven by beating satan at his own game.[14]

Theophilus is celebrated as a saint by the Catholic Church every February.

SEXUAL IMMORALITY, PROSTITUTION, AND MOLESTATION

This chapter still needs one more comparison to the other queen of heaven aliases. This is hard to include, because it is extremely heart breaking. It is with a very heavy heart that I write this section.

We have seen that prostitution, rape, molestation, homosexuality, physical abuse, abortion, and infanticide are all forms of worship to the queen of heaven. It is so much easier to read about these types of things happening thousands of years ago, but this is different because it occurring in our generation.

The recent evil behaviors committed against children by Catholic priests are not something new. They have been taking place for more than a thousand years. In *Vicars of Christ,* Peter De Rosa makes claims about the ninth century AD that are reminiscent of the ancient temples of Artemis, Isis, and Aphrodite.

> Many monasteries were the haunts of homosexuals, many convents were brothels in which babies were killed and buried. Since the end of the Roman Empire, historians say that infanticide was probably not practised in the West on any great scale - except in convents.

> The Council of Aix-la-Chapelle in the year 836 [AD] openly admitted it. As to the sex-starved secular clergy, they were so often accused of incest that they were at length forbidden even to have mothers, aunts or sisters living in their house. Children, the fruits of incest, were killed by the clergy, as many a French prelate put on record...The great Ivo of Chartres ([AD] 1040-1115) tells of whole convents with

inmates who were nuns only in name. They had often been abandoned by their families and were really prostitutes...

One reason for there being more prostitutes in Rome than in any other capital city was the large number of celibates. The convents were often brothels. Women sometimes took a dagger with them to confession to protect themselves against their confessor.

Chroniclers tell of clerics spending their days in taverns, their nights in the soft arms of their mistresses. 'The holiest hermit has his whore.' As St Bridget said to Pope Gregory: 'The clergy are less priests of God than pimps of the devil.'[15]

In the late 1990s, a leaked Vatican report claimed, "three out of every five nuns stated they were sexually victimized by a priest, nun, or other religious person."[16] CNN World reported that in 1998 Pope John Paul II apologized for this abuse of nuns and other victims by priests.

"Sexual abuse within the church is a profound contradiction of the teaching and witness of Jesus Christ," the pope said. "The synod fathers wished to apologise unreservedly to the victims for the pain and disillusionment caused to them."[17]

The same article also stated these facts:

–   In March 2000, the *National Catholic Reporter*...ran a series of stories on internal reports in the Vatican about the sexual abuse of nuns and other women by priests and bishops around the world.

- The internal reports said some priests and missionaries had forced nuns to have sex with them, and had in some cases committed rape and forced the victims to have abortions.
- The reports cited cases in 23 countries, including the United States.

The Public Broadcasting Station website for *Frontline* reported in 2014:

In the U.S. alone, 16,787 people have come forward to say that they were abused by priests as children between 1950 and 2012, according to the U.S. Conference of Catholic Bishops, the organization for the Catholic hierarchy in the country. Those figures are incomplete. The data excludes, for unclear reasons, any people who came forward in 2003. The conference also counts only allegations it determined were "not implausible" or "credible."[18]

In an article titled, "'Payout chart' for molestation: Secret archive held chilling details of clergy abuse" from March 2016, *The Washington Post* reported:

The [grand jury] report relied on a secret archive at the Altoona-Johnstown diocese, which dates back to the 1950s and was opened up this summer when authorities obtained a search warrant. The grand jury interviewed surviving priests and their alleged victims, and compiled a 147-page account detailing accusations against more than 50 religious leaders including priests and teachers.

One of the most startling pieces of evidence, among more than 115,000 documents seized from the secret archive, was a "payout chart" Adamec created to determine how much to pay victims who reported abuse.[19]

The payouts began at $10,000 and went up to $175,000 for the worst case of sexual abuse.

Priests and nuns have reportedly molested children throughout the United States. This is a very twisted form of prostitution since the victims could never be restored to their previous state of a peaceful conscience through any amount of money, and the majority of criminals never saw the inside of a courtroom or jail.

In the custom of the queen of heaven, these types of activities brought about sickness and the spread of disease. Sexually transmitted diseases were no strangers to the Catholic criminals. Unfortunately, in Africa, Catholic priests may have been instrumental in the spread of AIDS. This was due to the African Catholic clergy having had a unique understanding of what the term *celibacy* meant:

> In a report on her 1995 meeting with Cardinal Martínez in the Vatican, O'Donohue noted that celibacy may have different meanings in different cultures. For instance, she wrote in her report, a vicar general in one African diocese had talked "quite openly" about the view of celibacy in Africa, saying

that "celibacy in the African context means a priest does not get married but does not mean he does not have children."[20]

This meaning of *celibacy* replicates the meaning of the word *virgin* as used by many of the aliases in this book. Recall that in the chapter titled, "Ishtar" I said, "Her virginity was due to her freedom from never being married, not her sexual purity."

ENCOUNTER WITH MARIOLOGY

Less than a year after my throne room vision, I spoke publicly about the queen of heaven to an audience of mixed religious backgrounds. A brave Catholic woman stood up and challenged what I said about the Catholic Mary. Despite the confrontation, I had complete peace. I wanted to respond to the woman, but sensed God's desire for me to be silent. In awe, I stood there and listened as a few pastors kindly defended what I had just said.

This challenge did not surprise me. While doing research, and putting together my presentation, I was hesitant to include some of my discoveries because I knew that these assertions would be offensive to many people. In those moments, God would remind me, "For am I now seeking the favor of men, or of God? Or am I striving to please men? If I were still trying to please men, I would not be a bondservant of Christ" (Galatians 1:10). I am a bondservant of Christ; therefore, I left nothing out.

One thing said in my defense to that woman has stayed with me. A friend shared, "When I struggled with the New Age concepts that God was trying to clean out of my life, it was important that I held on to my relationship with God and not take on the burden to defend the entire New Age movement." I think this is the key to helping Catholics understand truth. It is not up to them to defend the entire Catholic Marian movement.

Figure 39. Catholic Mary with Jesus on a wooden cross [21]

I know there are Catholics who do not venerate Mary as prescribed by the *Catechism of the Catholic Church*. Although I do not claim to understand such things, it is obviously possible to worship Jesus Christ alone and be Catholic. This is what I am encouraging.

When the woman left the room, I wanted to run to her so we could talk alone, but I had to finish my speaking engagement. After the session ended, while packing my car, I heard the woman's voice calling my name. I was so happy she sought me out!

We had a pleasant conversation. My heart was full of love for her as she continued to insist that I was naïve about the Catholic

Mary. I asked her to teach me and gave her my number. We never did meet, but because of her, I put a lot of thought and research into how I would present the Catholic Mary in this book. I took her advice and searched out genuine Catholic resources.

Figure 40. Wooden idol of Catholic Mary with sunrays and the moon [22]

Although the experience was a bit unsettling, I can now say that if I had offended everyone in the room, I would do it again. My aim is to please the One who has brought me on this path, to please the One who has chosen me to voice this injustice, and to please the One who will stir the hearts of the offended. It is my prayer that God will stir them into pure devotion to Him alone.

THE BIBLICAL MARY IS NOT THE QUEEN OF HEAVEN

I find it ironic that Catholic theology understands the entire book of Revelation to be a figurative work, except for the following verses, which they interpret literally:

> A great sign appeared in heaven: a woman clothed with the sun, and the moon under her feet, and on her head a crown of twelve stars; and she was with child; and she cried out, being in labor and in pain to give birth. (Revelation 12:1-2)

Many works of art portray this literal interpretation of Mary standing on the moon with the sun behind her as shown in Figure 40.

STARS, SUN, MOON

Interpreting the verse figuratively instead is supported throughout Scripture where the stars, the sun, and the moon take on significant meaning. The first time the sun, moon, and stars are together symbolically is in young Joseph's dream. Joseph was the youngest son of Jacob (a.k.a. Israel). In Genesis 37, we find Joseph sharing his dream with his father, who provides an immediate interpretation.

> Lo, I have had still another dream; and behold, the sun and the moon and eleven stars were bowing down to me." He related it to his father and to his brothers; and his father rebuked him and said to him, "What is this dream that you have had? Shall I and your mother

and your brothers actually come to bow ourselves down before you to the ground? (Genesis 37:9)

Here the sun, moon, and stars are Jacob, Rachel, and the patriarchs of Israel's tribes.

Think about the sun that rises every morning, shines every day, and lets nothing escape its light. It is the brightest physical light in our existence and is a spiritual representation of Jesus. He is the sun all throughout Scripture, with attributes of the sun:

The Lord God is a sun. (Psalm 84:11)

The sun of righteousness will rise with healing in its wings. (Malachi 4:2)

Very early on the first day of the week, they came to the tomb when the sun had risen. (Mark 16:2)

Because the sun was obscured; and the veil of the temple was torn in two. (Luke 23:45)

He [Jesus] was transfigured before them; and His face shone like the sun, and His garments became as white as light. (Matthew 17:2)

His face was like the sun shining in its strength. (Revelation 1:16)

Therefore, we can conclude that Jesus is the sun in Revelation 12 just as He is the son of the nation of Israel. Another way to say, "a woman clothed with the sun" is found in Galatians 3:27, "For all of you who were baptized into Christ have clothed yourselves with

Christ." The woman clothed with Christ (sun) is a representation of the Messianic Jews.

It is clear from Joseph's dream that the twelve stars of the woman's crown represent the twelve tribes of Israel. I propose that the moon in Revelation represents the Bride of Christ who shines in spiritual darkness. If this is so, the eschatology of Isaiah may reveal deeper understanding. Chapter 30 is about God's graciousness toward Israel,

> The light of the moon will be as the light of the sun,
> and the light of the sun will be seven times brighter,
> like the light of seven days, on the day the LORD binds
> up the fracture of His people and heals the bruise He
> has inflicted. (Isaiah 30:26)

The light of the Bride of Christ will be as the light of Christ, and the light of Christ will be seven times brighter because the nation of Israel will be completely healed and restored of the fracture that was, in part, caused by the queen of heaven. Both Jesus and His bride will influence Israel at this point in time. In the following verse, the Hebrew word for *set* means "come" or "arrive" and *wane* means "gather."

> Your sun will no longer set, nor will your moon wane;
> For you will have the Lord for an everlasting light.
> (Isaiah 60:20, italics added)

Once Jesus is with us, we will never refer to His coming again (sun will no longer set) and the Bride of Christ will no longer have to hold gatherings (moon wane) because they will forever be all together with Christ.

Does the woman (Israel) in Revelation 12 who is standing on the moon (Bride of Christ) represent judgment in any way? The moon is in the sky along with the sun and stars, so this means that the moon is holding the woman up in the sky. She is not treading on it; she is being elevated by it. In the entire Bible story, Israel will be ultimately elevated when she realizes that Jesus Christ is her Messiah and becomes a part of the Bride of Christ.

The entire chapter of Revelation 12 also sits well with the woman figuratively being Israel, not Mary.

QUEEN MOTHER

Mary is also considered a queen in Catholicism because her son is a king. In AD 784, Ambrose of Autpert, who was a Frankish Benedictine monk said, "She is raised above the angels and reigns with Christ. It should suffice that she is truly called queen of heaven, because she has given birth to the King of Angels."

Used throughout the Old Testament, the term Queen Mother is a royal, official title. However, a closer look reveals that godly women never hold this title, but only women who are idolatrous. In 1 Kings 15, Asa, who was a godly king, removes the title of Queen Mother from his mother because of her Asherah. In Jeremiah, the king and the queen mother are to take lowly seats due to their worship of the queen of heaven (see Jeremiah 13:18). In 2 Kings 10, King Ahab and his Queen Mother were killed by Jehu for their worship of the queen of heaven (see chapter titled, "Asherah").

The women in Scripture who rightfully have the title of Queen were either head of a country or were married to kings. Despite Solomon honoring his mother with a throne, she is never called a queen as his wives were. Mary was not the wife of a king nor was she the leader of a country, therefore calling her a queen not biblical.

GOD HAS NO MOTHER

We have discovered that the queen of heaven is believed to be the *mother to all other gods*. The Catholic Mary is also called the Mother of God, but does God have a mother? Psalm 110:4 says that Jesus is a "priest forever according to the order of Melchizedek." Melchizedek was a

> king of righteousness, and then also king of Salem, which is king of peace. Without father, without mother, without genealogy, having neither beginning of days nor end of life, but made like the Son of God, he remains a priest perpetually. (Hebrews 7:2c-3)

Therefore Jesus, in His capacity as God, has neither a mother nor a date of birth. John's epistle clearly explains that Jesus existed long before He put on flesh.

> In the beginning was the Word [Jesus], and the Word was with God, and the Word was God. He was in the beginning with God. And the Word became flesh, and dwelt among us, and we saw His glory, glory as of the only begotten from the Father, full of grace and truth. (John 1:1-2, 14)

The man, Jesus, had a Father who was Holy Spirit and a mother who was Mary (see Matthew 1:18). However, the spirit being of Jesus has coexisted with Father God and Holy Spirit since before time began. This means that no human mother or human father created God. Therefore, to think that Mary currently exists in heaven as the "Mother of God" is blasphemous. Jesus is the one who created Mary, not the other way around.

CATHOLIC MARY IS A CREATION OF ROME

The Romans were famous for their worship of the queen of heaven. Recall this quote from the chapter titled, "Aphrodite":

> In her oldest known myth, her descendants ruled in Asia Minor, while the later development of this myth brings her son Aeneas and his family to Italy to found the Roman civilization. This ancient tradition was revitalized by the rulers of the Roman Empire ...Believing that their divine right to rule rested on an ancestral bond to the queen of heaven.[23]

Rome's pantheon of gods included Diana and Venus. The Christian conversion of the Roman Empire is described in *Literature, Science, Art, and Politics.*

> Constantine and his successors, converted by the sword; the people are baptized by force; their temples are turned into churches, and their priests into a Christian priesthood; their statues of gods and goddesses are converted into the likenesses of the various Apostles and saints; and, for images of the Virgin Mary, the statues of Venus afford an ample supply.[24]

In his book, *Miracle Workers, Reformers, and The New Mystics*, John Crowder tells of a group of Christians known as the Nestorians. Their church began in Persia through a missionary trip taken by Jude. When Emperor Constantine merged the Roman church with the state of Rome, the Eastern Church was not included and "were spared from a lot of spiritual abuses from a government church. The Eastern Church never merged with a military force, and they never persecuted other sects of Christians as the Romans did. The state never got a chance to water down their doctrine either.[25]

After Nestorius was given leadership over the Eastern Church in AD 427 he realized that they referred to Mary as the Mother of God. "He immediately began preaching against this, and said they should refer to her as the "Mother of Christ," since they were close to deifying her."[26] His opponents reacted:

> A sham council was set up at Ephesus, and...everybody started excommunicating one another. This marked the end of the Eastern church trying to work under the authority of Western bishops. They basically went independent, and were labeled "Nestorians" because they supported...Nestorius. To sum it up, it was the emperor who chose to boot Nestorius. So we see a secular politician affecting the largest church split in history to that date. The worldwide church was split in half. The Ephesian Council subsequently opened a gateway of devotion to Mary that still continues today. In the end, Nestorius was proven right about the Theotokis [Mother of God]. I will point out that the East never venerated icons or Mary either. On many points, they remained undefiled by what I believe to be Western errors.[27]

Clearly the Catholic Mary evolved into something that is not the same as the Mary in Scripture.

If it has not begun to happen already, you will now start to see the queen of heaven's manipulation where ever you are. Ignorance of the devil's most powerful weapon no longer holds you. This dark principality can no longer ruin you for your lack of knowledge! Now it is time to defeat the queen of heaven in your life and render her powerless in the lives of others.

¹ Valter Campanato/ABr, "File:Basilica of the National Shrine of Our Lady of Aparecida, 2007.jpg" [Online] https://commons.wikimedia.org/wiki/File:Basilica _of_the_National_Shrine_of_Our_Lady_of_Aparecida,_2007.jpg [2016, Dec].

² This black Madonna is one of hundreds that are found around the world including, Our Lady of Altötting [Bavaria, Germany]; Our Lady of the Hermits [Einsiedeln, Switzerland]; Our Lady of Guadalupe [Mexico City]; Our Lady of Jasna Gora [Czestochowa, Poland]; Our Lady of Montserrat [Spain]; and Our Lady of Tindari [Sicily].

³ Prof. Plinio Corrêa de Oliveira (October 12), "Our Lady Aparecida" [Online] http://www. traditioninaction.org /SOD/j227sd_OLAparecida_10-12.html [2014, Oct].

⁴ *Archaeological Study Bible,* 1573.

⁵ Jose Liuz, "File:Statue of Our Lady of Aparecida (replica) - Old Basilica of Aparecida - Aparecida 2014 (3).jpg" [Online] https://commons.wikimedia.org/wiki/File: Statue_of_Our_Lady_of_Aparecida_(replica)_-_Old_Basilica_of_ Aparecida_- _Aparecida_2014_(3).jpg [2016, Sep].

⁶ Wagner, *Confronting the Queen of Heaven,* 31 (also see "Ephesus, House of the Virgin Mary" [Online] http://www.ephesus.us/ephesus/ houseofvirginmary [2014, Oct].

⁷ Benjamin Soloway Alexandra Ellerbeck, National Catholic Reporter Religion News Service (Oct 17, 2014) "As Brazilians drift away from Catholicism, Virgin Mary procession as popular as ever" [Online] http://ncronline.org/news/global/ brazilians-drift-away-catholicism-virgin-mary-procession-popular-ever [2016, May].

⁸ Ibid.

⁹ Diego Velázquez, "File:Diego Velázquez - Coronation of the Virgin - Prado.jpg" [Online] https://commons.wikimedia.org/wiki/File:Diego_Vel%C3%A1zquez_- _Coronation_of_the_Virgin_-_Prado.jpg [2016, Sep].

¹⁰ "*AD CAELI REGINAM – ENCYCLICAL OF POPE PIUS XII ON PROCLAIM- ING THE QUEENSHIP OF MARY*" (Oct 11, 1954) [Online] http://w2.vatican.va

/content/pius-xii/en/encyclicals/documents/hf_p-xii_enc_ 11101954_ad-caeli-reginam.html [2016, Sep].

[11] Full text of "The Myroure of Oure Ladye : containing a devotional treatise on divine service, with a translation of the offices used by the sisters of the Brigittine monastery of Sion, at Isleworth, during the fifteenth and sixteenth centuries" [Online] https://archive.org/stream/themyroureofoure00unkwuoft/themyroure ofoure00unkwuoft_djvu.txt [2016, Dec].

[12] *"AD CAELI REGINAM – ENCYCLICAL OF POPE PIUS XII ON PROCLAIMING THE QUEENSHIP OF MARY."*

[13] Doctor Mellifluus, "Encyclical Of Pope Pius Xii On St. Bernard Of Clairvaux, The Last Of The Fathers To Our Venerable Brethren, The Patriarchs, Primates, Archbishops, Bishops, And Other Local Ordinaries In Peace And Communion With The Apostolic See "[Online] http://www.vatican.va/holy_father/pius_xii/encyclicals/documents/hf_p-xii_enc_24051953_doctor-mellifluus_en.html [2014, Oct].

[14] Benard, *Goddesses Who Rule*, 244. Kindle, Chapter 14, 95%.

[15] Rosa, *Vicars of Christ: The Dark Side of the Papacy*, 404, 408.

[16] Kennedy, *Lucifer's Lodge*, 181.

[17] CNN.com/WORLD (November 23, 2001) "Popes Web apology over sex abuse" [Online] .http://www.cnn.com/2001/WORLD/europe/11/22/pope.apology [2016, May].

[18] Sarah Childress, Frontline (February 25, 2014) "Secrets of the Vatican, What's the State of the Church's Child Abuse Crisis?" [Online] http://www.pbs.org/wgbh/frontline/article/whats-the-state-of-the-churchs-child-abuse-crisis/ [2016, May].

[19] Michelle Boorstein and Julie Zauzmer, The Washington Post (March 3, 2016) "'Payout chart' for molestation: Secret archive held chilling details of clergy abuse," [Online] https://www.washingtonpost.com/news/acts-of-faith/wp/2016 /03/03/abuse-survivor-advocates-see-hope-in-spotlight-and-in-new-report-alleging-widespread-cover-up/[2016, May].

[20] John L. Allen Jr and Pamela Schaeffer, National Catholic Reporter Online (March 16, 2001) "Reports of abuse AIDS exacerbates sexual exploitation of nuns, reports allege" [Online] http://natcath.org/NCR_Online/archives2/2001a/031601/031601a.htm [2016, May].

[21] Taken by author at St Martin's Cathedral in Rapid City, SD.

[22] Photo taken by the author.

[23] Benard, *Goddesses Who Rule*, 17-18.

[24] Fields, *Literature, Science, Art, and Politics*, 602.

[25] Crowder, *Miracle Workers, Reformers, and The New Mystics*, 125.

[26] Ibid., 126.
[27] Ibid., 127.

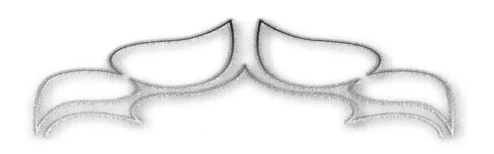

DEFEAT THE QUEEN OF HEAVEN

THE FACTS AND history presented about the queen of heaven are indisputable. You have read about how this demonic force demands worship that defiles God's prescribed commandments. You have learned how she moves through time and is in our culture today. You know her calling cards are sexual immorality, anger, child abuse, self-mutilation, sickness, violence, emotional strife, murderous rampages, gender confusion, and much else. You may have even discovered her subtle appearance in your own life.

Despite all this, it is clear that defeating the queen of heaven is possible by focusing our worship and devotion purely on God alone. We saw examples of this in our journey through the history of the kings. Those who had anything to do with the queen of heaven experienced trouble during their reigns (see 2 Kings 22:12). This is because the queen of heaven's aliases who fool many into thinking they are hospitable, kind, and good are nothing but demons who impersonate Jesus Christ, "They made Him [God] jealous with strange gods…They sacrificed to demons who were not God, to gods whom they have not known" (Deuteronomy 32:16a, 17a). The One True God is the only spiritual being who can truly know us and can truly be known by us.

The kings who worshiped God alone thrived and prospered. Consider King David who committed some very serious sins, yet God said, "David walked in integrity of heart and uprightness" (1 Kings 9:4). Although David repented for his sins, I do not believe this is the only reason why God honors him above all other kings. I believe it was because he never entertained the queen of heaven.

I am not saying that he was not faced with this demonic principality, for he certainly was. I am saying that when he recognized her influence, he either quickly repented or never acknowledged her to begin with.

The queen of heaven will suffer defeat:

> Sit silently, and go into darkness, O daughter of the
> Chaldeans, For you will no longer be called the queen
> of kingdoms. (Isaiah 47:5)

This defeat begins with each person allowing God's purification in his or her life:

> I will sprinkle clean water on you, and you will be
> clean; I will cleanse you from all your filthiness and
> from all your *idols*. Moreover, I will give you a new
> heart and put a new spirit within you; and I will
> remove the heart of stone from your flesh and give
> you a heart of flesh. I will put My Spirit within you

and cause you to walk in My statutes." (Ezekiel 36:25-27, italics added)

If the queen of heaven has been exposed in your life, the devil's goal is to make you feel condemned and in need of due punishment. It is important that you do not believe this lie! God wants to restore you and make you whole.

Think of it this way. If your child does something wrong, you do not stop loving them. You discipline them in order to restore them to goodness. You do not condemn them for the rest of their lives. Instead, you continue to love and provide for them. How much more does your Father in heaven love you through all your mistakes? He wants to restore you to His goodness.

PURIFY FAITH

One beautiful summer evening I was watching my husband shoot his bow. At first he was not shooting very well, which is unusual for him. A few minutes later, he began shooting the arrows in a tight group on the bull's eye. He then took a break, commenting to me on how he shoots so much better when he focuses his aim at the center point and does not just fling his arrows at the target.

Immediately, I realized this was a picture of how our worship with God can get defiled by the queen of heaven. Keeping our faith pure requires focus and aim. Flinging beliefs around occurs when we justify them with cultural norms instead of the Word of God.

When our devotion is in a tight group centered on Christ alone, we are in a position of God's favored attention. This is not a way of earning His love, but instead is a lifestyle of companionship with the One who loves us the most.

Purifying our faith is a two-step process. First, we renounce and put away all the influences of the queen of heaven that have left us naked and ashamed. Second, we put on the spiritually pure clothes of Christ. Jacob told his family to "put away the foreign gods which are among you, and purify yourselves and change your garments" (Genesis 35:2). Jerusalem, a representation of the Bride of Christ, is given the same command through the prophet Isaiah.

> Awake, awake, clothe yourself in your strength, O Zion; clothe yourself in your beautiful garments, O Jerusalem, the holy city; for the uncircumcised and the unclean will no longer come into you. Shake yourself from the dust, rise up, O captive Jerusalem; loose yourself from the chains around your neck, O captive daughter of Zion. For thus says the Lord, "You were sold for nothing and you will be redeemed without money." (Isaiah 52:1-3)

Jesus tells us the same thing. "I advise you to buy from Me...white garments so that you may clothe yourself, and that the shame of your nakedness will not be revealed" (Revelation 3:18). How do we pay for these beautiful, pure garments? We do it by ridding ourselves of all impure worship and giving our entire devotion and adoration to God alone.

If your faith is pure, then it will stand up to the fires of testing and bring about praise, honor, and glory to the One True God (see 1 Peter 1:7). Allow God's refining fire to purify you.

As sons and daughters of the Most High God, and as the bride of His Son Jesus Christ, we have authority over ALL dark powers. The following sections are specific ways to defeat the queen of heaven and diminish her power in the earth.

BREAK UNHEALTHY SOUL TIES

If you are struggling to let go of something that you read about in previous chapters, an unhealthy soul tie might be keeping it active in your life. An unhealthy soul tie is anything you attach yourself to that invites a demonic force that exalts itself above Jesus Christ. As horrific as that sounds it is very easy to have this happen. Ties can occur with things like yoga, video games, and even other people. Sometimes soul ties are healthy and needful, such as those that occur between a husband and wife in marriage. Sometimes healthy ties can become unhealthy.

Soul ties can also exist with physical objects like figurines. This is a result of an unholy emotional bond to the item. I experienced this myself with a beloved nativity set. On the *Christian Restoration in Ireland* website, Ken Symington explains the reason behind this.

> When people give reverence to an image in any shape or form, or talk to it, or place flowers at the base of it, or rub its feet, or bow before it, or pray to God through it, or to the person the statue represents, then know for certain that powers of darkness will attach themselves to that plaster cast figure or picture and lock the person to it. They will be joined to that life-less image which is being idolized. That is why, for instance, the thought of breaking a plaster and paint model used in such a manner is unthinkable to them. It is no longer neutral material because they have invested something of themselves into it.[1]

Know that your struggle is good because it serves as an indicator that you are willing to allow God to help you purify your devotion to

Him. I encourage you set aside some time in order to ask God if a soul tie is the source of the resistance you are feeling.

While praying, pay attention to anything that comes to mind, anything that you hear in your spirit, and the atmosphere with which the possible answer comes. If it comes with peace and understanding, you can trust that it is a revelation from God. On the other hand, if there is confusion, shame, or condemnation then the devil is trying to interfere. In the latter case, tell satan to leave and be persistent in asking God for an answer.

God may give you an immediate answer or it might come to you over time. Either way, once you start seeking God's help, He will respond. Be alert to what Holy Spirit prompts you to do. Obedience will bring the freedom you desire.

Months after following Holy Spirit's guidance in getting rid of my nativity, I still have feelings over the loss. However, I do not regret being obedient because I know undoubtedly that those figurines would have become a stronghold for the enemy in my life. If I had said no to what God wanted me to do, that nativity would have held more value to me than God Himself.

HEALING

We have discussed in many of the previous chapters how the queen of heaven inflicts sickness and injuries. Now is the time to change the common mindset of hopelessness when our body is attacked and good health is stolen from us. Our hope is that Jesus not only died for our sins, but He was severely beaten for our healing (see Isaiah 53:5).

During Jesus' earthly ministry and for the century that followed, people knew that demons caused behavioral problems, diseases, injuries, and sickness. They knew to call on the power of God to fight for them. Gradually belief in demonic activity changed and the use of divine healing faded.

In *Finding Victory When Healing Doesn't Happen*, Randy Clark says, "Spiritual warfare (or demonization) is less often talked about in religious settings and is often misinterpreted as a dysfunction of the mind and body, such as a physical or mental illness."[2]

Modern society's answer for sickness and behavioral problems is usually a pill. A person can conclude there are no complete cures by observing the pharmaceutical commercials on TV where a dark blob, big elephant, or something else representing the disease is lurking in the background even after the person takes a pill.

We give alcoholics the excuse that they are prone to the "disease" of alcoholism because it runs in their family. While it might be a family trait, many are blinded to the fact that satan can alter our physical body so that breaking an addiction seems impossible. *The Cross and the Switchblade* by David Wilkerson shares many stories of how God miraculously broke strong addictions.

Physical injuries are often a result of accidents, without the slightest thought of what might have spiritually caused the accident. Instead of immediately pronouncing healing, hopelessness sets in.

A close friend of mine once asked me to pray for her knee that was in excruciating pain. I had her sit down and invited God to come heal her as I commanded the muscles, ligaments and bones to be healed, and for the pain and excess fluid to leave. She felt heat (a sign of healing), so I thanked God and asked Him for more.

I had her bend her knee (it is always good to check on the healing progress) and she winced because it still hurt. Then, I asked her how she injured her knee. She said that she was standing doing dishes and it just went out.

Immediately I thought of two other friends who recently told me they were just walking or standing and it felt like someone punched them in the knee. I then switched gears in how I prayed, rebuking the demonic schemes released against her. I commanded the evil presence, and the pain it caused, to leave in the name of Jesus.

I asked my friend to get up and walk around. She did and the look on her face said it all! Her knee no longer hurt and she could put weight on that leg. She even sent me a text later in the day saying that she was so happy that her knee was fine! Praise God!

A month later, this same friend and I were at a prayer conference. One night we were standing around and chatting about God. Suddenly, both of my knees buckled! We immediately knew what was going on and rebuked the evil spirit. The pain soon left my knees and I have been fine ever since.

Seek out and chase healing until you get it, no matter how long it takes.

CUTTERS

We learned about the queen of heaven priests who cut themselves in the chapter about Asherah. Today depression is claimed to be the main cause for this behavior, not idol worship. Like I have said before, we may not all have little household idols or go out to Main Street to bow down before a large tree, but we still suffer from the same compulsive behaviors that surrounded the ancient idolizers. These compulsive behaviors are a form of worship.

A young woman at a quilt retreat I attended shared that she would like to have her hair braided. I offered to do it for her. As I brushed out her long brown hair, I noticed too many scars to count on her forearms. My heart broke for her. This sweet woman had succumbed to the same queen of heaven influence as the Asherah priests who Isaiah dealt with. Scripture says they cut themselves to shreds until their "blood gushed out." I had no doubt; from the amount of scars she had, that her blood had gushed out too.

I know it can be very soothing when someone else brushes my hair, and I sensed she felt the same. Therefore, I took my time with her hair as we talked. She told me about an anime (Japanese adult cartoon character) that she really liked. This character had qualities of being immortal and being able to cause harm to others by hurting himself. He could kill another by stabbing himself; he would live, but his enemy would die from the stab wound. The irony of it all deeply troubled me.

When I finished her hair, I gently put my hand on her scarred arm and said, "God can heal these scars along with the wounds in your heart. Can I pray for you?" She said "Yes." Do you know it is all in the "Yes?" This is where healing is found. It starts by saying "yes" to God when He wants you to brush someone's hair.

GENDER IDENTIFICATION

Today's society masculinizes women and in the process, emasculates men. How many TV shows and movies show women physically beating up on men? How many commercials and sitcoms show women verbally degrading men? Men are now even starting to take the last name of their wife in marriage.

Did you know that more men become women than the other way around? This may remind you of the eunuchs of old who served the queen of heaven as "she priests" and the goddesses who encouraged violence toward men.

The human race's only answer to the question of gender confusion is that the person who suffers from it must be right, that they were born as the wrong sex. Society applauds these individuals when they make physical changes and call them brave, but the emotional problems remain. No one is there for them when they are depressed or decide to commit suicide.

The reason people struggle with this issue is not because the assignment of their gender at birth was wrong, but rather the devil has stolen their entire identity. This loss of identity can be traced straight back to the Garden in Eden, where Adam and Eve were convinced by the devil that they did not know who they were.

They already knew good from evil, they knew God personally, and they were secure in their identity with God. Yet, through their own free will, and the influence of evil schemes, Adam and Eve allowed themselves to be convinced otherwise. In that process, they lost their identities.

Even secular institutions are beginning to realize that gender confusion is a matter of the mind:

> John Hopkins University hospital under the leadership of the famed psychiatrist Dr. Paul McHugh, discontinued sex-change surgery years ago…As McHugh observed (speaking of male-to-female surgery), "It is not obvious how this patient's feeling that he is a woman trapped in a man's body differs from the feeling of a patient with anorexia nervosa that she is obese despite her emaciated, cachectic state. We don't do liposuction on anorexics. Why amputate the genitals of these poor men? Surely, the fault is in the mind not the member."[3]

The precious, gender-confused people of today are in need of God's bountiful love for them, not a sex change. They do not need our judgment or condemnation; they need to encounter the mercy and compassion of the One True God who lives in us. Only God can successfully and permanently heal the mind by breaking the power of the queen of heaven over an individual.

When faced with someone who is confused, do not turn away in disgust, but instead hear what God has to say about them. If you have not already read my experience with a gender-confused friend in the chapter titled, "Inanna," then I encourage you to do so now.

ABORTION

Those who worshiped the queen of heaven practiced the abominable act of sacrificing live babies in an ancient ritual with fire. Sacrifices of the unborn are continuing today in the name of feminine rights, as discussed in the chapter titled, "Lilith."

The *Worldometers* website states, "According to WHO [World Health Organization], every year in the world there are an estimated 40-50 million abortions. This corresponds to approximately 125,000 abortions per day."[4]

The psychological effects on women who have an abortion have become so prevalent that there is now a medical term for it, Post Abortion Stress Syndrome. It is a form of Post-Traumatic Stress Disorder (PTSD) that troubles our military members who have seen combat.

Many godly organizations come alongside these hurting women to provide healing. The only way we can change this culture of abortion is by loving on those who have experienced the pain of abortion and bringing truth to those dear ones who are considering having the procedure.

If you know of a woman who has had an abortion, do not condemn her. Instead, ask God what you can do to memorialize her lost baby and honor her as a mother. Show her the love of Jesus.

If you have first-hand experience of abortion as a father or mother, I want you to know that your Daddy God loves you beyond measure and wants to heal you of this trauma. Take comfort in knowing that your little one is safe in His tender care.

---

[1] Ken Symington, Christian Restoration in Ireland, "Understanding Soul Ties" [Online] http://www.christian-restoration.com/soul%20ties.htm [2016, Aug].

[2] Clark, *Finding Victory When Healing Doesn't Happen*, 55.

[3] Michael Brown, "What the Sex-Change Industry Doesn't Tell You" 10/4/2013 [Online] http://www.charismanews.com/opinion/in-the-line-of-fire/41250-what-the-sex-change-industry-doesn-t-tell-you [2016, Apr].

[4] Wordometers.info/abortions [2016, Nov].

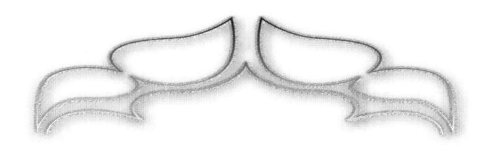

BONUS CHAPTER
THE FIG TREE

WHILE WRITING THE chapter about Asherah, I began to wonder about the 300-year-old asherim that Josiah chopped down and destroyed on the Mount of Destruction. This began my research into finding out that one of the oldest living trees on the earth today is a fig tree in Sri Lanka that is over 2,300 years old.

Botanists date the first cultivation of fig trees to about 6,000 years ago. They place their origins in Asia Minor, Iran, Syria, and the Arabian Peninsula.[1] With many unusual qualities, fig trees are of the genus *Ficus sycomorus,* specifically known as sycamore fig or fig mulberry.

A fig is a "false fruit" because the ovary of the flower does not form it. Fig tree flowers are not visible because they are inside the fig itself. Therefore, a fig is not really a fruit because it is composed of decayed flowers. "The tiny flowers never bloom, of course, because they never see the light, but they ripen inwards and...become something which is popularly known as the sweetest of fruits."[2]

There are two types of fig trees: self-pollinators and cross-pollinators, the latter need the help of fig wasps to pollinate. Self-pollinators have figs that appear twice a year: once in the spring before the leaves have come out and once again in the fall. The first fruit, known as *breba*, falls off before ripening and is usually inedible, although some people enjoy eating them. The fall fruit is tree ripened and very succulent.

LUXURIANT TREE

Just as a fig tree can bear fruit without leaves, as it does in the spring, it can also have a high abundance of leaves without bearing any fruit. The *Horticulturist and Journal of Rural Art and Rural Taste Volume 2*, written in 1847, says that the trees with too many leaves are troubling since, "*over-luxuriant trees* never bear abundant crops" (italics added).[3]

Figure 41. Morton Bay fig tree in Santa Barbara, California [4]

This type of tree is found in 1 Kings 14:23, "For they also built for themselves high places and sacred pillars and asherim on every high hill and beneath every *luxuriant tree*" (italics added).

FIGS TREES IN THE BIBLE

We know that at least one fig tree was in the Garden of Eden since Adam and Eve covered themselves with fig leaves. It is highly probable that the leaves were from the same tree of which they ate and sinned against God:

> When the woman saw that the tree was *good for food*,
> and that it was a *delight to the eyes*, and that the tree
> was desirable to *make one wise*, she took from its fruit
> and ate; and she gave also to her husband with her,
> and he ate. (Genesis 3:6, italics added)

As the bearer of the "sweetest of fruits," we have already discovered that a fig tree is *good for food*. The tree in Eden was most certainly much bigger than the largest fig tree in the United States today (see Figure 41), which is over 80 feet tall with a 198-foot spread canopy (over half the length of a football field).

Therefore, fig trees are definitely a *delight to the eyes*. The chapter titled, "Asherah," proved that a person worshiped asherim in hopes to *make one wise*. So the fig tree definitely fits the profile of the tree from which Adam and Eve ate.

God described this tree in Eden as "the tree of knowledge of good and evil." In the Bible, fig trees represent both good and evil. The first verse below identifies the fig tree as a symbol of prosperity (good) while the second links the fig tree with judgment coming upon those who worshiped the queen of heaven (evil):

> So Judah and Israel lived in safety, every man under
> his vine and his fig tree, from Dan even to Beersheba,
> all the days of Solomon. (1 Kings 4:25)

They will devour your harvest and your food; they will devour your sons and your daughters; they will devour your flocks and your herds; they will devour your vines and your fig trees; they will demolish with the sword your fortified cities in which you trust. (Jeremiah 5:17)

Just as the fig tree was key to the fall of man, it is also significant in the reconciliation of man to God. Jesus spoke a parable comparing the signs of when the kingdom of God is near, to the signs of when summer is nigh once the fig tree leaves come out (see Matthew 24:32). I believe when Jesus cursed the fig tree, he was demonstrating how Israel could be returned to a right relationship with God.

Jesus entered Jerusalem on a colt in the Hebrew month of Nisan in the springtime. The following day, Jesus cursed the fig tree:

On the next day, when they had left Bethany, He became hungry. Seeing at a distance a fig tree in leaf, He went to see if perhaps He would find anything on it; and when He came to it, He found nothing but leaves, for it was not the season for figs. He said to it, "May no one ever eat fruit from you again!" And at once the fig tree withered. (Mark 11:12-14; Matthew 21:19e)

Written from the disciple's point of view, these verses do not make it clear what Jesus was thinking. Matthew and Mark may have assumed Jesus was hungry and looking for something to eat, but it is doubtful that any man, let alone Jesus, would expect this tree to have edible figs in the springtime as the verse implies.

This fig tree should have had breba fruit and no leaves. Instead, this troublesome, luxuriant fig tree had leaves, but no fruit. Since the queen of heaven took on the form of a luxuriant tree, I propose that this fig tree was worshiped as an Asherah. Jesus cursed it so that no one would eat its spiritual fruit ever again.

The following day Jesus and His disciples passed by the dead tree and Jesus had a very strange response to Peter's observation.

> As they were passing by in the morning, they saw the fig tree withered from the roots up. Being reminded, Peter said to Him, "Rabbi, look, the fig tree which You cursed has withered." And Jesus answered saying to them, "Have faith in God. Truly I say to you, whoever says to *this mountain*, 'Be *taken up* and cast into the sea,' and does not doubt in his heart, but believes that what he says is going to happen, it will be granted him. Therefore I say to you, all things for which you pray and ask, believe that you have received them, and they will be granted you." (Mark 11:20-24, italics added)

They were looking at a dead fig tree, not a mountain. However, asherim were on "every high place" that were located in prominent locations. "This mountain" was a spiritual mountain where the queen of heaven was worshiped. The original Greek word for "taken up" also means to take away sin. Therefore, by taking up and throwing this mountain into the sea, they would be putting their faith purely in God alone.

When people worshiped the queen of heaven on the high places, their pleas were never answered. Their idols had no ears to hear with and no mouth to speak with (see Psalm 115:5-6). This was evident with the Asherah and Baal prophets that Elijah confronted on the mountaintop. They called out to their deities but there "was no voice, no one answered, and no one paid attention" (1 Kings 18:29).

However, in the above verses, Jesus said will not happen when they pray to God. There is no need for self-mutilation, travailing, or doubt. When you ask God to remove an evil spiritual mountain, you can count on His immediate action on your behalf. Jesus even said that once your heart is set to remove that mountain, God is already removing it before you ask.

ANCIENT & MODERN FIG ASHERIM

ISIS

Isis was known as the Lady of the Sycamore. "This title has been interpreted to relate to a specific and particularly old tree that once stood to the south of the Temple of Ptah at Memphis [Egypt] during the Old Kingdom."[5] There are some Egyptian hieroglyphs that show Isis as a tree where her legs are the trunk. The *Egyptian Book of the Dead*, which supposedly helps the deceased navigate the afterlife, says, "You shall sit under the branches of the tree of Hathor." Isis in this capacity was an Asherah fig tree.

HULUPPU TREE

Some think that the huluppu tree in the *Epic of Gilgamesh* (see chapters titled, "Inanna," "Lilith," and "Asherah") is a willow, but I disagree. The huluppu tree originally grew along the Euphrates River where sycamore fig trees grew and in one version of the poem, the word "fruitful" is used three times in relation to the tree (willows do not bear fruit). One version of the poem says, "The tree grew big, its trunk bore no foliage."[6] A tree with fruit and no foliage is a fig tree with breba fruit.

Figure 42. Eleuthera Banyan fig tree [7]

Additional lines in the poem reveal, "In its roots the snake who knows no charm set up its nest, in its crown the Imdugud-bird placed its young."[8] The roots of the fig tree are aerial which means they grow above the dirt and are a haven for snakes. It is also common for birds to nest in the crowns of the fig trees where they enjoy the figs.

BUDDHISM

The tradition of worshiping asherim is still in practice today all around the world at the sites of thousands of Buddhist temples. The temple in Bodh Gaya is where Buddha received his enlightenment under a fig tree, hence the name Tree of Enlightenment. Although the original tree was destroyed, a sapling from it stands in the same place today and is known as the Mahabodhi (Bodhi) tree.

The Bodhi tree's scientific name is *Ficus religiosa*, otherwise known as "a sacred fig tree" to the followers of Hinduism, Jainism, and Buddhism. Planted near Buddhist temples, these trees are the objects of devotion to millions of people as Buddha incarnate. Legend reveals that King Devanampiya Tissa received a sapling of the original Tree of Enlightenment in 245 BC and planted it in his home country of Sri Lanka.

> Ceremonies were performed in its honour and on the tenth day the sapling was placed on a chariot and taken, with pomp and pageantry, to Anuradhapura, the capital. There it was planted, with magnificent splendour and ceremony, in the Maha Megha garden, where it still flourishes, and receives the veneration of millions of devotees. It is also the oldest recorded tree in the world...The tree symbolizes, in a vivid way, the Enlightenment.[9]

This tree is nearly 2,300 years old, which would make the 300-year-old asherim that Josiah cut down on the Mount of Destruction very young!

CATHOLIC MARY

A *New York Times* article titled "A Tree Drooping with Its Ancient Burden of Faith," written in 2015, is about a sycamore fig tree in Cairo, Egypt that is beloved by many who worship the Catholic Mary.

This is the Virgin's Tree, whose site in north Cairo has been a place of Coptic pilgrimage for hundreds of years. Here, according to a legend carefully nurtured by these Egyptian Christians, Mary stopped and rested with Joseph and the infant Jesus during their travels in Egypt 2,000 years ago.[10]

The article makes it clear that people who visit the site must consider the tree to have some sort of power. One such visitor was witnessed by the author of the article:

With fierce concentration, he reached forward to stroke the nearest limb of the sycamore and passed the same hand over his head. He rubbed the tree again and again, each time massaging his face and his heart as if to absorb its essence. "To us, it's a miracle that a tree would stay here like this all these years," explained Mr. [removed]. Then he sighed. "It adds to my faith just to see it."[11]

From the Garden of Eden to Egypt, the fig tree has definitely played an important role in worship of the queen of heaven.

---

[1] Sutton, *Figs*, Kindle, Chapter 3, 21%.

[2] Ibid., Chapter 2, 18%.

[3] Downing, *Horticulturist and Journal of Rural Art and Rural Taste*, 527.

[4] "File:Moreton Bay Fig Tree.jpg"[Online] https://commons.wikimedia.org/ wiki/File: Moreton_Bay_Fig_Tree.jpg [2016,Nov].

[5] Jimmy Dunn "Tree Goddesses" [Online] http://www.touregypt.net/featurestories/ treegoddess.htm [2015, Oct].

[6] "The Huluppu Tree" [Online] http://www.piney.com/BabHulTree.html[2016, Nov].

[7] Taken by author on the island of Eleuthera, Bahamas.

[8] "The Huluppu Tree" [Online].

[9] Thera, *Collected Bodhi Leaves*, 360-361.

[10] Susan Sachs (Dec 2001), "Cairo Journal; A Tree Drooping with Its Ancient Burden of Faith" December 26, 2001 [Online] http://www.nytimes.com/2001/12/26/world/cairo-journal-a-tree-drooping-with-its-ancient-burden-of-faith.html [2015, Oct].

[11] Ibid.

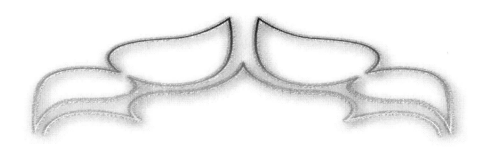

APPENDIX A
VISION ELEMENTS

IT WAS IMPORTANT for me to analyze the vision I had in order to determine if it conformed to Biblical truth. This appendix is the result of my study.

TIMING

I first had to determine when this royal event in my vision took place. Establishing this would be necessary in order to frame all the rest of the elements. The attributes of the bride, the characteristics of the King, and the absence of the King's crown all help to determine where this vision occurs on a biblical timeline.

When the King opened the doors, the bride did not come running: she was already present, alertly waiting for her Bridegroom. The following verses attest to how believers, who are the bride, are to be ready.

> Be on the alert then, for you do not know the day nor
> the hour. (Matthew 25:13)

> But you, brethren, are not in darkness, that the day
> would overtake you like a thief; for you are all sons of
> light and sons of day. We are not of night nor of
> darkness; so then let us not sleep as others do, but let
> us be alert and sober. (1 Thessalonians 5:4-6)

> Let us rejoice and be glad and give the glory to Him,
> for the marriage of the Lamb has come and His bride
> has made herself ready. (Revelation 19:7)

Of course, there is also the parable of the ten virgins that shows
how the bride is to be ready at any moment for her Bridegroom to
appear (see Matthew 25:1-13). The Bride of Christ is ready and
waiting to marry the Lamb, Jesus Christ; a glorious occasion that
happens before His second coming.

The physical layout of the vision closely resembled a church
wedding, but instead of the bride going down the aisle to meet her
groom, the King goes to meet her just as He does in Scripture.

> For the Lord Himself will descend from heaven with a
> shout, with the voice of the archangel and with the
> trumpet of God, and the dead in Christ will rise first.
> Then we who are alive and remain will be caught up
> together with them in the clouds to meet the Lord in
> the air, and so we shall always be with the Lord.
> (1 Thessalonians 4:16-17)

This seems to place the timing of the vision within the moments
before the marriage of the Lamb to His bride. The apparel of the

King supports this conclusion. In my vision, the King wore a military uniform that included a deep red shirt. When Jesus returns His garments will already be red from the blood of His wrath.

> Who is this who comes from Edom, with garments of glowing colors from Bozrah, this One who is majestic in His apparel, marching in the greatness of His strength? "It is I who speak in righteousness, mighty to save." Why is Your apparel red, and Your garments like the one who treads in the wine press?
>
> "I have trodden the wine trough alone, and from the peoples there was no man with Me. I also trod them in My anger and trampled them in My wrath; and their lifeblood is sprinkled on My garments, and I stained all My raiment. (Isaiah 63:1-3)

These verses from Isaiah occur on the day of God's wrath also known as "the Day of the Lord." It is a day of war, great destructtion, and bloodshed. The earth will be void of all men, animals, birds, and fish. This is why Jesus, our King, is dressed in red. Below is an interesting decree concerning God's loved ones (guests) on this horrible day:

> Be silent before the Lord God! For the day of the Lord is near, for the Lord has prepared a sacrifice, He has consecrated His guests. Then it will come about on the day of the Lord's sacrifice that I will punish the princes, the king's sons and all who clothe themselves with foreign garments. (Zephaniah 1:7-8)

Foreign garments are equivalent to what the man was wearing in the wedding parable, "But when the king came in to look over the dinner guests, he saw a man there who was not dressed in wedding clothes" (Matthew 22:11). Instead of wedding attire, which is the robe of righteousness received when we are clothed with Christ, the guests wore foreign garments.

First Thessalonians gives a New Covenant understanding for the Day of the Lord. The promise of safety for the Bride of Christ is evident during this terrible period. Notice that although we may not know the day or hour, it is *not* to overtake us like a thief.

> Now as to the times and the epochs, brethren, you have no need of anything to be written to you. For you yourselves know full well that the day of the Lord will come just like a thief in the night. While they are saying, "Peace and safety!" then destruction will come upon them suddenly like labor pains upon a woman with child, and they will not escape.
>
> *But you, brethren, are not in darkness, that the day would overtake you like a thief;* for you are all sons of light and sons of day. We are not of night nor of darkness; so then let us not sleep as others do, but let us be alert and sober...For God has not destined us for wrath, but for obtaining salvation through our Lord Jesus Christ, who died for us, so that whether we are awake or asleep, we will live together with Him. (1 Thessalonians 5:1-6, 9-11, italics added)

The wrath of the Day of the Lord occurs before the wedding, which is why Jesus' garments are red when He comes for His bride.

One more thing was significant in revealing the timing of my vision. The atmosphere in the vision was light and joyful because the King was so happy. Isaiah expresses Jesus' joy, "As the Bridegroom rejoices over the bride, so your God will rejoice over you" (Isaiah 62:5). Song of Solomon supports this, "Go forth, O daughters of Zion, and gaze on King Solomon with the crown with which his mother has crowned him on the day of his wedding, and on the day of his gladness of heart" (Song of Solomon 3:11).

Solomon's mother crowned him on the day of his wedding. In my vision, the King was not wearing a crown. In Scripture, Christ receives many crowns after He marries His bride, "I saw heaven opened, and behold, a white horse, and He who sat on it is called Faithful and True, and in righteousness He judges and wages war. His eyes are a flame of fire, and on His head are many diadems" (Revelation 19:11-12; see also Song of Solomon 3:11, Revelation 19:17-18).

Here is a summary of events in order to understand the timing more clearly as it involves the bride, the King, and the absence of crowns.

1. Jesus treads the wine press and his clothes are stained red on the Day of the Lord (see Zephaniah 1, Isaiah 63:1-3, Revelation 19:13).
2. He comes for His bride who is ready and waiting for Him (see Revelation 19:7-8). This was the event in my vision.
3. The marriage of the Lamb (see Revelation 19:7-8).
4. Jesus is crowned as King of kings and Lord of lords (see Revelation 19:16).
5. Jesus returns with His queen to the earth (see Revelation 19:11-16).

6. War and marriage supper: birds feast on the kings and their entourages who followed the beast (see Revelation 19:17-21).

It seems that the events in my vision occur after the Day of the Lord, but before Jesus is crowned (#2 above). With this established, it is easier to understand the rest of the elements of my vision.

BRIDE

A brilliant light poured out from around the bride accentuating her bright ivory gown. Keep in mind that the bride's gown is a wedding garment. The ivory colored gown bothered me immediately after having the vision because I thought that in Revelation the bride wore white. I was glad to find out I was wrong.

> Let us rejoice and be glad and give the glory to Him, for the marriage of the Lamb has come and His bride has made herself ready. It was given to her to clothe herself in fine linen, bright and clean; for the fine linen is the righteous acts of the saints. (Revelation 19:7-8, italics added)

Your Bible may say *white* instead of *clean*. The Greek word actually means, "clean." While searching Revelation for the word *white* I found that it describes the robes of the saints and the clothes of the armies that return to earth with Christ after the marriage. Let us consider these two types of robes—linen and white.

First, we will look at the white robes. Why are they white and who is wearing them? Revelation says, "These who are clothed in the white robes, who are they, and where have they come from...These are the ones who come out of the great tribulation, and they have washed their robes and made them white in the blood of the Lamb" (Revelation 7:14).

It is important to understand that *they have washed their robes and made them white in the blood of the Lamb* simply means these people are born again. In Galatians we find, "For all of you who were baptized into Christ have clothed yourselves with Christ" (Galatians 3:27). Washing one's robe is the simple decision to relinquish your life to Christ. The Greek word for white in this verse is *leukaino,* which means "to make white." So the robes of white are received through individual acts of initial salvation (see Galatians 3:28).[1]

Next, we will consider the linen robe. The bride is not an individual but the collective body of Christ made up of all born-again believers. The linen of the bride's wedding garment is clean and bright in its natural state. The Greek word for bright used in Revelation 19:8 is *lampros,* which means, "shining, bright, brilliant, transparent, luxuries or elegancies in dress or style."[2] Wikipedia states, "Linen fabrics have a high natural luster; their natural color ranges between shades of ivory, ecru, tan, or grey."[3]

The linen depicts the righteous acts of the saints. Isaiah 64:6 says, "All our righteous deeds are like a filthy garment." Without Christ, we create our own standard that falls short of what is right to God. Not usually done intentionally, acts of righteousness are a result of our love and adoration for God.

Jesus referred to righteous acts as good works, "Let your light shine before men in such a way that they may see your good works, and glorify your Father who is in heaven" (Matthew 5:16, italics added). This is the wedding garment of the bride as I saw it in the vision. In her relationship to Jesus, the Bridegroom, she was shining for all to see. Paul says the same thing in 1 Thessalonians, "But you, brethren, are not in darkness, that the day would overtake you like a thief; for you are all sons of light and sons of day" (1 Thessalonians 5:4-5).

Paul talks at length about good works in his letters, stating that one who practices good works is rich, proper, and of good repute. He is very clear in that we are not born again due to our good works, but we are equipped to do them after we are saved.

> For by grace you have been saved through faith; and that not of yourselves, it is the gift of God; not as a result of works, so that no one may boast. For we are His workmanship, created in Christ Jesus for good works, which God prepared beforehand so that we would walk in them. (Ephesians 2:8-10)

We are washed and righteous in the blood of the Lamb, not by our good works (righteous deeds). This is why the bride's wedding gown is not white; instead, it is bright and clean. It shines before men because of the bride's good works.

DOVE'S EYES

The Bridegroom and bride had an expression in their eyes that I do not have the words to describe. *Love* and a*doration* fall far short of the expression of deep emotion that held their gaze. Their eyes laid bare something within their souls that transcends time.

The one thing that came to my mind when I saw this was "doves' eyes" as mentioned in the Song of Solomon. The King describes his bride, "How beautiful you are, my darling, how beautiful you are! Your eyes are like doves" (Song of Solomon 1:15). The bride has something similar to say about her King, "His eyes are like doves beside streams of water, bathed in milk, and reposed in their setting" (Song of Solomon 5:12).

When King Solomon described his bride's eyes as that of a dove, he may have been thinking of the White-winged dove that has beautiful blue and red around its eyes. However, I wonder if He was also considering his bride's prowess against her enemies. A dove's field of view is only forty degrees short of a full circle and has a broader than normal area of sharp focus. Just as a dove is very well equipped to see oncoming predators, so is the bride able to discern the schemes of the devil.

WITNESSES

The many people on either side of the aisle in my vision represent Old Testament believers. Revelation clearly tells us that others are present at the wedding besides the King and his bride, "Write, 'Blessed are those who are invited to the marriage supper of the Lamb" (Revelation 19:9). The prophetic book, the Song of Solomon, also records that sixty mighty men are with the King on the day of his wedding (see Song of Solomon 3:7-8).

It is important to understand that Old Testament believers are not part of the Bride of Christ. God calls Himself the husband of Old Testament believers, not a bridegroom. "For your husband is your Maker, whose name is the LORD of Hosts" (Isaiah 54:5)

This is in contrast to the believers in the New Testament who are the Bride of Christ. Jesus, the King, is her Bridegroom. "For I am jealous for you with a godly jealousy; for I betrothed [engaged] you to one husband, so that to Christ I might present you as a pure virgin" (2 Corinthians 11:2). Notice God's name of Jealous in this verse and the bride's virginity, which is a reference to her freedom from idol worship.[4]

269

The resurrection of the Old Testament saints occurred in the moment Jesus died on the cross as the temple veil was torn.

> The veil of the temple was torn in two from top to bottom; and the earth shook and the rocks were split. The tombs were opened, and many bodies of the saints who had fallen asleep were raised; and coming out of the tombs after His resurrection they entered the holy city and appeared to many. (Matthew 27:51-53)

There are no verses that say how these saints left the earth in the first resurrection, but it is safe to assume they were carried up to heaven just as Jesus was. They are now considered the cloud of witnesses to New Testament believers (see Matthew 27:51-53; Luke 24:52; Hebrews 12:1).

In the vision, the witnesses were all in bright, gem-colored clothing similar to the colors around God's throne in the spirit realm.

> Behold, a throne was standing in heaven, and One sitting on the throne. And He who was sitting was like a jasper stone and a sardius in appearance; and there was a rainbow around the throne, like an emerald in appearance. (Revelation 4:2-3)

GOLD CARPET

A gold carpet ran the length of the throne room from the throne all the way to the door where the bride stood waiting. Revelation 21:21 describes the New Jerusalem as having a street made with "pure gold like transparent glass." Jeremiah 7:34 says that the voices of the bride and Bridegroom will cease to be heard in the streets of

Jerusalem because of the devotion to the queen of heaven. Here we can see that this street in Jerusalem is redeemed from horrendous abominations through pure worship to God as the Bride of Christ is given in marriage to her King (see Revelation 21:21).

More details of my vision correspond with the Bible, but these were sufficient for me to know it was from God.

---

[1] Blue Letter Bible, "Lexicon :: Strong's G3021 - leukainō " [Online] http://v3. blueletterbible.org/lang/lexicon/lexicon.cfm?Strongs=G3021&t=NASB_[2014, Jan].

[2] Ibid., "Lexicon :: Strong's G2986 – lampros."

[3] Wikipedia, "Linen" [Online]_http://en.wikipedia.org/wiki/Linen [2014, Jan].

[4] The term, idol, is used thirteen times in the books of Corinthians, more than any other book in the New Testament.

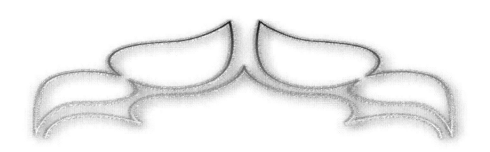

APPENDIX B
KINGS CHART

<u>KEY:</u>

( ) – duration of reign

* – king had direct contact with these prophets

Italics – allies

ALL CAPS – enemies

(J) – Judah

(I) – Israel

(Ar) – Aram (Syria)

(As) – Assyria

(B) – Babylon

(E) – Egypt

NORTHERN KINGDOM: ISRAEL

King	Prophets	Concurrent Kings	Worship
Jeroboam I (22 yrs) Son of Nebat Family killed by Baasha 1 Ki 11:26-14:20; 2 Chr 10:2-13:20	Ahijah* Iddo	REHOBOAM (J) ABIJAM (J) Asa (J) Ben-Hadad I (Ar) *Shishak* (E)	Evil Isis/Hathor Asherah
Nadab (2 yrs) Son of Jeroboam Killed by Baasha 1 Ki 15:25-31	Ahijah Iddo	ASA (J) Ben-Hadad I (Ar)	Evil Isis/Hathor Asherah
Baasha (24 yrs) Son of Ahijah Family killed by Zimri 1 Ki 15:16-16:13; 2 Chr 16:1-6	Ahijah Iddo Jehu	ASA (J) BEN-HADAD I (Ar)	Evil Isis/Hathor Asherah
Elah (2 yrs) Son of Baasha Killed by Zimri 1 Ki 16:8-14	Jehu	Asa (J) Ben-Hadad I (Ar)	Evil Isis/Hathor Asherah

King	Prophets	Concurrent Kings	Worship
Zimri (7 days) Servant of Baasha Suicide 1 Ki 16:9-20	Jehu	Asa (J) Ben-Hadad I (Ar)	Evil Isis/Hathor Asherah
Omri (12 yrs) 1 Ki 16:16-28; Mi 6:16	Jehu Elijah	Asa (J) Ben-Hadad I (Ar) Ben-Hadad II (Ar)	Evil Isis/Hathor Asherah
Ahab (22 yrs) Son of Omri Killed in battle 1 Ki 16:28-22:40; 2 Ki 10:1; 2 Chr 18:1-34; Mi 6:16	Jehu Elijah Micaiah*	Asa (J) *Jehoshaphat* (J) BEN-HADAD II (Ar) Shalmaneser II (As)	Evil Isis/Hathor Asherah Astarte
Ahaziah (2 yrs) Son of Ahab Married Athaliah Sickly death 1 Ki 22:40, 49; 2 Ki 1:1-18; 2 Chr 20:35-36	Elijah	*Jehoshaphat* (J) Ben-Hadad II (Ar)	Evil Isis/Hathor Asherah
Jehoram/ Joram (11 yrs) Son of Ahab Killed by Jehu 2 Ki 3:1- 9:26; 2 Chr 22:5-8	Elisha* Micaiah	*Jehoshaphat* (J) *Jehoram* (J) *Ahaziah* (J) *Athaliah* (J) *Edom King* BEN-HADAD II (Ar) HAZAEL (Ar) MESHA (Moab)	Evil Isis/Hathor Asherah

King	Prophets	Concurrent Kings	Worship
Jehu (28 yrs) Anointed by God 2 Ki 9:1-12:1; 2 Chr 22:7-8	Elisha	Athaliah (J) Joash (J) HAZAEL (Ar) Assur-Nazir I(As) Shalmaneser II (As)	Evil Isis/Hathor Asherah
Jehoahaz (17 yrs) Son of Jehu 2 Ki 10:35; 13:1-9, 22-23	Elisha	Joash (J) HAZAEL (Ar) BEN-HADAD III (Ar) Shalmaneser II (As)	Evil Isis/Hathor Asherah
Jehoash/Joash (16 yrs) Son of Jehoahaz 2 Ki 13:10-20, 24-25; 14:8-16; 2 Chr 25:17-24	Elisha* Jonah	Joash (J) AMAZIAH (J) Ben-Hadad III (Ar) Shalmaneser II (As)	Evil Isis/Hathor Asherah
Jeroboam II (41 yrs) Son of Joash Died by the sword 2 Ki 13:13; 14:15-29; Ho 1:1; Am 1:1; 7:7-13	Amos Jonah Hosea	Amaziah (J) Uzziah (J) Ben-Hadad III (Ar) Shalmaneser II (As) Samsi Vul IV (As) Tiglath-Pileser III (aka Pul) (As)	Evil Isis/Hathor Asherah
Zechariah (6 mos) Son of Jeroboam II Killed by Shallum 2 Ki 14:29; 15:8-11	Hosea	Uzziah (J) Tiglath-Pileser III (aka Pul) (As)	Evil Isis/Hathor Asherah

King	Prophets	Concurrent Kings	Worship
Shallum (1 mo) Son of Jabesh Killed by Menahem 2 Ki 15:10-15	Hosea	Azariah (J) Tiglath-Pileser III (aka Pul) (As)	Evil Isis/Hathor Asherah
Menahem (10 yrs) Son of Gadi 2 Ki 15:14-22	Hosea	Azariah (J) TIGLATH-PILESER III (aka Pul) (As)	Evil Isis/Hathor Asherah
Pekahiah (2 yrs) Son of Menahem Killed by Pekah 2 Ki 15:22-26	Hosea	Azariah (J) Tiglath-Pileser III (aka Pul) (As) Assur-Daan III	Evil Isis/Hathor Asherah
Pekah (20 yrs) Son of Remaliah Killed by Hoshea 2 Ki 15:25-31; 16:5-6; 2 Chr 28:5-15; Isa 7:1-6	Hosea Isaiah	JOTHAM (J) AHAZ (J) TIGLATH-PILESER III (aka Pul) (As) Assur-Daan III (As) Assur-Nirari II (As) *Rezin* (Ar)	Evil Isis/Hathor Asherah
Hoshea (9 yrs) Son of Elah Made king by Pul Taken captive by Shalmaneser 2 Ki 15:30; 17:1-18:12	Hosea	Jotham (J) Ahaz (J) Hezekiah (J) TIGLATH-PILESER III (aka Pul) (As) SHALMANESER IV (As) Assur-Daan III (As) SO (E)	Evil Isis/Hathor Asherah

SOUTHERN KINGDOM: JUDAH & BENJAMIN

King	Prophet	Concurrent Kings	Worship
Rehoboam (17 yrs) Son of Solomon 1 Ki 11:43-14:31; 2 Chr 9:31-12:16; 13:7	Shemaiah*	JEROBOAM (I) Ben-Hadad I (Ar) SHISHAK (E)	Good, later evil Ashtoreth on Mount of Destruction
Abijam/Abijah (3 yrs) Son of Rehoboam 1 Ki 14:31-15:8; 2 Chr 11:20, 22; 2:16-4:1	Shemaiah	JEROBOAM (I) *Ben-Hadad I (Ar)*	Not wholly devoted to God Asherah Ashtoreth
Asa (41 yrs) Diseased feet in old age 1 Ki; 15:8-24, 32; 2 Chr 14:1-16:14; Je 41:9	Shemaiah Azariah* Hanani*	Jeroboam (I) Nadab (I) BAASHA (I) Elah (I) Zimri (I) Omri (I) Ahab (I) BEN-HADAD I (Ar) Ben-Hadad II (Ar)	Dedicated to God, removed high places and asherim from Judah Asherah (later) Ashtoreth
Jehoshaphat (25 yrs) Son of Asa Married into Ahab's family 1 Ki 15:24; 22:2-50; 2 Ki 3:7-27; 8:16; 2 Chr 17:1-21:2	Jahaziel* Eliezer Jehu* Micaiah*	*Ahab (I)* *Ahaziah (I)* *Jehoram (I)* BEN-HADAD II (Ar) EDOM KING MESHA (Moab)	Dedicated to God, removed high places and asherim from Judah, but they were later replaced by the people Ashtoreth

King	Prophet	Concurrent Kings	Worship
Jehoram/Joram (8 yrs) Son of Jehoshaphat Incurable sickness, died in pain 1 Ki 22:50; 2 Ki 8:16-24; 2 Chr 21:1-20	Jahaziel Eliezer Elijah*	Jehoram (I) Ben-Hadad II (Ar) Hazael (Ar) EDOM KING	Evil Walked in the way of Israel Asherah Isis/Hathor Ashtoreth
Ahaziah/Jehoahaz (1 yr) Son of Jehoram Killed by Jehu 2 Ki 8:24-9:29; 10:13-14; 2 Chr 21:17; 22:1-9	Jahaziel	*Jehoram* (I) HAZAEL (Ar)	Evil Same as King Ahab Astarte Isis/Hathor Asherah Ashtoreth
Queen Athaliah (6 yrs) Daughter of Ahab Mother of Ahaziah 2 Ki 11:1-16, 20; 2 Chr 22:10-21	Jahaziel Obadiah	Jehu (I) Hazael (Ar)	Evil Astarte Isis/Hathor Asherah Ashtoreth
Joash\Jehoash 7yo (40 yrs) Son of Ahaziah Sickly, killed by his servants 2 Ki 11:21-12:21; 2 Chr 22:11-12; 24:27-25:25	Obadiah Joel Zechariah*	Jehu (I) Jehoahaz (I) JOASH (I) HAZAEL (Ar) Ben-Hadad III (Ar) Assur-Nazir (As) Shalmaneser II (As)	Dedicated to God but kept high places, Asherah (later) Ashtoreth

King	Prophet	Concurrent Kings	Worship
Amaziah (29 yrs) Son of Joash Chased and killed 2 Ki 12:21; 13:12; 14:1-20; 15:1; 2 Chr 24:27-25:28		JEHOASH (I) Jeroboam (I) Ben-Hadad III (Ar) Shalmaneser II (As) Samsi-vul IV (As)	Dedicated to God but kept high places Asherah Ashtoreth
Azariah/Uzziah 16 yo (52 yrs) Son of Amaziah Struck with leprosy 2 Ki 14:21-15:7; 2 Chr 26:1-23; Isa 1:1; Hos 1:1; Amos 1:1; Zec 14:5	Amos Hosea Zechariah* Isaiah	Jeroboam II (I) Zachariah (I) Shallum (I) Menahem (I) Pekahiah (I) Pekah (I) Ben-Hadad III (Ar) Samsi-vul IV (As) Tiglath-Pileser III (aka Pul)(As) Assur-Daan II (As)	Dedicated to God but kept high places Ashtoreth
Jotham (16 yrs) Son of Azariah 2 Kings 15:5, 7, 30-38; 2 Chr 26:21-27:9; Isa 1:1; Hos 1:1; Mi 1:1	Isaiah	PEKAH (I) Hoshea (I) REZIN (Ar) Assur-Daan III (As) Assur-Nirari II (As) Tiglath-Pileser III (aka Pul) (As) AMMON KING	Dedicated to God but kept high places Asherah (later) Ashtoreth
Ahaz (16 yrs) Son of Jotham 2 Ki 15:38, 16:1-17:1;2 Chr 27:9-28:27; 29: 19; Isa 1:1; 7:1-25; 14:28; Ho 1:1; Mi 1:1	Isaiah* Jothan Micah Obed	PEKAH (I) Hoshea (I) REZIN (Ar) TIGLATH-PILESER III (aka Pul)(As) Shalmaneser IV (As)	Evil Walked in ways of Israel Asherah Ashtoreth

King	Prophet	Concurrent Kings	Worship
Hezekiah (29 yrs) Son of Ahaz 2 Ki 16:20; 18:1- 20:21; 21:3; 2 Chr 28:27-32:33; 33:3; Pr 25:1; Isa 1:1; 36:1-39:8; Je 26:18-19; Ho 1:1; Mi 1:1	Isaiah Micah Obed	Hoshea (I) Israel taken captive SHALMANESER IV (As) SENNACHERIB (As) Berodach-baladan (B)	Dedicated to God, removed queen of heaven from Judah but not the Ashtoreth on Mount of Destruction
Manasseh 12 yo (55 yrs) Son of Hezekiah Captive by Assyria 2 Ki 20:21-21:18; 2 Chr 32:33-33:23; Je 15:4	Isaiah Nahum	Sennacherib (As) Esarhaddon (As) Assur-Banipal (aka Osnappar) (As)	Most evil king Asherah in God's temple Ashtoreth Later repented
Amon (2 yrs) Son of Manasseh Killed by servants 2 Ki 21:18-21:25; 2 Chr 33:20-25	Zephania Nahum	Assur-Banipal (aka Osnappar) (As)	Evil Asherah Ashtoreth
Josiah 8 yo (31 yrs) Son of Amon 2 Ki 21:24-23:30; 1 Chr 3:15; 2 Chr 33:25-35:27; Je 1:1-2; 3:6; 25:3	Jeremiah Zephaniah Huldah Nahum Habakkuk	Assur-Banipal (aka Osnappar) (As) Nineveh destroyed NECO (E)	Dedicated to God, cleansed queen of heaven from Judah and Israel, remov- ed Ashtoreth from Mount of Destruction

King	Prophet	Concurrent Kings	Worship
Jehoahaz II/ Shallum/Joahaz (3 mos) Josiah's fourth son Imprisoned in Egypt 2 Ki 23:30-23:34; 2 Chr 36:1-4; Je 22:11-17	Jeremiah Huldah	NECO (E)	Evil queen of heaven
Eliakim/Jehoiakim (11yrs) Josiah's second son Made king by Neco Captive to Babylon 2 Ki 23:24-24:6; 2 Chr 36:4-8; Je 1:3; 22:18-23; 26:20-23; 36:1-32; 25:1	Jeremiah Daniel Uriah*	NECO (E) NEBUCHADNEZZAR (B)	Evil queen of heaven
Jehoiachin/Coniah/ Jeconiah 18 yo (3 mos) Son of Eliakim Captive to Babylon 2 Ki 24:6-24:17; 25:27-30; 2 Chr 36:8-10; Je 22:24-30; 24:1; 28:4	Jeremiah Daniel Ezekiel	NEBUCHADNEZZAR (B)	Evil queen of heaven

King	Prophet	Concurrent Kings	Worship
Mattaniah/Zedekiah (11 yrs) Made king by Nebuchadnezzar Sons killed in front of him, tortured, captive to Babylon, died in prison 2 Ki 24:17-25:7; 2 Chr 36:10-20; Je 1:3; 21:1-22:10; 37:1-39:8; 24:8-10; 27:1-15; 28:1; 29:1, 15-20; 32:1-5; 34:2-11, 21; 37:1-39:8; 49:33; 52:1-11; Ez 17:11-21	Jeremiah Ezekiel Daniel	NEBUCHADNEZZAR (B)	Evil queen of heaven

Chart derived from the Bible and *Adam's Chart of Synchronological Chart Map of History*

BIBLIOGRAPHY

Abrahamsen, Valerie. Women and Worship at Philippi, Diana/Artamis and Other Cults in the Early Christian Era. Portland: Astarte Shell Press, 1995.

Adams, Hon SD. Adams Synchronological Chart Map of History. 1871.

Archaeological Study Bible, An Illustrated walk through Biblical History and Culture, KJV. Grand Rapids: Zondervan, 2010.

Arnold, Clinton E., ed. Zondervan Illustrated Bible Backgrounds Commentary. Vol. 2. Grand Rapids: Zondervan, 2002.

Benard, Elisabeth, ed. Goddesses Who Rule. New York: Oxford University Press, Inc. Used with permission., 2000.

Blue Letter Bible. n.d. <http://www.blueletterbible.org>.

Braund, David C. Augustus to Nero (Routledge Revivals): A Sourcebook on Roman History 31 BC - AD 68. New York: Routledge, 2014.

Bron, Christiane. "The Sword Dance for Artemis." The J. Paul Getty Museum Journal 24 (1996): 69-85.

Brown, Candy Gunther. The Healing Gods: Complementary and Alternative Medicine in Christian America. New York: Oxford University Press, 2013.

Budin, Stephanie Lynn. "A Reconsideration of the Aphrodite-Ashtart Syncretism." 2004. JSTOR. 31 March 2014 <http://www.jstor.org/discover/10.2307/3270523?uid=3739904&uid=2&uid=4&uid=3739256&sid=21103896503313>.

Calmet, Augustine, Charles Taylor and Edward Robinson. Dictionary of the Holy Bible. Boston: Crocker and Brewster, 1832.

Carlson, Ron. Fast Facts on False Teachings. Eugene: Harvest House Publishers, 1994.

Catechism of the Catholic Church with modifications from the Editio Typica. New York: Doubleday, 1995.

Clark, Randy and Craig Miller. Fiinding Victory When Healing Doesn't Happen. Mechanicsburg: Global Awakening, 2015.

Cornelius, Izak. The Many Faces of the Goddess: The Iconography of the Syro-Palestinian Goddesses Anat, Astarte, Qedeshet, and Asherah c. 1500-1000BCE. Saint-Paul Fribourg Switzerland: Academic Press Fribourg Vandenhoeck & Ruprecht Gottingen, 2004.

Crowder, John. Miracle Workers, Reformers, and The New Mystics. Shippensburg: Destiny Image Publishers, Inc, 2006.

D'Este, Sorita. Artemis Virgin Goddess of the Sun & Moon - A comprehensive study of the Greek goddess of the hunt, her powers, myths and worship. London: Avalonia, 2005.

Downing, A.J., ed. Horticulturist and Journal of Rural Art and Rural Taste Volume 2. Vol. 2. Albany: Luther Tucker, 1847.

Fields, Osgood, & Co. Literature, Science, Art, and Politics Volume XXIII. Boston: University Press: Welch, Bigelow, & Co. Cambridge, 1869.

Fischer-Hansen, Tobias and Birte Poulsen. From Artemis to Diana. The Goddess of Man and Beast. Ed. Acta Hyperborea. Vol. 12. Copenhagen: Museum Tusculanum Press, 2009.

Foss, Clive. Ephesus after Antiquity: A late antique, Byzantine and Turkish City. New York: Press Syndicate of the University of Cambridge, 1979.

Fragpane, Francis. The Three Battlegrounds. Cedar Rapids: Arrow Publications, 1977.

Franz, Gordon. "Nahum, Nineveh and Those Nasty Assyrians." Bible and Spade (2009).

Freeman, James M. The New Manners & Customs of the Bible, A complete guide to the origin and significance of our time-honored biblical tradition. North Brunswick: Bridge-Logos Publishers, 1998.

Good-Star, Quincy. The Blue Road, Jesus Fulfilled the Old Way. Rapid City: Miracle Center, 2013.

Grayson, Albert Kirk. Assyrian Royal Inscriptions. Wiesbaden: Otto Harrassowitz, 1972.

Hahn, Scott, Ph.D. and Leon Suprenant Jr. Catholic for a Reason. Steubenville: Emmaus Road Publishing, 1998.

Hall, Manly P. Lectures on Ancient Philosophy. London WC2R 0RL: Penguin Group, 2005.

Hamilton, Edith. Mythology. New York: Back Bay Books/Little, Brown and Company, 1942.

Harris, R. Laird, Gleason L. Archer Jr, Bruce K. Waltke. Theological Wordbook of the Old Testament. Vol. 1 & 2. Chicago: Moody Press, 1980.

Harrison, Jane. Myths of Greece and Rome. Ed. Matthew Vossler. Garden City: Doubleday, Doran & Company, Inc., 1928.

Herder, Peter. Babylon, The Resurgence of History's Most Infamous City. Kansas City: Forerunner Publishing, 2009.

Herodotus and G.C. Macaulay (translator). The History of Herodotus. 440 BC (July 2001).

Holliday, Pat. The Witchdoctor and the Man. Jacksonville: Agapepublishers, 2001.

Hunter, M. Kelley. Black Moon Lilith. Tempe: American Federation of Astrologiers, Inc., 2010.

—. Living Lilith: Four Dimensions of the Cosmic Feminine. Bournemouth: The Wessex Astrologer Ltd, 2009.

Hurwitz, Siegmund. Lilith the First Eve: Historical and Psychological Aspects of the Dark Feminine. Ed. Robert Hinshaw. EinSiedeln: Daimon Verlag, 2012.

Hynson, Colin. Ancient Civilizations, Mesopotamia. London: World Almanac Library, 2006.

Johnson, Buffie. Lady of the Beasts, The Goddess and Her Sacred Animals. Rochester: Inner Traditions International, 1994.

Kanco, Bishop Samuel Vagalas. Witch Doctor and the Man, Fourth Generation Witch Doctor Finds Christ. Jacksonville: Agape Publishing, 2000.

Kennedy, William H. Lucifer's Lodge: Satanic Ritual Abuse in the Catholic Church. Reviviscimus, 2004.

Kjos, Berit. A Twist of Faith, How feminist spirituality is changing the church and betraying the women it promised to heal. Green Forest: New Leaf Press, 1997.

Lamm, Maurice. The Jewish Way in Love & Marriage. Middle Village: Jonathan David Publishers, Inc., 1991.

Landau, Elaine. The Assyrians. Brookfield: The Millbrook Press, 1997.

—. The Babylonians. Brookfield: The Millbrook Press, Inc., 1997.

Leick, Gwendolyn. Sex and Eroticism in Mesopotamian Literature. London: Routledge Taylor & Francis Group, 1994.

Lucian (translated by Herbert A. Strong, M.A. LL.D). The Syrian Goddess (Original title - De Dea Syria). Ed. M.A. D.Sc. John Garstang. London: Constable & Company LTD, 1913.

Macoy, Robert. Illustrated History and Cyclopedia of Freemasonry: Containing an Elaborate Account of the Rise and Progress of Freemasonry. New York: Macoy Publishing and Masonic Supply Co., 1908.

McDowell, Josh and Don Steward. Handbook of Today's Religions. Nashville: Thomas Nelson Publishers, 1983.

Mozel, Philip. "The Cult Statue of Aphrodite at Palaepaphos: A Meteorite?" The Journal of the Royal Astronomical Society of Canada 100.4 (2006): 149-155.

Murty, Danuse. Story of the Bodhi Tree. n.d.

Nardo, Don. Life During the Great Civilizations, Ancient Persia. Farmington Hills: Black Birch Press, 2003.

—. Lost Civilizations, Empires of Mesopotamia. San Diego: Lucent Books, 1947.

National Geographic Partners, LLC. "The Most Influential Figures of Ancient History." National Geographic Time Inc. Specials (2016): 112.

"On the Threshold." Grand Lodge of the Most Ancient and Honorable Society of Free and Accepted Masons for the State of New Jersey. n.d.

Patai, Raphael. The Hebrew Goddess. Detroit: Wayne State University Press, 1967.

Porter, Barbara. "Ishtar of Nineveh and Her Colaborator, Ishtar of Arbela, in the Reign of Assubanipal." Papers of the 49th Rencontre Assyriologique Internationale, Part One 2004: 41-44.

Ragozin, Zenaide. The Rise and Fall of the Assyrian Empire. Didactic Press, 2014.

Reade, Julian. "The Ishtar Temple at Nineveh." Iraq, Nineveh Papers of the 49th Recontre Assyriologique 2005: 347-390.

Rosa, Peter De. Vicars of Christ: The Dark Side of the Papacy. New York: Crown Publishers, Inc., 1988.

Sayce, A.H. "The Astarte Papyrus and the Legend of the Sea." The Journal of Egyptian Archaeology 1 May 1933: 4.

Schomp, Virginia. People of the Ancient World, Ancient Mesopotamia, The Sumerisnas, Babylonians, and Assyrians. Scholastic Inc., 2004.

Shuter, Jane. Mesopotamia, Excavating the Past. Chicago: Heinemann Library, 2006.

Smith, William, LL.D., ed. Dictionary of the Bible, Comprising its Antiquities, Biography, Geography and Natural History. New York: Fleming H. Revell Company, 1884.

Spaulding, D.D., RT. Rev. F.S. Joseph Smith, Jr., As a Translator. New York: The National Council, 1912.

Spencer, Aida Besancon, Donna F.G. Hailson, Catherine Clark Kroeger, William David Spencer. The Goddess Revival, A Biblical Response to God(dess) Spirituality. Eugene: Used by permission of Wipf and Stock Publishers. www.wipfandstock.com, 2010.

Stone, Perry. How to Interpret Dreams and Vision, Understanding God's warnings and guidance. Lake Mary: Charisma House, 2011.

Sutton, David C. Figs, A Global History. Ed. Andrew F. Smith. London: Reaktion Books Ltd, 2014.

Tate, Karen. Sacred Places of Goddess, 108 Destinations. Consortuim of Collective Consciousness, 2006.

"The History of John, the son of Zebedee, the Apostle and Evangelist." Apocryphal Acts of the Apostles. Ed. LL.D., PH. D. W. Wright. Vol. 2. London: Williams and Norgate, 1871. 3-60.

Thera, Piyadassi. "The Story of the Mahinda, Sanghamitta and the Sri Maha-Bodhi." Collected Bodhi Leaves Volume II: Numbers 31-60. Sri Lanka: Buddhist Publication Society, 2010. 347-366.

Wagner, C. Peter. Confronting the Queen of Heaven. Colorado Springs: Wagner Institute for Practical Ministry, 1998.

Whiston, William. Josephus The Complete Works. Nashville: Thomas Nelson Publishers, 1998.

Wilkinson, Richard H. The Complete Gods and Goddesses of Ancient Egypt. New York: Thames and Hudson Inc, 2003.

Wolkstein, Diane, and Samuel Noah Kramer. Inanna, Queen of Heaven and Earth, Her stories and hymns from Sumer. New York: Harper and Row, Publishers, Inc., 1983.

Wroe, Ann. <u>Pontius Pilate</u>. London: Random House UK, 1999.

Zodhiates, Spiros, ed. <u>AMG Complete Word Study Dictionary</u>. Cedar Rapids: Laridian, n.d.

—. <u>The Complete Word Study Dictionary New Testament</u>. Ed. Spiros Zodhiates. Chattanooga: AMG Publishers, 1994.

INDEX

Thank you for reading my book. Please share your story of how our Jealous God helped you overcome the queen of heaven by sending your story to contact@kellyjeanwhitaker.com

Please consider leaving this first-time author a favorable review on Amazon. Thank you!

#JealousYVWH

KellyJeanWhitaker.com

https://www.facebook.com/JealousYVWH